How to Keep Your Company Out of Court:
The Practical Legal Guide for Growing Businesses

Paul A. Allen, Editor

E 70

Prentice-Hall, Inc.
Englewood Cliffs, New Jersey

Prentice-Hall International, Inc., *London*
Prentice-Hall of Australia, Pty. Ltd., *Sydney*
Prentice-Hall Canada Inc., *Toronto*
Prentice-Hall of India Private Ltd., *New Delhi*
Prentice-Hall of Japan, Inc., *Tokyo*
Prentice-Hall of Southeast Asia Pte. Ltd., *Singapore*
Whitehall Books, Ltd., *Wellington, New Zealand*
Editora Prentice-Hall do Brasil Ltda., *Rio de Janeiro*

© 1984 by

PRENTICE-HALL, INC.

Englewood Cliffs, NJ

346, 0652
H847

Library of Congress Cataloging in Publication Data

Main entry under title:

How to keep your company out of court.

Includes index.
1. Small business—Law and legislation—United States.
2. Compromise (Law)—United States.   I. Allen, Paul A.
ISBN 0-13-411132-X
ISBN 0-13-411140-0 {PBK}

PRINTED IN THE UNITED STATES OF AMERICA

ABOUT THE AUTHOR

Paul A. Allen is General Counsel of Plus System, Inc., a joint venture of banks that established and operates a nationwide electronic funds transfer switching network. Plus System, whose members are located throughout the country, operates a service system of automated teller machines. The company's headquarters are in Denver, Colorado.

Before becoming General Counsel of PLUS, Mr. Allen spent more than seven years in private law practice in Washington, D.C. Mr. Allen has experience in all phases of antitrust and related litigation as well as counseling on a variety of antitrust, franchising, regulatory, and commercial matters.

Mr. Allen is a graduate of the New York University Law School (J.D. with honors, 1974) and the Johns Hopkins University. He has been a contributor to *Inc.* magazine's law column and has published other articles in the *Legal Times of Washington* and the *China Business Review.*

Mr. Allen has been a speaker, moderator, or chairman of law related conferences sponsored by the American Bar Association, the Federal Bar Association, and other organizations. He has been a guest lecturer at the Georgetown University Law School and the George Washington University School of Government and Business Administration. He is admitted to the District of Columbia and Maryland bars and is a member of local and national bar associations.

CONTRIBUTING EDITORS

J. Robert Brame, III

Mr. Brame, a graduate of Vanderbilt University (1964) and the Yale Law School (1967), is a partner in the Richmond, Virginia office of McGuire, Woods, and Battle. He was defense counsel in *Gilbert v. General Electric* (U.S. Sup. Ct. 1976) and *Dillard v. Industrial Commission of Virginia* (U.S. Sup. Ct. 1974). Mr. Brame is a charter member of the Labor Law Section of the Virginia Bar Association and the EEO Law Committee of the Defense Research Institute. He is also a member of the EEO Committee of the Labor Law Section of the American Bar Association and has been a faculty member at a National Institute of Trial Advocacy. Mr. Brame has spoken to legal and management groups on union organizing campaigns, class actions, discrimination, and labor law of the future.

Sheldon S. Cohen

Mr. Cohen is a partner in the Washington, D.C. law firm of Cohen and Uretz. He served as Chief Counsel of the Internal Revenue Service between 1963 and 1964, and he was Commissioner of Internal Revenue from 1965 to 1969.

Jay Gary Finkelstein

Mr. Finkelstein is associated with the Washington, D.C. office of Piper & Marbury, where he specializes in general corporate and securities matters. He is a graduate (magna cum laude) of Princeton University (1975) and the Harvard Law School (1978). From 1978 to 1979 he served as law clerk for the Honorable Frank A. Kaufman, now Chief Judge of the U.S. District Court for the District of Maryland.

Jon F. Hartung

Mr. Hartung is a partner in the San Francisco law firm of Farella, Braun & Martel where he specializes in banking and real estate matters. He holds an undergraduate degree from Yale University and a J.D. from the University of California, Berkeley.

Cannon Y. Harvey

Mr. Harvey is a partner in the Denver law firm of Holme, Roberts & Owen. He holds a bachelor's degree from the University of Missouri (1962), an

M.A. from Harvard University (1963), and an LL.B from the Harvard Law School (1966). Mr. Harvey has been a law school teacher of securities and corporate law. He is the coauthor (with Harold S. Bloomenthal and Samuel E. Wing) of the 1982 and 1983 *Going Public Handbook* (Clark Boardman and Co., Ltd.). He has extensive experience in securities matters and is a frequent speaker on the securities laws.

Alan J. Kasper

Mr. Kasper has been Patent Counsel for the Communications Satellite Corporation (COMSAT) in Washington, D.C. since 1971. Previously, he was an Examiner in the U.S. Patent and Trademark Office. Mr. Kasper is a graduate of the Georgetown Law Center, and he holds a degree in Electronics Engineering from the State University of New York at Buffalo. He has lectured on intellectual property topics and serves on committees of the Patent, Trademark, and Copyright Section of the American Bar Association as well as the American Patent Law Association.

Howard H. Lewis

Mr. Lewis, a graduate of Harvard College (1956) and the Harvard Law School (1962), is a partner in the Philadelphia law firm of Obermayer, Rebmann, Maxwell and Hippel. He has over twenty years' experience in general corporate practice and business litigation. For nine years he represented the Reading Company in its reorganization under Section 77 of the Bankruptcy Act.

Michele D. Stratton

Ms. Stratton is an associate at Farella, Braun & Martel. Her practice involves advising banking and business clients on a wide variety of corporate, commercial, and financial planning matters. Ms. Stratton received her J.D. from the University of California, Berkeley, her B.A. from Harvard University, and an M.C.P. from the Massachusetts Institute of Technology.

Arthur Wineburg

Mr. Wineburg is Chief of the Patent Branch, Unfair Imports Investigation Division, of the International Trade Commission in Washington, D.C. Before that, he practiced for more than ten years in Washington where his practice primarily centered on counseling and litigating on antitrust and trade regulation questions. He earned his law degree at George Washington University; he has a Masters in Economics from the University of Minnesota and a B.A. from Bard College. He has lectured and written on economic as well as legal issues.

Robert Joel Zakroff

Mr. Zakroff, a graduate of Temple University (1969) and the Washington College of Law at American University (1972), is the senior attorney at the Law Offices of Robert Joel Zakroff and Associates in Washington, D.C. He has extensive experience representing creditors in bankruptcy proceedings, and since 1975 he has served as Trustee in Bankruptcy in over 1250 cases. He has administered State insolvency proceedings as Assignee for Benefit of Creditors and has also represented debtors in Bankruptcy. He has often lectured and spoken on creditor and debtor issues

Introduction

This book will help your company avoid costly legal disputes. Designed for executives, managers, and financial and legal advisers in small and growing companies, its 13 chapters provide practical advice for preventing litigation with the company clan, such as its employees and stockholders, and with outsiders, such as competitors, customers, or suppliers.

Both content and style distinguish this volume from others you may have seen. *Content:* We describe and suggest solutions for legal problems that are the most common or that pose the greatest risks to businesses today. *Style:* We use standard English prose, tips, rules, examples, and even a few charts; we left the legal jargon and case citations for the law library. The book is designed to be read straight through or used only as a reference when you need help on resolving a particular problem.

Beyond its legal significance, our advice makes good business sense. For example, our suggestions for adopting a sound labor relations program can increase productivity while reducing legal risks; the recommendations for protecting your innovations or trade secrets can protect your competitive position; the rules for keeping peace within the corporate family can prevent the unraveling of the business; and the tips for extending credit and repaying debts can help your firm remain solvent in tough economic times.

The time is right for a book like this: as we suggest in chapter 1, the law is so pervasive that successful managers must be conversant with it as well as the traditional fields of finance, marketing, and human resource and information management. The law need not be among the apparently unmanageable new challenges that American business faces in the 1980s:

- Persistent and perplexing problems of inflation and recession.

- The technological revolution that will have a dramatic effect on our economic, political, and social life.

- Foreign and domestic competition that is increasing and creating greater demand for the scarce economic, human, and natural resources that any company must have to survive and grow.

- Interdependence of world economies that allows economic diseases to spread rapidly around the globe.

- Larger, more visible role of American business, particularly as the 50-year dominance of government is being questioned and reduced. Yes, this *is* a challenge.

- Increasingly intense competition for management positions—and good jobs generally—as the post-World War II baby-boom generation approaches middle age and demands more income.

These trends will produce increased tension, competition, and conflict. Who doubts that they will also generate new legal problems and lawsuits? If they do, these are some of the consequences:

1. *There are enormous "opportunity costs" when businessmen spend time on courtroom and legal matters instead of corporate planning, product development, or marketing.* Managers rarely put a price on their diverted, unproductive time, but the general counsel of one of the ten largest companies in the country says lost management time is his firm's biggest litigation "cost." According to a recent survey of chief executive officers of America's largest corporations, 60 percent spend between 5 percent and 25 percent of their time on legal problems.[1] But this may be a low estimate because managers don't carefully account for the time they spend on legal problems, so it mounts up quickly before they are aware of it.

2. *The direct out-of-pocket cost of litigation is rising.* There seems to be no dampening of the litigation explosion and with it the cost of legal services. According to one estimate, in 30 years there will be more than ten million cases in the federal courts of the country and over forty million state court cases in California alone. The average cost of retaining outside counsel is almost $80.00 per hour—double the cost of providing these services by an "in-house" lawyer.[2] While big companies can absorb these expenses, smaller firms feel the pinch because their cash must go to satisfy more pressing needs such as product development, marketing, loans, or overhead.

3. *Litigation can severely disrupt a company's operations and destroy its business plan.* The diversion of management resources from running the company to running a lawsuit can doom the carefully constructed business plan: it can delay for months or years the introduction of a new product. It can also damage employee morale, slow production, and disrupt customer relations. Even worse, the disruption can increase management's psychological investment in a case, and that clouds an objective analysis of the dispute. In short, when a company is a defendant in a lawsuit it is not attacking the competition or developing new markets; it is merely defending its flanks.

4. *Litigation can be bad public relations.* Every company gets occasional

---

[1]*Harvard Business Review*, Corporate Legal Decision Making Survey.

[2]Stichnoth and Dolan, "Management Strategies for the Corporate Counsel," *Legal Economics*, Jan.–Feb., 1982, p. 16.

customer complaints, but who needs to worry about bad press reports based on courtroom testimony?

5. *Litigation can be good news for your competitors.* Important and "confidential" business information often is made public during pre-trial maneuvering. Your product plans, accounts, and customer data can help your competitors and hurt your competitive position.

6. *Litigation can produce bad results.* Managing a legal dispute is like much business planning generally—there is no absolute "best" alternative, only a number from which you must select the one that's preferred. Too often, lawyers and clients alike assume that litigation is the only way to resolve a dispute. (In chapter 2 we show that's not true.) But the problem with a lawsuit is that the judge or jury decides, and neither one may know much about your business or industry. The result is certainly less predictable and often less creative because the courtroom is not conducive to devising options or making trade-offs.

7. *Litigation may signal a bigger problem.* A lawsuit may be a harbinger of worse things to come. For example, if it's a dispute about the quality or performance of a product, it may mean there are other customers who are just as dissatisfied as the fellow who sued you. Litigation is often a red flag—it alerts you to what may be bigger problems later.

The new challenges of the '80s and the more conventional perils of litigation confirm what every businessman or woman already knows—it's usually best to avoid court. In the 1980s this will be more important than ever because the risks are so much higher. This book tells you which legal problems you should worry about and how to manage them in a practical, business-like way:

- *Lawyers.* Every company has legal problems of one sort or another. Chapter 1 tells you how to be a better consumer of legal services: it offers five principles of legal cost control, tips for keeping counsel reined in, and six traits to look for when hiring a lawyer in the first place.

- *Out-of-Court Resolution.* Even if you have a legal dispute, you need not resolve it in court. It's best if the business antagonists can resolve the matter themselves free of third parties such as judges or juries. In chapter 2 we describe six techniques for resolving disputes out of court and pose ten questions to answer as you decide which, if any, technique to use.

- *Organization.* If you are not careful when organizing a business, you may choose the wrong form of legal enterprise or fail to satisfy the owners' desire for power and money. Chapter 3 lists the pros and cons of four business types and shows how one of them—the corporation—can satisfy all the owners' interests.

- *Corporate Operations.* Smart management of the corporation's internal legal affairs preserves harmony. Chapter 4 offers rules for keeping peace in the corporate family and tips for avoiding personal liability as a stockholder, director, or officer.

- *Contracts.* Contracts are essential to and common in the operation of all businesses. Chapter 5 gives you some everyday rules for buying and selling goods, six principles of contract law, and the most common sources of contract disputes.

- *Product Liability.* Manufacturers shudder at the prospect of being sued for personal injuries sustained by users of their products. Chapter 6 starts with a product liability primer and then describes in detail a nine-point plan for managing product liability risks.

- *Labor.* The workers of the 1980s are more aggressive, ambitious, and less inclined to accept the edicts of management. Chapter 7 gives you rules for selecting employees, rules for managing them, rules for discipline, and practical suggestions for handling the challenge of unionization.

- *Intellectual Property.* Technology-based and service-oriented companies are more numerous than ever, and all of them must protect their inventions, innovations, secrets, and commercial names. Chapter 8 deals with the vital subjects of patents, trade secrets, trademarks, and copyrights; it describes creative ways to protect your valuable commercial property.

- *Antitrust.* You must efficiently distribute products, yet not run afoul of the antitrust laws. Chapter 9 offers tips for managing these laws, warns of the risks of trade associations, tells you how to legally restrict your dealers' or distributors' sales territory or customers, and offers a checklist for wisely selecting and terminating dealers.

- *Financing.* Obtaining affordable financing is the number one business problem for many growing companies. Chapter 10 explains the rules of borrowing and the many forms of bank financing, tells you how to properly make a loan request, and identifies the most common borrowing mistakes.

- *Taxes.* What executive is not aware of the perils of the tax laws? In Chapter 11 we tell you how to handle a tax audit and how to avoid the most common tax problems in closely held corporations, such as excessive compensation of officers, constructive dividends, the penalty taxes, and the payroll taxes.

- *Securities.* Fast-growing companies inevitably think of "going public." In Chapter 12 we give you the pros and cons of going public, warn of the expansive meaning of a "security," tell you about registration and disclosure, and suggest how to structure a capital offering so you can legally avoid federal registration.

- *Credit.* Virtually every company extends credit and incurs debts. Chapter 13 tells you how to extend credit wisely and protect your security, what to do when your debtor files for bankruptcy, and what action you can take when the debt burden on your company becomes excessive.

There are two reasons why we chose these issues and excluded others: each one is a common legal problem that is also likely to pose risks or create exposure for the company. You will often see the word "exposure" in this book. Used narrowly, it means the amount of money that a company stands to lose in the event there is an adverse outcome. Example: Manufacturers of asbestos may have an exposure of billions of dollars in the thousands of products liability cases filed against them. More broadly, exposure refers to the other "costs" a company incurs in litigation—the bad publicity, the management time spent on the case, and the effect on employee morale.

If followed, the suggestions in these chapters will reduce your exposure: You will learn to anticipate legal and business problems and deal with them quickly, competently, and efficiently.

Though each chapter presents a unique set of issues, there is a common thread woven throughout. It is this: Many legal disputes can be prevented in the first instance, or resolved in the second, with judgment, common sense, and preparation. Although perhaps not a revelation, this aphorism can still do as much to reduce your legal exposure as the best lawyer in town. Judgment, the ability to decide objectively, authoritatively, and wisely; common sense, an intuitive sense for making the right decision without regard to specialized (as in the law) knowledge; and preparation, being ready with the necessary facts before finally acting or deciding. This book does not teach common sense but it will prepare you for the legal challenges ahead. That will improve your judgment and, we hope, keep you out of court.

Paul A. Allen
Editor

ACKNOWLEDGMENTS

I must first thank the Contributing Editors for their fine work and the considerable patience they displayed during the months when this manuscript was being prepared. They were always alert to legal detail as well as the unique needs of the book's readers.

The one person to whom I owe the largest debt is Sharon Harvin; her skill, hard work, and support made the entire project possible. One would be hard pressed to find a more capable and loyal assistant.

Several other people helped a great deal along the way. Jay Gary Finkelstein, one of the Contributing Editors, provided valuable assistance in the early design of the book and later by reviewing certain chapters. Bradley S. Waterman, of the Washington law firm Cohen and Uretz, and Arthur Wineburg, a Contributing Editor, reviewed portions of the manuscript and made several valuable suggestions. Two of my former colleagues, Jeffrey L. Kestler and Barbara C. Stergis, also reviewed parts of the book and I thank them as well.

I am also indebted to Rosewell Page, III of the Richmond, Virginia law firm of McGuire, Woods, and Battle. Mr. Page has extensive experience in the defense of product liability cases and he developed the Risk Management Plan described in chapter six.

Finally, I must thank the people at *Inc.*, particularly the magazine's Managing Editor, Roberta W. Shell, for giving me an early opportunity to write about the law for a business audience.

My contribution to this book is dedicated to the memory of an inspired and able writer, my grandmother, Lillian DeWaters.

Paul A. Allen
Editor

Contents

1. How to Be a Smart Consumer of Legal Services: Controlling Legal Fees and Lawyers

by PAUL A. ALLEN

In law, nothing is certain but the expense.
—Samuel Butler

Few experienced businessmen would challenge Butler's maxim. A lawyer's advice may be equivocal but its high cost is rarely in doubt.

More companies are paying more money for legal fees than ever before. According to the United States Department of Commerce, total legal fees in 1980 were an astonishing $23.4 billion, more than 1 percent of the country's Gross National Product. Between 1972 and 1976 legal fees increased at a rate three times greater than corporate profits. Some companies now spend as much as 30 percent of their after-tax profits for legal services.

As a federal judge recently recommended, it is time to treat lawyers like suppliers of commercial products. Managers must be smart, tough, educated consumers of legal services in order to obtain sound legal advice at a fair price. This will permit them to turn the law from a drag on corporate profits to a booster of the company's business goals.

Your company cannot avoid destructive and costly legal disputes unless you know how to use a lawyer properly; that is, how to make him an effective and economically efficient part of your business team. This requires mastery of the art of "legal cost controls." You will learn these and more in this chapter:

- The three grim realities of law and business today;
- What you have a right to expect from a lawyer;
- Six characteristics to look for when selecting a lawyer;
- The five principles of legal cost control;
- Tips to keep counsel reined in; and
- When it is cost-effective to hire a full-time, in-house lawyer for your company

THREE GRIM REALITIES OF LAW AND BUSINESS

Though you may resent it, legal constraints are ubiquitous. The result is a complex and high stakes game of legal poker. As we show throughout this book, it is foolish and potentially disastrous to ignore the rules of this game in the vain hope that you will ultimately beat the house. It rarely happens.

Successful businessmen are realistic, practical, and shrewd; they understand "the realities of the market." The realities of the law and business market are brutal and unpleasant, but they characterize the environment in which you must operate.

Reality 1: You Do Business in an Increasingly Regulated and Commercially Complex Society

Why is there so much litigation and why are your legal bills so high? Consider the following facts:

- There are over 85 federal agencies with significant regulatory power over private economic activity.
- The cost of federal regulation alone is over $200 billion per year, an amount equal to about 10 percent of the country's Gross National Product.[1]
- All 50 states regulate myriad commercial activities. There are also the statutes and rules and regulations of counties, cities, municipalities, and townships. Finally, there is that amorphous code of state conduct known as the "common law." All states have it, and if you have been sued for negligence because a customer slipped and was injured on your business premises, you know what it can cost you or your insurer.

You conduct business in a society of enormous commercial complexity. Be prepared to walk nimbly through the minefield.

---

[1]Buhler, "The Origins and Costs of Regulation," Proceedings of the Private Costs of Regulation, Marketing Science Institute and U. of N. Carolina School of Bus. Admin., May 31–June 2, 1978.

Reality 2: Americans Love a Good Fight: We Are Prone to Conflicts, Disputes, and Litigation

In this day and age, anybody can sue and usually does.
—William Fishman, Chairman and Chief Executive Officer,
ARA Services (Wall Street Journal, Sept. 30, 1981)[2]

Americans have always been an aggressive and contentious lot. Years ago, disputes between merchants were settled with fists and brute force. That violent method has been replaced with litigation, something as commonplace today as fist fights once were. It seems that antagonists still prefer a good fight to discourse and settlement. As one chief executive says, litigation is our new national pastime. Many are playing the game:

- In 1974 there were 62,000 civil suits filed in the New York trial court—equal to one lawsuit for each lawyer in the state.
- Between 1960 and 1975 the caseload in federal trial courts increased 106 percent.
- Between 1940 and 1981 the number of new civil cases in lower federal courts increased six times faster than did the population.
- Between 1967 and 1976 the number of new civil cases filed in state trial courts increased twice as fast as the population.
- If rates continue to rise, in the year 2010 there will be 10 million new federal cases in the United States and 40 million new cases in California alone.[3]

The litigation gusher has flooded the nation's court system. In 13 urban areas, it now takes an average of over one year to get a case to trial. (Remember that when you tell your lawyer to "sue the bastards.") With the typical federal court trial judge now responsible for 350 cases, it's no wonder that 90 percent of all cases filed are settled before trial.

Litigation is often a mild symptom of a serious disease—deep and widespread dissension. One expert claims that senior managers spend almost one-fourth of their time dealing with company conflicts of one sort or another.[4] Some senior executives spend far more: In 1979 the president of the Kellogg Company, the huge cereal concern, devoted fully 40 percent of his time to legal and government matters.[5] If you feel besieged with customer complaints, employee

---

[2]Reprinted with permission, Dow Jones and Company © 1981.

[3]*The Business Lawyer*, Jan. 1982, p. 689.

[4]Gordon L. Lippitt, Ph.D., Professor of Behavioral Science, School of Government and Business Administration, the George Washington University.

[5]© 1979 by The New York Times Company. Reprinted by permission. The "Business and Law" column, Aug. 10, 1979.

disputes, conflicts with government agencies, and litigation, take solace from the knowledge that your predicament is a common one among the businessmen and women in America.

Reality 3: You Are Surrounded By an Army of Lawyers

The third reality of the market is the surfeit of lawyers. The numbers tell the tale. In 1981 there were 575,000 lawyers in the country, twice the number 20 years earlier.[6] This is equal to 1 lawyer for every 600 people. (The ratio in Japan is 1:12,000.) The ratio is even worse in many of the major industrial and commercial states: it is 1:272 in New York, 1:298 in California, 1:323 in Illinois, and 1:354 in Florida. Cringe at the ratio for the District of Columbia, 1:18.[7]

Ratios don't tell the whole story. A new survey by the American Bar Association (the lawyers' trade association) finds that "litigation/trial practice" became in 1982 the number one specialty of America's lawyers. It edged out the less clamorous "corporate/business" specialty that had been number one.[8]

This great army of lawyers is composed of many different combat divisions—law firms (over 40,000 at last count), government agencies, corporate legal departments, and solo practitioners. But the size and growth rate of in-house legal staffs is particularly revealing because it reflects the increasing need for counseling and litigation expertise as well as the high cost of outside lawyers. The biggest companies and those in highly regulated industries have the most lawyers. Consider the following 1981 figures from the *Legal Times of Washington*:

Company	Number of Lawyers
AT&T	895
Exxon	450
General Electric	340
Sears, Roebuck & Co.	146
IBM	141

The astute executive understands the changing business environment in which he operates and adopts a business plan to deal with it. The realities of law and business today are that our society is increasingly complex in regulatory and commercial matters; that we are awash in business conflicts and lawsuits; and that there is a legal army awaiting the opportunity to demonstrate its combat skills.

---

[6]*American Bar Assoc. Journal*, Vol. 67, pp. 1098–99.
[7]Ibid., Vol. 68, p. 898.
[8]Ibid., p. 800.

WHAT YOU HAVE A RIGHT TO EXPECT FROM A LAWYER

Know what you have a right to expect from your lawyer:

- Legal advice that is fast, sound and practical.
- Good judgment.
- Cost efficient service.

Annually evaluate the cost and quality of the legal services you have received so you can determine whether your counsel measures up. Attorney failures in this regard may be due to inadequate instructions from you, incompetence, or even a simple misunderstanding. For guidance in making these judgments, look to the important criteria discussed next for choosing a lawyer.

SIX CHARACTERISTICS TO LOOK FOR WHEN SELECTING A LAWYER

We got outlawyered. I feel they represented us inadequately.
—Harry A. Merlo, Chairman of Louisiana Pacific Corporation, after an adverse jury decision and then a settlement that cost his company $5.3 million. (Wall Street Journal, Aug. 9, 1982.)[9]

You would not buy from the first product supplier who sent you a bid, or appoint the first distributor to visit your office, or hire the first financial officer who sent you a resume. Be equally selective when hiring lawyers.

There are six essential characteristics to look for. The relative importance of each one varies according to your own needs and resources and the lawyer's precise role, particularly whether he is to serve as your general counsel or a one-time litigator. (The importance of properly defining the role is discussed on p. 33.) For most companies most of the time this is what's important:

1. Personal Compatibility

This is the key to a productive, healthy, and useful relationship with your lawyer. It is essential for the lawyer who serves as the general counselor and business adviser to the company, though it is less important for the litigation specialist hired for occasional courtroom work. You are likely to talk with the general counselor frequently, perhaps on a daily or weekly basis; you might see far less of the specially hired litigator.

---

[9]Reprinted with permission, Dow Jones and Company © 1982.

While lawyers do not usually rank personal compatibility high, many small companies do. A recent survey of subscribers to *Inc.* magazine (a monthly business publication for small and growing companies) found that "personal contact with members of the firm" is the most important factor in choosing a law firm. More than half the survey's respondents rated it number one.[10]

There is good reason for such a high ranking. Management and counsel must have personalities that mesh; they must be able to speak openly, freely, and candidly. Without this rapport, you won't ask advice as often as you should, nor will you volunteer potentially vital information on your industry, company, or employees. Your lawyer will be reticent too; he will not have a psychological stake in the success of the company, and he may not be able to appreciate your management style or the corporate culture.

A lawyer must have solid information and a complete understanding of the company and its problems. When a lawyer acts as a general business counselor, he should offer guidance, suggest alternatives to proposed actions, and anticipate (and in that way prevent) legal problems. This is often called the "preventive" or "anticipatory" role of lawyers. But an attorney will fail at that role unless he and the company's managers have high regard and empathy for each other, eagerly listen to each other's views, develop a mutual attitude of tolerance and acceptance, and are able to work harmoniously together. You need a lawyer who listens, understands, and advises; not someone who pontificates and lectures.

2. Good Judgment

The quintessential attribute of excellent lawyers and businessmen is their ability to make a decision or form an opinion with objectivity, authority, and wisdom. Companies demand good judgment from their executives; they should do the same from their counsel.

Lawyers with judgment (and there are ways, as we shall see in a moment, to locate them) are more than mere legal technicians who draft contracts, prepare leases, and write corporate documents only from legal form books. In addition to being personally compatible with you, they:

- Offer practical advice, not abstruse theories;
- Develop reasonable alternatives for you to consider;
- Understand the nature of your business, its market, and customers;
- Work within your financial and staff limits;
- Are flexible and responsive to your changing needs;
- Know the importance and value of time; and

---

[10]"You and Your Attorney," by Bradford W. Ketchum, Jr., *Inc.*, June 1982, copyright © 1982, Inc. Publishing Company.

- Are prepared to offer reasoned decisions and judgments, not knee-jerk answers.

Lawyers with judgment understand tactics and strategy, have foresight and intellectual breadth, and tend to have a reliable "gut feeling" about the tough issues. While large, cash-rich companies can afford a legal general who lays seige to his opponent with an army of lawyers, growing companies with better uses for their money must use a better strategy. They must win another way: they must conserve resources, use surprise and stratagems, carefully consider all options, take prudent risks, and as in war concentrate forces at the weakest point of defense. Lawyers with judgment know that strategy changes with each client.

3. Thorough Preparation

As with most of the other five characteristics, this one is not unique to the top quality lawyer; thorough preparation is as essential in business as it is in law. Your adviser's broad knowledge of a general field (whether it's patent law or corporate finance) is not much help if he is not adequately prepared for that important meeting or planning session. Preparation means learning the particular facts about the matter under discussion, taking time to review the plans and papers before the meeting, or simply going into the session (be it a board meeting or court hearing) with the important points on the tip of the tongue rather than in the file at the office. It also means spending time with management so the lawyer can get a "feel" for the company; that is, understand the corporate culture, the first principle of legal cost control. (See p. 32.)

Preparation is not a substitute for good judgment, but judgment alone does not win legal battles; the forces must be prepared or they cannot properly execute the battle plan.

4. Technical Expertise

If your lawyer has judgment, he probably has legal expertise; but if he has the latter, there's no guarantee he has the former. No doubt a lawyer must have a working knowledge of the laws and regulations that affect your business. In the *Inc.* survey, lawyers ranked expertise as the most important criterion a company should look for when hiring an attorney. But lawyers can overemphasize expertise and downplay judgment.

Expertise is particularly important for companies in heavily regulated industries such as broadcasting and energy. But all growing companies face an array of business and legal issues that demand technical knowledge. For example, you may need a specialist for pension planning, complex tax matters, securities issues, labor matters, and patent and trade secret protection. Such lawyers often have useful experience in several industries. On the other hand, you might find it helpful to hire someone who is an expert in your particular industry; some lawyers specialize in serving clients in such fields as computer hardware and software, real estate, or financial services.

A person's legal expertise, like his knowledge of most other subjects, is not absolute; it is only a point on a continuum. In consultation with the lawyer, determine two things—how much expertise you really need (and can afford), and how much the lawyer has. Where, in short, are your needs and the lawyer's expertise on that continuum? Make an appropriate match and you will pay only for the level of skill you actually need. But use foresight; today's simple securities or corporate law problem may become much tougher questions as the business grows. You don't want to search for another lawyer every time the issue gets more complicated. Full service, quality law firms should be able to solve this problem by matching your needs with their attorneys' different levels of expertise.

5. Good Service

Find a lawyer who will provide prompt personal legal service. There is nothing more frustrating than an inaccessible lawyer or one who takes days to advise you on an urgent business problem. In fact, in *Inc.'s* survey of its subscribers, "timely service" was the number one source of dissatisfaction with lawyers.

Good service is easier to promise than deliver. Be prepared to ask tough questions when measuring this quality. Does the attorney have clients of comparable size or in a similar industry and have they received satisfactory service? Ask them. Does the attorney often travel, for example, handling litigation around the country, or is he generally in the office? Does this matter to you? Does he have colleagues of comparable skill who can substitute for him? Did he take enough time with you at the initial meeting or was he too rushed? Will you be a "significant" client? If not, will he treat you as one anyway?

If prompt responses are particularly important for your business, say that up front or make it a term if there is a written agreement between you and the lawyer. A simple clause requiring the attorney to use his "best efforts" to provide prompt legal advice may be just the leverage you need. If that doesn't work, hire another lawyer.

6. Reasonable Fees

Unless you have an unlimited operating expense budget, you will want a lawyer whose fees are reasonable. (Beginning on p. 34 we tell you how to control fees once you retain counsel.) Shop around, but be wary of exceptionally high or low rates. Ultimately, the test for what is "reasonable" is to measure actual performance against dollar cost, but that's far easier to do *after* you have worked with the attorney.

Remember that fees are only one of six characteristics, and that low rates can't make up for bad legal service; in fact, bad legal service may be worse than none at all. It is difficult to rank the five other traits, but many lawyers would place judgment and preparation at the top of the list. Without them, legal advice will not be first-rate.

Investigate Before Hiring

Now that you know what to look for, how do you find it? If you are a Florida businessman, how do you find the right lawyer among the 27,498 licensed to practice law there,[11] and how do you know if he or she has "judgment"?

Get References. Whether you are searching for your first lawyer, switching to a new one, or adding a specialist to the team, look first to personal recommendations and references. Businessmen such as accountants and bankers who have worked with attorneys are in a good position to suggest names. Companies of similar size or in related industries can also be helpful. Tap your industry trade association and your counterparts in local business organizations such as the local Chamber of Commerce or government economic development organizations.

Ask the Bar Association. Local or state bar associations can provide help, but their recommendations are not based on firsthand, working experience with the lawyer. Many states now list lawyers by specialty or their avowed interest such as securities or tax. As a last resort, bar association and many public libraries have the Martindale–Hubbell Law Directory, which provides biographical sketches of most lawyers. The *American Lawyer*, a monthly publication about the legal community, publishes a two-volume description of the largest U.S. law firms.

Before you approach a lawyer, have a good idea from personal recommendations how he or she measures up to the six criteria just discussed. Next, interview the lawyer (obviously, no fee should be charged) while keeping the traits in mind. Ask for more references, and feel free to get names of other clients so you can have their opinion of the attorney's performance.

FIVE PRINCIPLES OF LEGAL COST CONTROL

For many business people I meet around town or in airports and taxis, high legal bills and the weather are two of the few subjects we can easily talk about.

—Ralph Nader

Avoiding courtroom battles will save you money. But the means and end can be reversed: reducing legal costs will help you to avoid court. How can it work both ways? Because unnecessary litigation is unlikely if you rigorously follow the Five Principles of Legal Cost Control.

---

[11]*American Bar Assoc. Journal*, Vol. 68, p. 898.

Principle 1: Tell Your Lawyer About Corporate Goals and the Corporate Culture

A lawyer can offer wise, appropriate, readily accepted advice only if he has a clear understanding of (1) your corporate goals and objectives and (2) the nature of the risks your company is willing to take. In a word, the lawyer must understand your "corporate culture"—your firm's goals, values, and beliefs. Otherwise, the legal advice will be inapt or wrong.

If you don't know where you want to take your company and how you are going to get there, your lawyer has no basis for formulating appropriate recommendations. Counseling and litigation involve measuring risks and making judgments. This process is not an abstraction; it occurs (or should) in a particular corporate setting, at one point in time, and within a defined industry.

Consider how important it is for a lawyer to understand the different corporate cultures of two hypothetical companies, Future Software and Midwest Tool Works. The first is a 3-year-old company whose 32-year-old founder, president, and principal stockholder is a brilliant software designer and marketer. Company sales have soared from zero to $20 million largely due to product innovations and mushrooming sales of personal computers. The founder is an agreeable fellow who is supremely confident that his new products will set industry sales records.

Midwest Tool is an old, established company whose stock is held by third-generation executives as well as several family trust funds. The company has a protected niche in a segment of the specialized toolmaking market, a position it can maintain with conservative management.

The corporate goals and acceptable risk levels of Future Software and Midwest Tool are very different, and the style and advice of their lawyers must reflect these differences. Future Software's founder is an aggressive risk taker with, so he believes, little to lose by plunging boldly ahead. No doubt he would defiantly take business and legal risks that would be promptly rejected by Midwest Tool. That company wants to maintain profits, retain market share, and conserve stockholders' equity. Unlike Future Software, it wants its lawyer to cross every legal "t" and dot every "i" and it is willing to pay for that luxury.

The two companies have unique legal needs. Midwest is protective of its pension fund and vigilant on labor matters, both of little concern to Future Software. But even with common issues (legal problems with customers, for example) the perspective and final decision will be quite different. A lawyer must understand the source of such differences—the company's goals, objectives, and level of acceptable risk. If he does not, there will be unnecessarily high legal fees, inappropriate legal advice, and an uneasy working relationship.

Principle 2: Define the Lawyer's Role

When you hire a lawyer you must also carefully define his role.

In Litigation. Hiring a lawyer for one lawsuit presents a relatively easy problem of role definition. Instruct him to defend (or prosecute) the company's case after adopting a strategy (see chapter 2) and establishing cost control guidelines (see page 34). Also determine whether additional advice is appropriate. Suppose, for example, that you were sued by an employee you fired. Perhaps the same events or faulty procedures leading to his termination and the lawsuit might cause disputes with other employees. If so, changes are surely in order. But without proper guidance the lawyer will not know whether an investigation of these matters and a recommendation is part of the role.

Most companies first use lawyers not in litigation, but in counseling. Here, you must be scrupulous in defining the role in order to avoid "sticker shock" when the bill arrives.

For Counseling. If you hire a lawyer for the limited purpose of preparing incorporation papers and writing sales or supply contracts, make sure the lawyer understands this and sticks to it. On the other hand, you might want counsel to provide general business advice and to become a part of the central management and strategy team. If so, say it at the beginning of the relationship.

This broader role, common in many small and large corporations, is said to involve two functions: *reacting* to problems as they arise and *anticipating* corporate needs.[12] (The latter can be done only by following Principle 1.) A broad role costs more money and requires technical legal skill as well as excellent judgment. But over the long term it can save money if legal problems are in that way anticipated and avoided.

If you fail to define the lawyer's role, you run the risk that it will be too broad (and therefore too expensive in the short run) or too narrow (and therefore too expensive in the long run). Make the choice yourself; do not assume the attorney you hire will define the role as you would.

Principle 3: Monitor the Lawyer's Performance

After you define the lawyer's role, be prepared to regularly and carefully monitor his performance and cost and to talk with him about both. Surprisingly, this rule is often ignored by busy managers. You should regularly receive copies of all correspondence and pleadings and look them over. If you are too busy for this, appoint another executive to maintain regular contact with the lawyer and

---

[12]See Stichnoth & Dolan, "Management Strategies for the Corporate Counsel," *Legal Economics*, Jan.–Feb., 1982, p. 13.

do it for you. Is the attorney doing precisely *what* you want *when* you want it? Are all the papers there? Was the work done on time? Is the lawyer accessible? Does he regularly suggest options and business alternatives for the company to consider? Do you have confidence in him and welcome his judgment or do you only reluctantly and warily hear him out?

By monitoring attorney performance you are more likely to get what you pay for even if you are not paying very much. You want and deserve value and the way to get it, as with other services, is to demand performance at the right price. If you're not getting it, hire a new lawyer.

Principle 4: Set Controls on Fees and Billing

When you select an attorney, agree on controls and procedures to keep fees reasonable.

Will You Go First-Class or Coach?

Before you define the attorney's role or assign a particular task, determine how good a job you really need. This should be routine if you have a clear picture of your corporate goals and culture. Don't be afraid to make trade-offs in the law as you do in business. You may not need the best contract money can draft if the value of the deal it covers is only a few hundred, or even a few thousand, dollars.

Press your lawyer to give you cost estimates according to the resources he or his firm would devote to the matter. No client expects to lose, and for this as well as ethical reasons attorneys often feel constrained to go first-class all the time. That's not always necessary. One big New York firm now will give estimates for its litigation services in at least three classes—first-class, coach, and tourist. The dollar differences are big, and the savings can be worthwhile if you are willing to assume some additional risk.

Whatever level of service you choose, discuss the various fee arrangements—hourly, by project, or retainer (p. 36)—and determine which one will work out best for you. (Contingent fees—payment of a percentage of the money recovered in a judgment—are not appropriate in counseling or when defending a lawsuit.) When you settle on an arrangement, put the terms in a written agreement.

The Relationship of Attorney's Role and Cost

The cost rises as the attorney's role expands. That's why a careful—but not necessarily narrow—definition of role is so important.

If you have a discrete project where the lawyer's role is limited, such as the preparation of an employment agreement or lease, you should request a "project fee" estimate. This is the flat rate cost to do the job. If you solicit estimates from more than one lawyer, be sure they are for the same legal product; custom agreements that fit your specific business are more expensive than standard, form-book contracts.

This process of soliciting bids, while shocking to legal traditionalists, is becoming more common. This is exactly what is done by the general counsel of Container Corporation of America (a unit of Mobil, ranked second on *Fortune* magazine's list of the 500 largest industrial corporations). Of course, he uses this procedure only on selected issues and among top quality law firms. The technique may yield even bigger dividends in coming years if the lawyer glut combines with client pressures to increase competition and reduce legal costs.

Know the Hourly Rates and the Legal Staff

Growing companies often need help on matters of uncertain length and scope. If this means paying hourly rates, first determine who will staff your matter or case. You should always hire a lawyer and not a law firm; the six characteristics we described earlier are found in individual lawyers, not their firms. Of course, every lawyer inevitably must call on his partners, an associate, or perhaps a paralegal for assistance. Know these people too—their backgrounds and experience, how much they charge, and under what circumstances they would be used.

Companies often want a team of lawyers available, particularly if they frequently demand advice on short notice. But beware of "pyramiding"—overstaffing a case with another partner *and* an associate or paralegal. While such teams are frequently necessary, they are sometimes used to train an associate or cushion a partner's workload at the client's expense. Be alert for lawyers who travel in pairs. In small cases, this can increase the bill considerably, but it may not add to the quality of the representation you receive.

One caution on hourly rates: don't be misled by high or low numbers, because it's the total bill that counts. You may be able to negotiate a cap or ceiling on the total fee, particularly if you are a new client for the lawyer or a start-up company. Try to get a ceiling or reduced rates for the next year as well.

Ask About Hidden Costs; Matters of Style

Always ask about secondary charges and hidden costs. How much does the firm charge for photocopying, secretarial overtime, computer time (such as for legal research), word processing, messenger services? These "disbursements" can add significantly to your total bill, particularly if the firm adds a surcharge (read "profit"). Request a schedule of these charges and impose limits on them if you think they are unreasonable. For example, consider refusing to pay for secretarial overtime except under unique circumstances.

Be alert for law firms with excessive overhead; they may have sumptuous carpets in the reception area, lavish facilities, and museum artwork. Someone must pay for this, so their legal fees are usually high. There is a role for these firms, but it may not be one for which you are always willing to pay. Law firms, like retail businesses such as Sears and Bloomingdale's, have their own style; you must decide which one suits you best. Sometimes you may want to pay these prices, but other times not. Do the attorneys always fly first-class, stay in the best hotels, and indulge in $70 steak dinners? If that is what you do and you don't mind paying the bill, then it's all right.

Consider the Retainer

One potentially valuable alternative to hourly rates and the project or flat fee is the retainer. This requires the client to pay a fixed fee for legal services that are rendered over a period of time, usually for one year. Attorneys often put a ceiling on the number of hours they will provide for the fee, but the effective per hour rate under a retainer should be lower than it would otherwise be.

The retainer has one advantage to both you and the lawyer—predictability. You know the budget for legal fees and the attorney knows what revenues to expect from his client.

There is also a psychological bonus. You are far more likely to call the attorney for advice, even about routine matters, if you know that the meter is not running every time you pick up the phone. This can prevent serious legal problems from ever arising.

Get Detailed Bills

Insist upon an itemized monthly or quarterly bill. Demand that it reflect the hours worked, by whom, and on what. Disbursements should be itemized as well. This allows you to monitor the costs of services on a current basis and to resolve squabbles promptly. It also will enable you to spot "demand charges." Example: If an attorney keeps track of his time in quarter-hour increments, even a two-minute call may be logged as 15 minutes. If his hourly rate is $80 an hour, that two-minute call can cost you $20.

A Word on Stock Interests

Attorneys can accept a stock interest in a company as compensation for legal work they perform for it. Some entrepreneurs at the start-up phase of their business prefer to pay lawyers in this way because they believe the lawyer's ownership interest in the company guarantees that he will go out of his way to give quality legal advice. Such an arrangement has the effect of making the lawyer a corporate insider and a member of the management team.

Not all lawyers are willing to accept stock in lieu of fees and many law firms find that it presents a nettlesome political problem. But if you are willing to give up some ownership interest, if you are short of cash at the start-up phase, and if you have confidence in the attorney's judgment, payment in stock may be an advantage.

Principle 5: Consider Alternatives to Litigation

There are many ways to resolve disputes before you reach the courtroom. These practical techniques conserve management time, often produce better results, and cost less than litigation. Always consider these alternatives, discussed in the next chapter.

TIPS FOR KEEPING COUNSEL REINED IN

These other tips will help you control legal fees:

1. Don't be intimidated by "prestigious" law firms. Remember, no matter how well known a lawyer may be, he is still working for you and you are paying the bill. Prestigious firms can bend more than they would lead you to believe. If you're not happy, find someone else.

2. The quality of legal work is not necessarily a function of a law firm's size or its geographical location. If you are not happy with a big firm, try smaller specialized firms. One corporate giant, FMC Corporation, reports that it has saved hundreds of thousands of dollars by using many small firms rather than one large one.[13] Furthermore, top-quality firms—large and small—are found throughout the country and are not limited to places such as New York, Chicago, and Los Angeles.

3. Be alert to the "Law Review Syndrome." When rendering a legal opinion, some firms will spend hours researching trivia; then they will polish and rewrite memoranda through seven or eight drafts. It is not usually necessary to dot every "i" and cross every "t" in internal memos. On matters that are not vital to the company, require the firm to provide you with a draft of the memo or put a cap on the amount of money you're willing to spend.

4. Does a memo already exist? When requesting advice that requires legal research, ask if the firm has already researched the matter and if the memo is in the firm's files. Of course, legal ethics prevents the lawyer from giving you a copy of a memo written for another client, but its existence should reduce research costs.

5. Be prudent when changing attorneys. By all means, change lawyers if you are unhappy, but don't continually jump around: you will have to re-educate each new lawyer.

6. Maintain leverage over your lawyer. Convince the lawyer that you are important to him and his business; he will give you better service. If you are not a big client in dollar terms, convince him you're important in other ways such as your future billings; your contacts, reputation, and references in the community; or as a toehold for him in your new, growing industry or business.

---

[13]*National Law Journal*, Oct. 27, 1980, p. 1.

7. For complex matters, use law firm partners rather than associates. Many businessmen think they can save money by getting legal advice from the cheapest law firm associate. But think how many hours it takes for a $60 per hour associate to research a problem and give you an answer. Often it's cheaper to use a partner who bills at a higher rate but who may be able to provide the advice with little or no research.

8. Be alert to price differentials for good results. Some firms will charge a premium above their hourly rate if they win the case or get another good result for you. Pin this down in your retainer agreement.

9. Conduct yearly evaluations of attorney performance and the attorney-company relationship. Take the time to talk with your lawyer, to review how well things went, and if necessary to institute reforms for the next year.

10. Draft documents in-house. You can save money by preparing drafts of some papers and sending them to your lawyer for rewriting.

11. Consolidate issues for discussion. Don't call your lawyer if you have only one question. Unless they are urgent, save your questions so you can review several matters at one time.

12. Use telephone calls whenever possible. Personal conferences with attorneys inevitably last longer than telephone calls. You will be charged for this luxury.

13. Stay informed of new developments in your industry. Your lawyer may be willing to keep you up to date for free. With this knowledge you can often avoid legal and business problems.

14. Charge legal fees to the appropriate operating division, not the legal department generally. This technique is advocated by many business executives, but it's a two-edged sword. It does have the effect of reducing legal fees because it puts pressure on the division manager; but a timid, insecure, or fearful manager may be afraid to incur any legal expenses even for pressing legal matters. Use this technique only if you have strong division managers.

15. Tell your lawyer the nature of the legal risks you are prepared to assume. Executives take business risks every day and they should be prepared to do the same when it comes to the law. Some lawyers fail to understand this, as well as the concept of declining marginal returns—that you pay a great deal for that last measure of legal protection.

16. Don't be a Legal Middleman. Sometimes, companies must pay legal fees but have no control over expenditures. For example, companies making use of industrial revenue bonds must use and pay for the services of the bond counsel retained by the municipality. These companies have no control over their legal fees. Avoid these situations or reach an understanding (in this case with the municipality) that you want an itemized bill.

ARE YOU SPENDING TOO MUCH FOR LEGAL SERVICES?

Monitor your legal expenditures as carefully as you do all other corporate expenses. The yearly review of attorney performance should include a scrutiny of legal fees. It is hard to know if you are paying too much, but here are some guidelines.

First, go through the Five Principles of Legal Cost Control and the Tips for Keeping Counsel Reined In to see how your attorney measures up.

Second, compare your legal overhead with companies comparable in size or line of business. If you are a member of an industry trade association, see if it has data on legal expenditures. Ask business associates, friends, or your accountant for their experience.

Finally, you can look for the results of surveys occasionally conducted by universities or business magazines. In June of 1982, for example, *Inc.* magazine published the results of its readership survey on legal services. The survey reported average annual legal fees for companies up to $25 million in size.

Remember that the "reasonableness" of the fees you pay will be a function of many unique factors such as the maturity of your business, the amount of government regulation of it, the role you have assigned your lawyer, the products you make, the services you demand, the kind of lawyers you hire, and the risks you take.

ARE YOU READY FOR IN-HOUSE COUNSEL?

It may surprise you to learn that companies as small as $30 million in sales can save money by hiring their own company lawyer. In-house counsel can be cheaper than retained lawyers and they offer other intangible benefits.

Economics will no doubt control your decision. According to estimates by the *Wall Street Journal*, in-house lawyers cost 35 to 50 percent less than retained counsel.[14] In fact, the average hourly cost of in-house counsel is approximately $41 per hour but outside counsel is $79 per hour.[15] (Hourly rates for outside counsel typically range from $60 to $250 for partners, and $35 to $125 for associates.)

The economics of lawyering is such that small companies (those with less than $100 million in sales) often can hire a general counsel for $50,000 to $80,000 per year. Adding 20 percent for fringe benefits and 50 percent for overhead, total corporate cost will come to $85,000 to $136,000.

---

[14]*Wall Street Journal*, March 1, 1982, p. 25. Reprinted by permission, Dow Jones and Co., © 1982.

[15]Stichnoth and Dolan, "Management Strategies for the Corporate Counsel," *Legal Economics*, Jan.–Feb., 1982.

You are ready to hire an in-house lawyer if your annual legal fees (generally excluding litigation) are within 25 percent of these total corporate costs. Next year you are likely to need more legal help (because of the company's growth and the increasing complexity of commercial and regulatory matters) and legal salaries will have risen in the interim. Also, the early addition of a lawyer to the management team gives him a deeper understanding of the company and its problems *before* a crisis develops. A versatile lawyer can be assigned nonlegal matters as well. In short, your first in-house lawyer is more an investment in the future; you may not get dramatic, immediate savings.

There are intangible benefits in having the company lawyer next door rather than miles away:

1. You don't need to reexplain the business to an outside lawyer every time a new matter comes up.

2. There is little educational downtime. In-house lawyers are more familiar with your company and the industry and are therefore economically more efficient.

3. In-house lawyers are accessible, can deliver the legal product when needed, and are not distracted from the needs of other clients.

4. In-house lawyers become part of the corporate team with attendant benefits such as esprit de corps and dedication to corporate goals.

5. In-house lawyers may be better at anticipating the company's legal problems and suggesting regulatory and legal initiatives to achieve corporate goals.

6. In-house lawyers generally have a bigger financial and psychological investment in the company's success.

7. Corporate legal costs can be more easily controlled.

8. Responses of an in-house lawyer tend to be more consistent and predictable than responses elicited from several outside lawyers.

Smart corporate consumers of legal services receive high quality legal advice at a fair price. These companies understand the Three Realities of Law and Business and know what they have a right to expect from a lawyer. They also choose lawyers who are personally compatible, exercise good judgment, are well prepared, have technical expertise, provide prompt service, and charge reasonable fees. Legal costs can be contained by following the Five Principles of Legal Cost Control and the Tips for Keeping Counsel Reined In.

Remember, the real value in selecting and using the right lawyer is in getting the best advice for a fair price at the right time so you can avoid problems that may be more costly to solve later. Money spent on the right lawyer can be among your best company investments.

2. How to Resolve Disputes Out of Court: The Practical Techniques and Benefits

by PAUL A. ALLEN

As a litigant, I should dread a lawsuit beyond almost anything short of sickness or death.

—Judge Learned Hand (1872–1961)

The Judge's fear is widely shared by sage and prudent businessmen and women. Disputes are inevitable between and within companies, and society's forum for resolving them is the courtroom. Or is it? Are the courts the only institution?

Companies hard pressed by the high cost of litigation and the endless delays in getting *any* decision are demanding new ways to solve commercial disputes. In this chapter you will learn:

- Six techniques for resolving disputes out of court;
- How these techniques can save time and money; and
- Ten questions to answer when deciding which, if any, technique to use.

THE ADR TECHNIQUES

The courts are always available for the particularly intractable dispute or the one that strikes at the very heart of your business. But for many disputes, there are other methods, and if you know what they are and how to use them you will see that the courts are merely one weapon in a large and diverse arsenal. A lawsuit should never be the first volley; it should be a second generation weapon used only if your goals cannot be met in another way.

These legal weapons are termed "ADR"—Alternate Methods of Dispute Resolution. ADR is a voluntary technique for conclusively resolving disputes out of court. While we discuss six techniques in this chapter, there are truly an infinite number because an ADR can and should be custom tailored to fit the dispute and the parties to it.

ADR is best understood as an infinite number of techniques resting on a continuum. As one moves from left to right on the continuum, the ADR is increasingly complex, more formal and structured, more time consuming and costly, and increasingly dependent upon persons other than the two business contestants.

At the far left end of the continuum is negotiation, which is flexible, unstructured, and involves the fewest problem solvers (just the two businessmen). By contrast, litigation at the far right end is a complex, formalistic, rigid, time consuming, and costly method for resolving business disputes and one whose principal "problem solvers" are agents or neutrals—lawyers and judges. The point is simply this: Based on the selected models we discuss in this chapter, you can devise your own dispute resolution method. The particular one devised should be a function of facts such as the nature of the dispute, the relationship among the contestants, the companies' financial resources, and the importance of a prompt solution.

The six models are:

1. Negotiation and Settlement
2. Neutral Facilitator
3. Neutral Substantive Expert
4. Trial by Management
5. Arbitration
6. Private Judging

SOME ADVANTAGES OF AN ADR

While each ADR is unique, as a class they have characteristics that set them apart from traditional litigation. These traits often make an ADR a better choice than the courtroom for resolving company disputes. As we identify these characteristics below, ask yourself how important each one was to the last serious dispute your company had, either with another company or with an employee.

1. ADR Deals with the Real Issue

A characteristic of most ADRs is that the businessmen, not the courts, devise the solution to the problem. This means that everyone devotes their full energy to the business dispute and not, as in litigation, to the "sport of lawyering"—the procedural motions, hearings, depositions, interrogatories, and pre-trial conferences.

2. ADR Offers Greater Expertise

The problem-solvers with ADR are the real experts, the businessmen or sometimes company-selected third parties, not the judges or lawyers who may be ignorant of the technical aspects of the dispute. With complex business arrangements or sophisticated engineering matters, it is often better to have the dispute resolved by the people who have the requisite working knowledge.

3. ADR Is Flexible

Judges can't devise unconventional, creative solutions to commercial disputes; the narrow dictates of the law, the spectre of appellate review, and other institutional barriers simply prevent it. Judges must limit themselves to finding the facts and applying the law. But in the give and take of most ADR problem solving, you can make trade-offs, decide for yourself what's important and what isn't, and fashion creative solutions to the problem. In short, ADR is flexible on two counts: in the choice of problem-solving method and in the crafting of the solution itself.

4. ADR Is Cheaper and Faster

ADR is generally cheaper than the courtroom, often enormously so, because it is so much faster. You set your own schedule and need not worry about the judge's. Your energies are devoted to the real issue, not the legal and procedural technicalities. You don't have to rely on lawyers as much, and that can save money.

5. ADR Solutions May Be Better

Because an ADR solution is a creation of the business antagonists, its legitimacy is unquestioned by either side; it is probably more sensible, creative, credible, and authoritative than a judicial pronouncement. By contrast, court decisions are often appealed, partly because the losing side has truly "lost." Psychologists and game theorists say that the courtroom is a classic "win-lose" or zero-sum game; your loss is the other fellow's gain. On the other hand, in most ADR resolutions, *both* parties gain ("win-win") because *both* must accept the outcome. If one side does not benefit in some way, why would he agree to the solution? And as we have seen, both sides can "win" because they make trade-offs during the problem-solving process.

6. ADR Is Confidential

Court proceedings and all the legal "discovery" (the motions, depositions, and interrogatory answers) are invariably public. But an ADR is confidential; only you and your antagonist know the facts and the outcome. Sometimes this can have a positive bottom-line effect, as in a trade secret dispute with an employee. A public airing of that matter might make available to your competitors your own valuable proprietary information. ADR also allows you to resolve a problem without setting a public precedent, a useful way to retain flexibility in responding to similar problems in the future.

7. ADR and Business Strategy

Court battles should always be conducted with attention to the company's goals and overall business strategy. But litigation often takes on a life of its own; with platoons of lawyers, experts, and judges milling about the front, the legal war can continue without purpose or plan.

By contrast, business considerations dominate the ADR process because there is only one goal and it is a dollars and cents commercial one: to resolve the dispute conclusively in a way that is consistent with the company's business strategy. The problem-solving process is not saddled with the heavy procedural baggage of the courtroom. The result is likely to be a better quality solution for both sides.

SIX SELECTED ADR TECHNIQUES

Discourage litigation. Persuade your neighbors to compromise whenever you can. Point out to them how the nominal winner is often a real loser—in fees, expenses, and waste of time.

—Abraham Lincoln

Any of these six ADRs make a good model for precise tailoring to your particular dispute.

1. Negotiation and Settlement

There is a paradox about negotiation and settlement: it's an obvious, prudent, and cunning first step, yet it sometimes is not thought of and used when a serious commercial dispute first arises. Perhaps this is due to the popular misconception that the first person to suggest it or another non-litigation technique has the weaker case, limited financial resources, greater legal exposure, or a paralyzing fear of battle. But a desire to negotiate and settle may mean you are the smarter contestant, not necessarily the weaker one.

Negotiation is essentially a bargaining process between the business contestants. It is especially effective in a commercial context, when the parties have dealt with each other before, when the number of participants is limited (it's tough to negotiate a settlement among ten companies), and when what's at stake is not a matter of fundamental value to anyone.

Negotiation tends to go much faster and to produce better results when it is not, as the game theorists would say, a zero-sum game; that is, where one side's loss is the other's gain. Put another way, if each side can win something, if both can benefit in some way, then negotiation is likely to succeed. But if there is one totally dominant party, if in short there is no "countervailing power," trade-offs are not possible and there will probably be a stalemate.

In recent years there have been hundreds of seminars given and many books written on negotiating skills and theories. (The book by Fisher and Ury, *Getting to Yes: Negotiating Agreement Without Giving In* is particularly readable.) Since this chapter is designed only to inform you of out-of-court options, we will not discuss negotiating techniques. But remember that negotiation and early settlement should be a part of your early strategy for resolving disputes and that you should discuss it at the earliest possible time with your attorney. Keep these other tips in mind:

- Consider putting a clause in your contracts requiring both sides to engage in one month (or another time period) of good faith negotiation before a lawsuit is filed. You can also require that the two executives who made the contract in the first place be the subsequent negotiators in the event of a dispute.

- If negotiation is not provided for by contract, think through (preferably with your lawyer) who will initiate the negotiations and how they will be conducted. While a willingness to negotiate is not necessarily a sign of weakness, an early tactical blunder can do serious damage.

- Work out with your lawyer in advance your overall strategy. Evaluate the dispute according to the issues identified on page 50.

- Try to get an idea of the costs, in dollars and lost management time, of not settling through negotiation. How important is the existing relationship (if any) with the other side?

Above all, recognize that lawyers resolve 90 percent of their cases through negotiation and settlement. As one corporate general counsel said, "like in horseshoes and hand grenades, close is often good enough."

2. Use of a Neutral Facilitator or Mediator

This technique is somewhat more complicated than pure negotiation. Its essential feature is the introduction into the negotiation and settlement process of a neutral party—a facilitator or mediator—whose job is to accelerate the negotiations. When the two-party negotiations stall or break down a facilitator can keep the dialogue going. The business contestants still make the decisions, but the facilitators speed up the process by identifying the parties' goals and interests, not particular solutions.

Negotiations often bog down in debates over "solutions"; particularly because one side's solution (take back these defective machines) flatly precludes the other side's solution (I will repair them in two weeks). But a facilitator or mediator focuses, not on each side's proposed *solution* to the problem, but on the *process* of trying to reach agreement. By improving the process there is a greater probability of success. The facilitator does this by:

- Managing or stroking the key participants;
- Isolating the interests and values of each side; determining, in short, what's really important, not what each side says is important; and
- Keeping the parties' emotions and efforts focused on solving the problem, not on posturing.

Note that the mediator is exactly what the name implies; he has no power to force the parties to do anything or even (unless you confer it) the power to make a recommendation. As a former director of the Federal Mediation and Conciliation Service said, "the most important power that a mediator has is none at all."

Of course, the success of this technique is largely determined by the same facts as negotiation—the parties must be willing to make concessions, be in a position of some "power" over the other, and be willing to resolve the dispute short of the courthouse steps.

Mediation has long been used in labor negotiations; you can get similar help to resolve conventional commercial disputes. For example, part-time facilitators are available through universities and trade associations; private consultants (such as EnDispute in Washington, D.C.) can mediate or recommend another procedure; and some organizations mediate in particular industries (such as the National Academy of Conciliators in the construction industry). Of course, if you and the company with which you are wrangling can agree on a neutral third party, that's all it takes.

Warning: When you hire a facilitator, be sure to put the ground rules in writing. Spell out exactly what he can do, his powers and responsibilities. This will avoid a dispute about the dispute.

3. The Use of a Neutral Substantive Expert

Instead of hiring a facilitator, you may want to go further: with your business antagonist, hire an expert in the matter at issue (whether it's patents, chemical or electrical processes, or software) and have the expert investigate the facts and perhaps make a report as well. This "statement of the case" may be enough to break a negotiating impasse because it serves as the foundation for further discussions. You might also ask the expert to make a recommendation or propose a solution.

Suppose you have a dispute about the performance of your newly installed, several hundred thousand dollar central computer system. You have new hardware and software but it doesn't perform as warranted: it can't do the inventory, or it's too slow. If it's a technically complex matter, where there may be truth in each side's position, a neutral computer software expert may be able to investigate the matter, make a recommendation, and resolve it short of further legal wrangling or a court action. If the neutral is qualified and respected, his recommendation is likely to be accepted; if he was asked only to compile all the facts, that in itself may be a breakthrough for the parties often have a hard time agreeing on the basic facts in technically complex disputes.

As with the facilitator, be sure the neutral expert is operating under specific written instructions previously agreed to by both sides.

4. Trial by Management ("Mini-Trial")

If these informal processes do not resolve the dispute, there is a more sophisticated and complex procedure that still leaves the final decision in the hands of the business contestants: Trial by Management or the Mini-Trial. It is an out-of-court, nonbinding, voluntary, and confidential method of dispute resolution, but its more formal procedures allow for a full airing of the dispute. Its essential features are:

- Full but informal presentation of the issues and each side's version of the facts at an "Information Exchange."
- The information exchange takes place before a panel composed of one executive from each side. The executive must have the authority to resolve the dispute—that is, to bind the company.
- If there is a third member of the panel, he is a neutral party whose role is not to decide the case but to preside at the information exchange.

It is important to recognize that the two persons (the business antagonists) or three persons (those two plus a neutral) on the panel do not actually render a decision as would a panel of judges or arbitrators. Instead, after the informal presentations and questioning by both sides (the "trial"), the parties attempt to work out a voluntary settlement.

There are several reasons why this approach can succeed even after previous negotiations have failed. The top-level executives see, perhaps for the first time, all the chinks in their own armor as well as the strength of their opponent's case; the actual decision-makers (not just their lawyers) meet face to face with a common foundation of facts on which to negotiate; and the issues are narrowed so there is a dialogue on the merits, not on legal technicalities.

A mini-trial usually makes sense only when the dollars at stake are substantial; in fact, that is when it has been most often used. One of the first and now best known examples was a patent infringement case between TRW, Inc. and Telecredit, Inc. Both companies had been involved in the development of computerized check verification systems. After three years of litigation and several hundred thousand dollars in legal fees, the case went to the mini-trial format. The information exchange took two days, but when management met at the end of the exchange they resolved the dispute in 30 minutes.

More recently, TRW again used the mini-trial, this time in a dispute with NASA but without a neutral adviser. TRW was the subcontractor on a special satellite system carried by the space shuttle and to be used for both military and commercial purposes. A dispute arose about a NASA requirement that the system remain operational if one satellite went out of orbit. In TRW's view, the requirement was not in the original specifications; to add it would cost another $26 million, and tens of millions more were at stake if the project was further delayed.

A "trial by management" involved the decision-makers as well as technical experts. The head of the Goddard Space Flight Center, the Deputy Administrator of NASA, and the responsible TRW division vice president participated. The dispute was settled within one day.

The Role of the Neutral Adviser. At the information exchange, the neutral adviser can ask questions designed to display the strengths and weaknesses of each side's case. The adviser would not initially participate with the company executives at their post-exchange conference, but if they could not immediately work out a settlement, the neutral might be asked for his view of how a judge or jury would decide the case. For this reason, the neutral is usually a lawyer; but he might also be a technical expert if that seemed more appropriate.

The Information Exchange. As our examples illustrate, the information exchange or informal hearing is just that—informal. It is usually quite short, ranging from only two hours to two days. Each side makes a presentation, perhaps involving the executives or other company personnel who have expertise in the matter. Questioning is allowed, but courtroom rules of evidence do not apply.

Preparation Is Essential. If the information exchange is to succeed, each side must be prepared. Ideally, the contestants will have exchanged papers setting out their position. Furthermore, the entire procedure must be spelled out in a written agreement among the parties. It should address such issues as the documents to be exchanged, the company personnel who will be involved, the deadlines and time schedule, and the authority of the neutral.

The mini-trial is not for all companies or all disputes. You surely would not set one up where the issue is insignificant or the financial stake small. It is likely to be most effective where the dispute is a relatively sophisticated one and where the two sides have a good working relationship or at least they see the advantage of promptly resolving the matter.

5. Arbitration

This is a well-known ADR. A federal statute authorizes the enforcement of arbitration awards and permits the arbitrator to exercise judge-like authority to obtain documents important to the case. Furthermore, many states now have "court annexed" arbitration—arbitration of small claims (usually up to $25,000) under the general supervision of the court. Compared to litigation, these court-approved arbitration procedures require as little as one-fifth of the hearing time and they cost about one-half as much in attorneys' fees. And if the experience of the District of Columbia and California is any indication, very few of these arbitration decisions are later challenged in court. Of course, you can fashion your own arbitration procedure if you and your opponent can agree on arbitrators and procedures.

Warning: There are two essential differences between arbitration and the four techniques previously discussed: in the former, you no longer make the decision, and the decision itself is binding. *First*, an arbitrator (not the two parties) decides the issue and he often "splits the difference" between the positions. The solution is not based on each side's trade-offs; instead, it may literally be one-half of what each wants. *Second*, an arbitration is binding on both sides and, except in extraordinary situations, it cannot be changed by a judge. But the previous four techniques are not binding; that is, the parties need not agree on anything if they don't want to.

In short, arbitration tends not to be as creative or ultimately as satisfying to both sides as the four voluntary techniques. Nevertheless, it has marked advantages over litigation.

6. Private Judging

Private judging is analogous to arbitration by one person, although with even more legal trappings. Several states, including New York and California, have statutes that permit the parties to have their case, or any particular issues in it, resolved by a court-appointed referee whom they select. The referee hears the case, decides the issues, and the findings become the court's judgment.

The advantages of this procedure are its low cost (compared to a full-blown trial), speed, the parties' freedom to select their own decision-maker, convenience (the parties and referee set the schedule, not the court), and privacy (less is exposed in court files). But as with arbitration, private judging is binding on the parties and the decision itself is made by someone other than the two business antagonists. Nevertheless, if the other techniques are not appropriate, private judging can save time and money and resolve a dispute more quickly than a conventional trial.

HOW TO DECIDE AMONG THE ADRs

These six techniques have one thing in common: they are alternatives to full-blown courtroom litigation. Some are innovative, others are traditional; some are components of our public justice system while others are not. How would you decide which technique to use and when to use it? The decision process is more art than science, and probably no one can tell you exactly which one is best at any one time. But here are ten questions to ask before you decide.[1]

1. What Kind of Dispute Is It?

There are two elements to this. First, is this mainly a dispute about facts or law? If it's mostly facts, an ADR may be better than a courtroom. If it's mostly a dispute about what the law is, only a judge can tell you that.

Second, what is the subject matter of this dispute? If it's a highly complex and technical issue, such as patent rights or computer software capability, it may be more suitable to out-of-court resolution. Judges apply the law to the facts; they cannot be technical experts on every issue that comes before them.

2. How Much Money Is Involved?

The answer to this question is important, but it doesn't automatically point to or away from the courtroom. If a lot of money is at stake, you want to win or at least come out with an acceptable settlement. The more money at stake, the greater the investment you should be prepared to make. This may mean litigation or a mini-trial is appropriate; you probably wouldn't use either one for a case worth very little.

3. How Strong Is Your Case?

If you are clearly right, you should have the upper hand with most ADRs as well as litigation, but arbitrators sometimes "split the difference" even when the

---

[1]This section of the chapter is based on an article the author wrote for *Inc.* magazine, August, 1982.

arguments are not equally strong. Where both sides have good arguments, the mini-trial, facilitators, and substantive experts can help you reach a fair solution.

4. Is There a Vital Corporate Issue at Stake?

You should not compromise on a vital corporate policy, such as the legality of your product distribution system, your patent rights that have been licensed to others, or the legality of your securities disclosures. In these cases, litigation may be the only prudent course.

5. What Is the Role of Precedent?

Do you want to set a public precedent on this issue? Assuming you win, you may want the world at large to know that "this is the way things will be." If you want the right to terminate your distributors or your employees under specified conditions, a court precedent will permit you to exercise these rights without further interference. But in answering this question, be sure to figure your odds of winning; the precedent will be set even if you lose.

6. What Is Your Relationship with the Other Side?

If your opponent is a long-time antagonist, you don't care if sparks fly during the courtroom battles. But if you have a disagreement with a valuable customer or supplier, you may not want to jeopardize the commercial relationship with litigation. In that event, the concilliatory out-of-court techniques are more appropriate.

7. How Flexible Is the Other Side?

If the antagonist is likely to be flexible, accommodating, and perceptive of the need to develop options and to work things out, negotiation (with or without experts) and the mini-trial should be good bets. But these techniques will not work with stubborn antagonists or those who are in the battle for reasons of pride.

8. Is Secrecy Important?

Except in unusual situations, all the records of a legal battle are open to the public. If the dispute is about something you don't want publicly aired—such as trade secrets or a seamy squabble with a top-level executive—try an ADR. (The first four alternate methods are more secret than the last two; some material may be made public even with private judging and arbitration.)

9. How Old Is the Dispute?

The negotiation technique can be used as soon as the dispute begins; but it may not be possible, or even wise, to call for a neutral substantive expert at the same time. First try to work things out without one. Mini-trials have generally been used after the parties have already spent large sums of money in legal fees or after the case has dragged on for months or years. You need not wait that long, but don't suggest a mini-trial the moment you receive the complaint letter; try negotiation first.

10. How Much Will Litigation Cost?

Try to measure litigation costs in both dollars and lost management time. Lawyers hate to be pinned down on this but try to get estimates, perhaps using different sets of assumptions, on likely legal fees and out-of-pocket costs. Also try to figure the amount and effect of lost management time. The other side may take many depositions of your company employees, file "interrogatories" your lawyers will have to answer with your assistance, and request that you turn over company files for their inspection. This takes managers away from running the company. How much will this cost you and for how long?

WHEN A DISPUTE BEGINS . . .

When a dispute begins, talk with your lawyer and together analyze your predicament to determine whether an ADR is appropriate. Even if you decide that the time is not yet right, periodically reevaluate the decision. Don't get bogged down in costly, time-consuming litigation simply because you have erroneously assumed there is no alternative. And don't let a lawyer's ignorance of ADRs force you into protracted litigation. Have him learn about the techniques or find someone else who can help you.

Keep in mind too that the six methods we have discussed are not rigid or finely prescribed. Flexibility is the watchword; each one is suitable in different situations and all but two (arbitration and private judging) can be designed in precisely the way you and the other side want.

WHY ADRs DON'T ALWAYS WORK

A fair question is, if ADRs are so good, why are they infrequently used? While ADRs are certainly much more common today than they were even two years ago, traditional litigation is still the most common method for resolving serious commercial disputes. But accurately measuring the popularity of all ADRs together, including negotiation, is like trying to determine how many cases of the flu are annually prevented with flu shots. We know when prevention fails and we can measure that failure with great precision—there are, after all, public records of lawsuits and influenza cases—but we rarely hear about the *absence* of litigation or disease. Furthermore, we are not always sure whether that absence is directly attributable to the preventive technique, be it an available ADR or flu shot, or an independent variable. In short, the question itself may be unfair; it may be that ADRs are used frequently but there *still* is a great deal of litigation.

A fairer question is, why aren't ADRs *more* frequently used? There are essentially two answers.

First, they are inappropriate techniques in resolving many commercial disputes. Despite the advantages of ADRs that we enumerated at the beginning of this chapter, there are often other, overriding considerations. Traditional litigation might be preferable for tactical reasons: a vital corporate policy may be at stake, settlement might encourage additional claims on the company, your opponent might be intractable or unrealistic, the matter at issue may not be susceptible to compromise at all, or the odds of prevailing may simply be greater by continuing to litigate. In short, the judgment of management and their lawyers may be that the company's interests are better served by using the court system.

An historical vignette illustrates the egregious case where one side sees litigation as its best strategy. The Roman general, Fabius Maximus, Cunctator (the Delayer) won most of his battles by adopting a curious strategy: he avoided them. Instead, he cunningly allowed his enemies to flail about and exhaust themselves through maneuvers that were designed to force the Cunctator to fight. His strategy gave birth to the term "cunctation"—the act of delaying. Today, lawyers and their prosperous (or profligate) clients occasionally use a similar strategy when they know that their resources are greater than their opponent's. The strategy calls for numerous delaying tactics consisting of court motions, depositions, legal briefs, hearings, and requests to turn over reams of documents. Like Fabius Maximus, the goal is to exhaust the opponent and avoid a final, decisive resolution of the matter.

While legal "cunctation" may be distasteful and while many lawyers would never adopt such a strategy, others have used it with great success. In sum, management and their counsel may decide, rightly or wrongly, that delay best serves the interests of the company and shareholders; in that event, prolonged litigation may be the choice over the swifter ADR.

There is a second reason why ADRs are not more frequently used: apart from questions of strategy, companies and their counsel may be reluctant to use an ADR because of ignorance, inertia, or the fear of taking a risk with a novel dispute resolution method such as the mini-trial. Recall that since the ADRs we have discussed require that both sides consent to their use, either side can force the dispute to court.

Litigation can be the product of a reasoned strategic decision or merely ignorance and inertia. But litigation is inevitably preceded by a serious dispute of some kind, and in the remaining chapters we show you how to avoid such disputes in the first place.

3. How to Organize the Business to Stay Out of Court

by HOWARD H. LEWIS

Poor business planning and short-sighted judgments at a company's birth cause hundreds of lawsuits every year. Understandably, it is the myriad business issues that consume the organizers of a new company, but this is no reason to slight the vital legal questions that must be answered at the same time. As you will see throughout this book, there is no fine line that separates "business" from "law" and the executive or lawyer who fails to understand this will endanger his company or client.

This chapter will tell you about the important legal and business decisions you must make at the inception of your company. You will learn:

- The pros and cons of each of the four types of business organization;
- How the corporate form of business can satisfy the investors' dual goals of money and power; and
- The basic steps in forming a corporation.

For most businessmen, the corporation is the best type of business enterprise. So, the second half of this chapter and all of the next describe corporate legal problems, particularly those that can cost a company a great deal of money or lost management time. The issues in these two chapters are at the corporate apex: they are the problems of managing relations among the company's owners (stockholders), directors, and officers. Other chapters in this book offer guidance for resolving problems at a different level in the firm, as with employees (chapter 7), financial institutions and the capital markets (chapters 10 and 12), and the Internal Revenue Service (chapter 11). Before we get that far, we will first look at the pros and cons of the four types of business enterprise.

HOW TO CHOOSE AMONG THE FOUR TYPES OF BUSINESS ENTERPRISE

The first question that must be answered by anyone planning to engage in a business is, what form should the enterprise take? There are basically four types: sole proprietorship, partnership, limited partnership, and corporation. The pros and cons of each are summarized in a chart on page 61.

Sole Proprietorship: Flexible but Risky

Advantages

1. *Maximum Flexibility.* A sole proprietorship is you doing business on your own. The business operates under your own name or a fictitious one (such as "Jones Used Cars") which must be registered with the state or states where you do business. Since you are on your own, you operate the business as you see fit.

2. *The Business Is Not Separately Taxed.* The financial success or failure of your business will be reflected on your individual state and federal tax returns.

3. *No Formalities of Operation.* There is no required paperwork: no minutebook, stock certificates, separate business returns, or reports.

Disadvantages

1. *No Limitation of Liability.* Since you and the company are one and the same, the business debts are your own personal debts. A sole proprietorship can't hide behind a corporate shield. (See the first Advantage under Corporations.)

2. *No Ability to Accumulate Assets in the Business.* Unlike a corporation, a sole proprietorship can't accumulate property or profits in the business without paying a premium in the form of higher personal taxes. Corporations are taxed at a lower rate than individuals so more money is available to plough back into the business. (See the second Advantage under Corporations.)

3. *Inability to Involve Others in Ownership or Funding of the Business.* Since the business is yours, everyone else is involved only as an employee; and since there aren't any shareholders or partners, your personal credit (which

includes the assets of the business) is the sole basis for raising money. This often shackles a company's growth.

4. *Inability to Take Advantage of Some Corporate Tax Benefits.* There are some tax deductions that are not available to individuals but are available to corporations. (Most of these are "fringe benefits.") In addition, the tax rates are higher for individuals (12–50 percent) than for corporations (16–46 percent).

Partnership: Flexible, Some Risk, but No Tax

A partnership is an association of two or more persons who carry on as co-owners of a business for profit. A partnership can exist without a formal agreement, though we don't advise you to operate that way.

Advantages

1. *No State or Federal Tax on the Business.* As in a sole proprietorship, the business of a partnership is not subject to a separate tax on income. Instead, each partner reports his pro rata share of income or loss on his own personal tax return. (The pro rata share is a function of the partner's percentage interest in the partnership. For example, each of four equal partners is entitled to 25 percent of partnership profits.) The partnership must file a federal information return and it may be required to file a return under the laws of some states, but the partnership doesn't pay a tax because the income "passes through" to each partner.

Warning: Although the principle seems simple, the tax laws for large sophisticated business partnerships are more complex than they are for corporations. This is particularly true for such matters as depreciation recapture and investment tax credits. Be sure to seek professional help for such returns.

2. *Flexibility and Lack of Formality.* There are few formal requirements for setting up or operating a partnership. Exceptions include the registration of the partnership name as a "fictitious name" and the filing of informational tax returns. Most states have adopted the Uniform Partnership Act (UPA), which sets general legal standards for partnership affairs. Unlike corporate laws, it does not lay down detailed rules for conducting the business, but it does establish a "fiduciary relationship" among partners. This is the highest standard there is in the law, and it means that a partner must act for the whole partnership's benefit, not his own. This standard cannot be changed by the partnership agreement although many other provisions in the UPA can be.

3. *Ability to Involve Others in the Business.* A partnership differs from a sole proprietorship in that others (the partners) share in the risks and rewards. This means a partnership has more than one source of additional capital.

Disadvantages

1. *No Limitation of Liability.* Each partner is individually liable for all the debts of the partnership, not just his proportionate share. (A partner with only a

10 percent interest in the partnership, for example, is still liable for 100 percent of its debts.) This risk can be minimized to some extent by the purchase of insurance but it cannot be entirely eliminated.

2. *The Necessity of Self-Government.* Although partnerships are operationally more flexible and less formal than corporations, this is not an unmixed blessing. It means the partners must write their own rules in the partnership agreement. That document typically addresses such issues as the term of the partnership; how to protect the other partners from the attachment of one partner's interest in the event of divorce, death, bankruptcy or other creditor proceeding; how to expel a partner; and how to provide for a partner's retirement or withdrawal from the partnership. While some of these matters are also common to corporations, they frequently are harder to resolve in a partnership because the rules are made by the partnership, not set down in statutes. Sometimes partnerships discover to their chagrin that everyone failed to anticipate a particular issue so the rules must be cobbled on the spot.

3. *Inability to Accumulate Assets.* Partnerships are treated less favorably than corporations when they accumulate property and profits. Partners, as individuals, pay taxes because the partnership's income passes through to them. Partnerships also have somewhat less flexibility in disposing of their assets.

4. *Inability to Take Advantage of Other Tax Benefits.* Partnerships can't take certain business deductions available to corporations and as we mentioned are subject to higher tax rates.

Limited Partnership: Just an Investment Device

The distinguishing features of a limited partnership are twofold: unless provided otherwise by contract, the liability of at least one of the partners (the Limited Partner) is limited to the amount of money he has contributed, and the limited partner cannot participate in the management of the business. By contrast, at least one of the other partners (the General Partner) is liable for all the partnership debts and he participates in the management of the partnership. Most states have adopted a version of the Uniform Limited Partnership Act that governs these enterprises. In practice, a limited partner is often an investor while the general partner operates the business. In fact, the best known limited partnerships are tax shelters or fund-raising entities with interests in real estate and oil drilling.

Advantages

1. *Partial Limited Liability.* As stated, the limited partner's liability for partnership debts is limited to the amount of his investment.

2. *Other Advantages.* The other advantages to this form of organization are the same as for general partnerships.

Disadvantages

1. *Greater Formality Required.* Unlike a general partnership, a limited partnership cannot be created simply by an oral or written agreement among the partners. Virtually all states require that the limited partnership agreement or a declaration of limited partnership or both be filed with the Secretary of State or the Corporation Bureau of the state in which the business is located. The limited liability of the limited partners generally is not available without such a filing.

2. *Other Disadvantages.* The other disadvantages of this form of organization are the same as for general partnerships.

Corporation: Low-Risk and Versatile

Most readers are probably familiar with the corporate form of business enterprise. It is surely the most common one today, and for most businesses it offers non-tax and tax advantages over the most likely alternative, the partnership.

Advantages

1. *Limitation of Liability.* If the corporation is properly formed and operated (see the next chapter), the shareholders will not be liable for the general debts of the corporation, only for the amount of their investment. This is the well-known "corporate shield."

Warning: This advantage will not be available if the shareholders abuse the corporate form. See "Limiting Shareholder Liability," chapter 4, p. 78. There is another wrinkle as well: banks and other financial institutions often require shareholder guarantees before they will loan money to small corporations. This removes the corporate shield for those loans because the shareholder is personally liable for the debt. See "Guaranty," chapter 10, p. 203. However, even if they have given a personal guarantee, the shareholders will still be shielded from the company's ordinary trade creditors.

2. *Financing and Accommodating Diverse Interests.* It is far easier to obtain external financing as a corporation than as a partnership. Along with limited liability, this is the preeminent reason for choosing the corporate form. Corporations are generally exempt from the usury laws; they can always get loans if they are willing to pay the price.

More importantly, the corporation is a versatile structure that can accommodate businessmen with diverse objectives—passive investors who contribute only capital, the "idea people" who devised the business plan, and the implementers who will devote their lives to the business and be compensated immediately with salary and bonuses. This versatility breeds a strong, dynamic company. It's all accomplished through the sale of different kinds of stock (such as common, nonvoting common, and preferred) and the creative use of other legal devices we discuss beginning on page 64.

3. *Centralized Management.* For all but the smallest and most specialized businesses, the corporate form has several management advantages over the partnership. Corporate management is centralized in a Board of Directors that acts for and binds the company. By contrast, general partners in a partnership have equal rights in the management and conduct of the partnership's business. This can produce intolerable delays in decision making. Conversely, any one partner can bind the partnership (for example, by signing a lease) but a shareholder can't do that for a corporation. Finally, lines of authority are much clearer in a corporation than in a partnership.

4. *Transferable Interests.* Corporate interests are easy to transfer but partnership interests are not: generally you can sell stock, but you can't transfer your interest in a partnership unless the other partners agree. Of course, there may not be a market for shares in a small, closely held company, but this problem should be anticipated with a stock redemption agreement (which requires the corporation to buy back the stock) or a cross-purchase plan (which requires the shareholders to do likewise). These devices are discussed further below. Not surprisingly, the relative ease with which stock can be transferred, as well as the market for it, is one of the features that attracts investors to corporations.

5. *Continued Life.* A corporation is said to have a "perpetual" existence; that is, the death or withdrawal of a shareholder will not legally terminate the corporation. By contrast, when a general partner dies, withdraws, or goes bankrupt the partnership technically dissolves. Usually this is not as bad as it sounds, but it has the potential for creating serious mischief.

6. *Tax Advantages.* Besides these operational benefits, there are some tax advantages that corporations alone enjoy. While these can be significant, the nontax considerations are probably more important in selecting among the four types of business enterprise. See chapter 11 for a detailed discussion of the most common corporate tax problems.

As noted before, corporate tax rates are somewhat lower than individual rates. This means a corporation can retain a modest amount of earnings (up to $100,000, for example) while paying a low tax on it. (For 1982 the company would pay 16% on the first $25,000 in net taxable income, 19% on the next $25,000, 30% on the next, and 40% on the last $25,000. The rate is 46% for income over $100,000. In 1983 the rates are 15%, 18%, 30%, 40%, 46%.)

Until recently, a corporation enjoyed many tax advantages in the operation of its pension or retirement plan. But the Tax Equity and Fiscal Responsibility Act of 1982 reduced (for the 1983 tax year) and eliminated (for tax year 1984 and later) most of them. Nevertheless, other advantages remain, including the ability to deduct as corporate expenses wages, salaries, and such health-related items as medical disability and group term life insurance; and to accumulate property or profits in the corporation subject to the lower corporate tax rates. The property or profits can later be enjoyed at the lower capital gain rates if the business is sold to another company or to the public in a secondary stock offering. *Warning:* There are limits on the amount of money that can be accumulated in this manner without the imposition of penalty taxes.

When to Go "Sub S." There is another tax advantage available to small corporations only, "Subchapter S" status. The Internal Revenue Code permits qualifying corporations to elect special tax treatment: no tax on the corporation itself. Instead, corporate income and losses (to the extent of one's investment) "pass through" to the shareholders just as they do to the partners in a partnership. All other features of the corporate form are retained. Sub S status is particularly attractive when the stockholders have high incomes and expect the company to incur large losses in its early years; the company losses become personal deductions of the stockholders. It is also used to allocate corporate income to low-income family members who get corporate profits that would otherwise be taxed at higher rates. But the IRS scrutinizes transactions of this nature.

You should evaluate Sub S status at the inception of the corporation because the Internal Revenue Code permits it on certain conditions only. There can be only one class of stock and no more than 35 shareholders. There are special rules on the time when an election of Sub S treatment must be made, and in some cases there are limits on the amount of allowable passive investment income (from royalties, rents, dividends, etc.). Under the right circumstances, Sub S status can offer the advantages of both a partnership and a corporation.

Disadvantages

1. *Double Taxation and How to Avoid It.* As we have seen, the Internal Revenue Code imposes a tax on the income of a corporation. But there is a second tax as well. If that after-tax income is then distributed to the shareholders as a dividend, the shareholders as individual taxpayers must pay tax on the money because it is part of their income. In effect, the corporate income is taxed twice. But there are ways to mitigate the effects of this double tax.

First, since a corporation may deduct salaries as a business expense, it could try to distribute corporate income to the shareholders in the form of salaries. *Warning:* If the salaries aren't "reasonable," the IRS treats them as dividends ("constructive dividends"). See page 212 of chapter 11 for a full discussion of this problem. Second, a Sub S corporation avoids the constructive dividend problem because it does not pay any tax on its corporate income. Finally, a shareholder can receive payments in other forms and some of these are deductible by the corporation. Examples: rent payments on property the shareholder leases to the company and interest on funds loaned to it. *Warning:* The corporation must receive fair consideration in such arrangements or there will be a "constructive dividend," a term explained in chapter 11.

2. *Formalities and Paper Work.* A corporation is burdened with many formalities unknown to partnerships, such as shareholder and board of directors' meetings; requirements for books, records, and board of directors' resolutions; and restrictions on the sale and issuance of stock. For these and other reasons, it is much more cumbersome to allocate profits and losses in a corporation than in a partnership. These formalities must be observed or the shareholders and directors will lose the protection of the corporate shield.

This Scorecard summarizes the pros and cons of each business enterprise we have discussed.

BUSINESS ENTERPRISE SCORECARD

Sole Proprietorship

Pros	Cons
—maximum flexibility	—no limits on liability
—no operational formalities	—tax disadvantage to asset accumulation
	—can't involve others in funding or ownership
	—no corporate tax benefits

Partnership

Pros	Cons
—few operational formalities	—no limits on liability
—others involved in business	—cumbersome self-government
	—can't accumulate assets
	—few business deductions

Limited Partnership

Pros	Cons
—partial limited liability	—generally an investment vehicle only
—see other partnership advantages	—more formalities than partnership

Corporations

Pros	Cons
—limited liability	—double taxation for dividends
—accommodates diverse ownership interests	—formalities and paper work
—easier to raise money	
—centralized management	
—transferable interests	
—perpetual life	
—tax deductions and lower rates	

Which Form Is Best?

The answer to that question turns on such facts as the nature of your business, your financial needs, and the number of business colleagues you have. A sole proprietorship is simply you conducting the business in the same legal sense as you do the rest of your affairs. A partnership is so particular and individual as to preclude generalization. Limited partnerships are specialized and uncommon; they usually are designed to generate tax losses as oil and gas syndications, real estate ventures, and equipment leasing operations.

While there is no "best" for all purposes, most readers of this book will opt for the straight corporation or its Sub S cousin because the advantages are many and the disadvantages few.

HOW TO FORM A CORPORATION

Suppose you have evaluated the four basic forms of business enterprise and concluded that a corporation is best. What's next?

Since a corporation is a creature of state law, you must comply with the pertinent statutory requirements in your state. If you don't, you run the risk that later a disgruntled shareholder or creditor will sue you *personally* on the ground that the corporation was never legitimately formed; in effect, that the corporation never existed. If you lose the suit, you will also lose all corporate advantages including lower tax rates and limited liability.

The first three steps to take when forming a corporation are to select and reserve a corporate name; file articles of incorporation; and convene the initial meetings of incorporator(s), shareholder(s) and director(s).

1. Select and Reserve a Distinctive Corporate Name

Your first step is to decide what you would like to call your corporation. The name you select must end with a word such as "Incorporated," "Company,"

"Limited," "Corporation," or their abbreviations, "Inc.," "Co.," "Ltd.," or "Corp." These tell the public that it is dealing with a business with limited liability. If a term of incorporation is not included in the name, you stand a good chance of losing the benefit of limited liability in the event of a lawsuit by a trade creditor.

After you have decided what you would like to call your company, the next step is to determine whether you can legally use the chosen name in the state where you want to incorporate. The Corporation Bureau in every state maintains lists of names of companies that have been incorporated in their state; most also have names of companies incorporated elsewhere but registered to do business in the state. These lists must be checked because a state will not allow two companies with identical corporate names to operate in its jurisdiction. Often a telephone call or a short letter, perhaps with a nominal fee, will enable you to find out if the name you chose is available.

Certain names are traditionally associated with a particular business, such as "fidelity" and "fiduciary" for a bank or a common first name ("Frank's _____") for a small service establishment. Try to avoid such commonplace names: a distinctive name is a valuable marketing tool and its selection should be made with great care. The more unique the name, the less likely it is to have been previously registered, either in the state where you incorporate or in other states where you later conduct business. There is yet another reason for choosing a distinctive name: you will avoid lawsuits by creditors or others who have disputes, not with you, but with a company whose name is identical or similar to yours. For a more extensive discussion of trade names and how to select them, see our discussion in chapter 8.

2. Select a State of Incorporation

Most companies incorporate in the state where their business operations are located. But some find it desirable to incorporate in a different state because of an apparently favorable law or tax ruling. In the past, Delaware was the chosen state of incorporation for many firms even though they had no substantial operations there. This is less true today. Your lawyer can advise you whether it makes sense to incorporate outside your own state.

Warning: If your firm conducts business beyond the boundaries of the state where it is incorporated, it must be "registered to do business" in those other states. If it fails to do so, the shareholders can be personally liable for the company's acts. See "Qualifying to Do Business" in the next chapter.

3. File the Necessary Forms

After you have selected and reserved a corporate name and chosen the state of incorporation, you must file "articles of incorporation" with the state's Department of State, Corporation Bureau, or similar office. This is the corporation's charter, its basic governing document. In most cases it is not difficult to prepare the articles since each jurisdiction has standard forms you can follow. But if the articles are not properly completed and filed, a creditor could later claim that a valid corporation was never created. You would then lose the important benefits you had hoped to gain from the corporate structure. Furthermore, some special matters must be handled in the articles (such as number of shares of stock, classes of stock, and voting rights), so it's important to talk with a lawyer to make sure these have been taken care of.

4. Hold the Required Meetings

After you file articles of incorporation, you must comply with certain other formal requirements such as the election of directors at the shareholders meeting, adoption of a corporate seal, adoption of bylaws, and convening an initial meeting of the board of directors. Once again, it is important to abide by these formalities to preserve the advantages of incorporation.

HOW TO SATISFY DIVERSE SHAREHOLDER INTERESTS: MONEY AND POWER

We said that the cardinal strength of the corporate structure is its capacity to accommodate diverse shareholder goals and investment objectives. The benefits are twofold: you can satisfy the needs of the organizers who already want to be stockholders, and you can attract new investors. The corporate form nurtures the business financing process by creatively allocating money and power, two essential goals for most investors.

There are an infinite number of ways to divide money and power in a corporation but there are only a few legal means to do it. You should be conversant with four that are used at the company's inception.

Marketing Your Stock: The Buy-Sell Agreement

Suppose you want to start a business to which you will contribute a modest amount of money as well as something more valuable—a patent, unpatented invention, a process, or simply a marketing or selling technique. You also have two friends, Baker and Daniels, who are willing to support the enterprise financially. Baker is willing to risk his money, perhaps even to lose it all, but if the business succeeds he wants his money back and a share of the profits as well. Baker is a passive investor, since he has no desire to work at the business. Daniels is a passive investor too, but unlike Baker he wants a current return on his investment *and* a chance to participate in any corporate success. You and your friends have different objectives but the corporate form can take care of them all. One solution is to do the following.

First, the corporation issues 51 percent of its common stock to you since it's your idea and you are contributing some money. As majority stockholder, you control the corporation.

Second, the corporation issues less than 50 percent of its common stock to Baker along with an obligation to repurchase it over a period of time at a formula value or to piggyback the shares in a subsequent offering to the public.

Stock Repurchase. The stock repurchase feature is called a "buy-sell" agreement or, more precisely, a "stock redemption" agreement. It might work this way. The corporation agrees to repurchase Baker's shares at book value over five years beginning on the third anniversary of incorporation. This will give the corporation the benefit of Baker's capital for the initial period of company growth and it will give Baker the opportunity to realize a gain on his investment. Baker gains when the corporation buys back the stock beginning in year three because the book value of the stock will have risen if the company prospered during those three years.

Piggyback. Baker might also make money on his initial investment in the event the company's shares are sold to the public: Baker's shares would be "piggybacked" and publicly offered along with the new shares, but the proceeds from the sale of Baker's stock would go to Baker, not the corporation.

What about Daniels? Unlike Baker, Daniels wants to see a payback immediately, so he is given preferred stock on which dividends would be paid. The stock could even be "cumulative preferred": if the dividend is not paid in any one year, it accumulates and must be paid before any dividend is paid on the common stock. Daniels now has some assurance that he will see an early return on his investment. Finally, his desire to share in the growth of the business can be satisfied by giving him a small amount of common stock redeemable as in the case of Baker's stock.

This example illustrates the versatility of the corporation as well as the complications that arise when planning its initial funding or "capitalization." Diverse interests can be accommodated, but it requires a clear understanding of them and the available legal techniques.

The Subscription Agreement: It Reduces Litigation Risks

A subscription agreement is a contract that obligates those who sign it (the "subscribers") to purchase shares in a corporation yet to be formed. Typically, the organizers of a corporation prepare and sign such an agreement as they plan the business and its capital structure.

The subscription agreement can be a simple document, merely reciting that Jones subscribes for 10 shares of stock at $10 per share. But in the example with Baker and Daniels, it should be more comprehensive: it should recite what property, ideas, or money you are contributing; the number of shares you will buy; and that you will own a majority of the voting common stock. It should also describe the cash contributions of Baker and Daniels as well as the stock and benefits they will receive in exchange.

The purpose of such an agreement is to avoid subsequent disputes and litigation. In our example, you contribute important ideas and products so you get voting control. But you don't make much of a cash contribution. By describing exactly what you contribute and what you get in return, the subscription agreement reduces the possibility that Baker or Daniels can later accuse you of fraud or securities violations for failing to tell them how much you were getting for so little.

The Shareholder Agreement: Allocating Money and Power

As in our Baker-Daniels example, there is often inherent tension in the goals, interests, and expectations of would-be company owners, and this is true even after the pre-incorporation period covered by the subscription agreement. This tension can be alleviated without litigation by preparing a shareholders' agreement. This is a document the shareholders sign, usually at the time of their first meeting. It's impossible to describe all the appropriate terms in a shareholders' agreement because they vary according to the company, business plan, and investor objectives. But our example suggests at least three problems that might arise and the ways to anticipate and resolve them.

Salaries and Profits. Recall that you are the genius of the business—it's your idea or product—so you have a majority ownership interest. Baker and Daniels want to be sure you don't abuse this by draining off all the profits to yourself or paying yourself or family members exorbitant salaries. The solution is to insert a provision in the shareholders' agreement that limits your salary and perhaps the salary of the other executives as well. The fear about draining profits can be alleviated with a bylaw provision that describes the vote required to declare a dividend.

Management. Despite Baker's and Daniels' wish to be passive investors, if the business doesn't do well they will want to have a voice in running it and they might even want to take over daily operations. Baker will do so because his investment return drops as book value drops; and Daniels will be fretful if he doesn't receive his quarterly dividends. (In fact, preferred stock sometimes provides for a voice in management if dividends are not paid.) Both these concerns can be handled in the shareholders' agreement.

The Buy-Out. Baker's buy-out by the corporation at "book value" raises this question: What is it and who determines it? Since the term is defined within the accounting profession, the real issue is the second one. While you will want to establish this figure with your own bookkeeper, Baker might want it determined by an independent certified public accountant. Such experts are expensive and inconvenient, but that's a small price to pay to avoid a lawsuit. For this reason, the shareholders' agreement should provide that book value will be determined by an independent accountant, someone whose figures Baker is not likely to challenge. (There are other ways to value stock, and they are discussed on page 76 in the next chapter.)

The shareholders' agreement might also deal with buy-out provisions in the event of the death or bankruptcy of a stockholder. These are also discussed in the next chapter.

Special Bylaw Provisions: Preserving Your Share

Special provisions in the company's bylaws can either supplement or substitute for a shareholders' agreement. Bylaws are not usually as versatile or as easily amended as a shareholders' agreement and for this reason they are perhaps a less desirable method for defining the relationship among the shareholders. Nevertheless, there are times when bylaws must be used.

Most stockholders in a closely-held corporation want to maintain their percentage interest (such as your 51 percent in our example) even if new stock is issued at a later date. You can do this if you have a "preemptive right"—the right to buy enough newly issued stock (in preference to nonstockholders) so that you keep your percentage interest. Baker and Daniels also would want this right in order to protect their investment. Many states require that preemptive rights be in the Articles of Incorporation or bylaws, so it's important to think about these issues early in the planning process.

CHECKLIST OF OTHER CORPORATE PLANNING ISSUES

A lawyer experienced in setting up and counseling corporations should review with you other important issues to think about during the planning process. Remember, these must be considered *before* you incorporate, or at least at the first meeting of stockholders and directors. Planning and forethought can prevent disputes from mushrooming into lawsuits. These are some of the more important issues:

1. Liability of Promoters

A promoter is someone who undertakes to form a corporation by obtaining essentials such as capital, an office lease, or a supply contract. When the corporation is later formed, it assumes the liability on any contracts a promoter has signed, but the promoter is not legally released from the contract unless all parties express an intention to do so by signing a new contract. If you act as a promoter, make sure you are clear of any liability on contracts you may have signed before the corporation was formed.

2. Class and Amount of Stock to Be Issued

As we mentioned, the corporation can issue different types, classes, and amounts of stock. Be candid with your lawyer and explain the goals and interests of the company's future stockholders so together you can figure out what the best capital structure would be. Control of the corporation is best manipulated by using classes of stock—some with voting rights and others without.

3. Stock Restrictions

Closely-held companies and family businesses generally don't want their stock sold to outsiders. If this is your preference, tell your lawyer before the stock is issued. Then you can restrict the sale of the stock so that others will not get an ownership interest in the company. This is discussed in detail in the next chapter.

4. Debt-Equity Ratios

Except to the extent it may raise tax problems (see chapter 11), the capital structure of the business is outside the scope of this book. Talk with your lawyer and accountant to determine the proper mix of debt and equity.

5. Subchapter S Status

As we said, a corporation may elect special tax treatment under Subchapter S of the Internal Revenue Code. This means there is (except in unusual circumstances) no tax on the corporate entity, corporate income passes through and is taxed to the individual stockholders, and any company losses (to the amount of the shareholder's investment) may be taken as individual losses. But Sub S status must be planned for because there are numerous preconditions associated with it.

6. § 1244 Stock

The Internal Revenue Code has an important provision that can benefit investors in small companies. Section 1244 of the Code provides that an original investor in common stock of a domestic corporation may take an ordinary loss up to $50,000 for specially qualifying stock ($100,000 for husband and wife filing jointly). This is an advantage over losses in nonqualifying stock because they are capital losses which are deducted from capital gains, not from income as are § 1244 stock losses. There are special requirements for this stock, but you should issue it if there is a substantial risk the company might fail.

7. Voting Power of Directors

Consider carefully what vote it should take for action by the Board of Directors. Along with money, the control issue is paramount in corporations, and you don't want to discover later that a bare majority is taking actions that are unacceptable to you.

8. Before Closing the Deal . . .

No doubt you will need an attorney to advise you and prepare the corporate papers. In most cases, the attorney represents either one of the shareholders or the corporation. To avoid later arguments that the shareholders were deceived in some way, insist that their own personal lawyers review all the corporate documents before anything is signed.

WHAT TO DO WHEN YOU NEED MORE MONEY

The business will probably need more money whether it thrives or withers. It can obtain debt financing from many sources and in many forms; these are discussed in detail in chapter 10. It can also raise money by selling stock; the problems of the securities laws are explored in chapter 12. But there are two particular issues pertaining to new stock that you should be aware of.

First, if the business is prospering, you may have the chance to raise new capital at a price that is several times higher than the amount per share you paid for the stock. In order to avoid charges of fraud and securities violations from the new buyers of stock when they discover how little you and the other initial investors paid, you should fully disclose in the subscription agreement how much you paid for it.

Conversely, if the company doesn't do well, there may be a desperate need for new capital in order to stave off collapse. Usually the only source for this capital is the existing shareholders, those already on board, and often only one or two of them will be able to make the necessary contribution. If so, they will likely demand a lot of stock for the money, or warrants or options to buy the company's stock at low prices. Again, it is important that all the shareholders be informed of the grave financial needs of the company and the terms of the investment so that charges of unfairness do not later arise in the event the company recovers and the new investment multiplies in value.

GOOD PLANNING IS ESSENTIAL

In this chapter we have examined the forms a business enterprise can take and the creative ways in which different stockholder objectives can be accommodated through allocations of money and power. What should be clear from this discussion is the need for careful planning and sound professional advice at the company's inception. Without it, the corporation runs a great risk of future litigation and attendant costs in dollars and management time. At no other point in a corporation's life is care and good legal advice more essential.

4. How to Avoid Lawsuits Over Corporate Operations

by HOWARD H. LEWIS

Good business planning at a company's inception can do much to reduce the risk of corporate disputes and litigation. But the same foresight is necessary throughout a corporation's life: tension and conflict within the firm are inevitable even if sales and profits are high, and there is always the danger the corporation or its employees will act illegally. In this chapter you will learn:

- Seven rules for keeping peace in the corporate family;
- How to avoid personal liability as an officer, director, or shareholder;
- The corporation's responsibility for the acts of its employees; and
- Why you may want to set up a corporate subsidiary.

This chapter describes those areas of corporate operations that present the greatest legal risks and it suggests ways to reduce the personal and corporate exposure. As with the preceding chapter, most of these problems arise in the closely held company; that is, the firm, be it large or small, with relatively few stockholders. Another central legal issue for both the publicly traded and the closely held company is compliance with securities laws; this is dealt with in chapter 12. In addition, several important corporate tax and accounting issues are discussed in chapter 11.

SEVEN RULES FOR KEEPING PEACE
IN THE CORPORATE FAMILY

At the corporation's birth, the founders are usually in high spirits and in general agreement on company operations and strategy. As time passes and the corporation faces new challenges—which can take the form of success *or* failure—the harmony may vanish. Too often, it is replaced by shareholder or director threats of court action. Common sense, fairness, and decency within the corporate family should prevent most disputes from escalating into litigation. But there are some specific rules of corporate behavior that can reduce the likelihood of court action or mitigate its consequences in the event a lawsuit is filed.

Rule 1: Observe Corporate Formalities

As we explained previously, corporations are creatures of statute so they must observe certain operational formalities required by state law or the firm's own bylaws. Businessmen in closely held companies are particularly tempted to ignore these rituals; the shareholders, directors and officers are often the same people, so the legal niceties seem artificial and wasteful. But that's a shortsighted and dangerous attitude for three reasons.

First, the failure to observe formalities and maintain records makes it more difficult to obtain loans or other forms of financing. *Second*, dissident shareholders and directors can use these derelictions as a basis to try to remove management. *Third*, outsiders such as trade creditors may be able to claim successfully that the failure to observe formalities means the business is no longer a corporation and is not entitled to the limited liability of the corporate shield discussed in chapter 3. Either way, management stands to lose—either power or money.

Tips for Observing Corporate Formalities:

- Hold regular meetings of the board of directors and the annual meeting of shareholders; keep accurate minutes.
- Make sure important corporate actions receive board approval and are reflected in a board resolution; this is particularly important for changes in officer salaries.
- Run the corporation as a distinct financial unit with its own books and records.
- Don't commingle corporate and personal assets.
- Make sure corporate contracts are in the corporation's name (see page 81).

- Provide the corporation with enough assets so it has a reasonable chance of success.

Rule 2: Be Fair in Dealings with Shareholders

As we discussed in the preceding chapter, a corporation is a distinct legal entity from the shareholders; in fact, the corporation represents its owners (the shareholders) in all matters within the corporation's powers. In many cases, particularly where the stock is held by many investors or where no one person has a large amount of stock, a shareholder's functions are limited: to vote at the annual meeting of shareholders but do little else. In that event, the shareholder has no special duty or obligation to the corporation or its directors; indeed, as we shall see in a moment, it is the directors who are held to a high legal standard.

Duty of the Majority. The duties and obligations of the majority stockholders are quite different. Whether in a large or small company, the majority stockholder or group of stockholders has a special duty to the minority: to act in good faith and to use care and diligence to protect the minority stockholder's financial and managerial interests. The majority must act in the best interests of the corporation as a whole when it manages the company's affairs and sets policies through the election of directors. The majority is a fiduciary—the person or persons to whom the corporate property is entrusted for the benefit of *all* stockholders.

This special duty most often comes into play in the closely held company where a majority of the stock may be held by one person or a small group of investors. If members of the majority are also officers and directors, they may be especially tempted to ride roughshod over the minority. This can breach the legal standard and expose the majority to personal liability. The best way to avoid such problems is to deal fairly and honestly with all stockholders.

Rule 3: Don't Squeeze Out the Minority

This is a corollary of the preceding rule. A "squeeze-out" (also called a "freeze-out") is an attempt by the majority shareholders, directors, and officers to manipulate the reins of corporate control in order to eliminate the minority stockholders or reduce their power or income. In a squeeze-out the minority is not fairly compensated for its losses. While some states do not automatically condemn these acts, squeeze-out schemes in many states are illegal if they breach the duty of good faith that the majority owes to the minority. Although the majority has legal control of the corporation, it should not be permitted to be predatory, to appropriate a minority shareholder's property (his interest in the corporation) without fair compensation.

Squeeze-out schemes take many different forms, but these are the most common:

- Diluting the minority's interest by issuing a great deal of new stock at an inadequate price. If the minority has a preemptive right (the right to purchase the shares), the stock will be issued when the minority is unable to pay for it.

- Paying exorbitant salaries to the majority shareholders–officers, but refusing to pay dividends to the minority stockholders who are usually not officers and are therefore unsalaried.

- Selling the corporate assets to the majority for a very low price. This is also a problem of self-dealing. (See page 80.)

- Merging with another company under a plan that adversely affects the minority.

Be particularly alert for squeeze-outs in companies where the stock is not widely held. If you are a majority stockholder or a member of a group of stockholders with a controlling interest, watch out for actions that the minority may *interpret* as a squeeze-out; if you are in the minority, insist that stockholder and board actions benefit the entire corporation, not just those in control.

Rule 4: Satisfy the Shareholder's Financial Interests

It is certainly easier to keep peace in the corporate family if the business is making money. *How* your company makes money is beyond the scope of this book, but *if* the company is making money a sensible plan for compensating all the company's owners—*all* its stockholders—will go a long way toward preserving amity. There are several ways to do it.

Pay a Salary

If some or all of the shareholders are also officers, the obvious way of compensating them is by paying a salary. Of course, the amount of the salary will depend upon the company's health and the services of the stockholder–employee. *Warning:* There are adverse tax consequences for paying excessive compensation to an owner–employee. In chapter 11 we offer some helpful guidelines for setting what the IRS terms "reasonable" levels of executive compensation.

Employment Agreement. Usually the majority stockholders and the other key people in a firm have no trouble negotiating their own salaries. But an investor who would be a minority stockholder may not believe he will be adequately compensated for his investment through dividends alone. One solution is to offer the minority investor an employment contract with the corporation by which he would be granted a salary at a specified rate, for a defined period of time, and with particular remedies in the event of a breach.

Warning: This course of action is not recommended in all cases. Unless the minority shareholder is interested in contributing to the business operations, is useful, and is compatible with the rest of management, an employment agreement with a passive investor does not make sense.

Of course, even senior company officers and holders of larger amounts of stock may want an employment agreement as insurance against unanticipated changes in the ownership of the firm. But any employment agreement should deal with at least one contingency—the employee's departure. Most companies want to be sure the departed employee does not immediately compete with it. A legal noncompetition clause must be limited in time and the geographic area it covers. (See chapter 8, page 159.)

Pay Dividends

The payment of dividends on stock is the obvious way of compensating a corporate investor. But as we noted in the previous chapter and as we will discuss again in chapter 10, a dividend is an expensive way to distribute corporate profits because it is paid out of "after-tax" dollars: unlike salaries, the corporation cannot take a tax deduction for dividend payments it makes.

The board of directors has great discretion in paying dividends; it can pay them or not as it sees fit provided that the payment does not impair the company's capital.

Warning: A corporation cannot withhold dividends in bad faith; that is, directors cannot intentionally refuse to authorize dividend payments where business conditions clearly warrant them, or as a way of punishing or oppressing minority stockholders. Although it's a short-term solution, a minority stockholder can sue the directors and corporation and require them to pay the dividend.

One way to satisfy a minority investor's interest is to adopt a guaranteed dividend policy. If this is done, the formula must be written so that dividends will not be paid until the corporation has adequate working capital to ensure steady growth. In addition, the dividend pay-out should permit some accumulation of earnings. (See chapter 11 for an explanation of the accumulated earnings tax, which is imposed when the converse happens—not enough dividends are paid out.)

Redeem Stock

Several of the suggestions in this Rule have focused on the minority stockholders. The reason is one of power and risk; power because the majority has it and can take care of itself, risk because disgruntled minority stockholders are an endless source of litigation. While the minority has less money at risk, it is just as interested as the controlling stockholders in realizing a fair return on its investment. The courts are exacerbating this problem: there is an emerging body of law that declares that the majority owes a duty to the minority to assure it a return on its investment in some way, whether by paying dividends or using some other technique.

That other technique is often stock redemption, the repurchase of the minority's stock by the corporation or the other stockholders. Assuming a fair value is established for the stock, the minority investor will be compensated in the event he no longer wants to be an owner of the company. Indeed, if the company has prospered in the years since he made the investment, he may make a substantial profit when the stock is redeemed. Such a redemption can be provided for in the shareholders' agreement, which is signed when the corporation is formed. Make sure all the details are spelled out, but allow for contingencies too: a redemption cannot beggar the company.

Go Public

Another method of satisfying the minority's thirst for a return on investment is a commitment on the part of the majority to "take the company public" and to "piggyback" the minority's shares in any such public offering. This means the corporation would sell new shares to the general public to raise additional capital while offering the minority's shares at the same time. Proceeds from the minority's shares would go to the minority, not the corporation. This is a special way of redeeming the minority's interest in the company, but through a stock purchase by the public rather than by the company. Of course, this technique works only when the company can go public, and that is not always possible even for a successful firm.

Tip: Majority shareholders in particular should exercise caution in dealing with the minority. Understand the nature of your special duty, the minority's interest in a financial return, and the many ways it can be satisfied.

Rule 5: Keep Stock in the Family

A universal goal in closely held companies is to prevent the ownership of the company—as evidenced by the stock—from passing into the hands of investors who may be anathema to the remaining owners. Attaining this goal calls for "restricting" the transfer of the stock and there are many reasons for doing it:

- Preventing outsiders from obtaining a management position in the company;
- Preserving harmony within the company;
- Qualifying for an exempt securities offering under the federal securities laws (see chapter 12); and
- Preserving the special tax status of a Subchapter S corporation (see chapter 3).

The most common reasons are the first two, which boil down to the stockholder's desire to maintain control. The issue is joined when a stockholder dies, goes bankrupt, has his assets attached by creditors, or simply tries to sell his stock. Unless these events are anticipated, there can be litigation with heirs, creditors, the selling stockholder, and the stock purchaser.

Before attempting to restrict the disposition of company stock, have your lawyer carefully check the laws of the state where the company is incorporated; a restriction that's valid in one state may not be valid in another. There are an infinite number of stock restrictions but the following are the most common:

- First Option: This gives the corporation or the other shareholders the right to buy back some or all of the stock during a defined period of time (perhaps as long as 90 days) upon the occurrence of a particular event such as the disability, insolvency, death, or departure of the shareholder.

- Buy-out: This provides for the automatic transfer of the shares at a set price upon the death (or sometimes disability) of the stockholder.

- Consent: This requires the consent of the other shareholders or a specified percentage of the voting stock before a sale can be made to outsiders.

That horribly ambiguous word in the law, "reasonable," is what governs the legality of stock transfer restrictions; only reasonable restrictions are lawful. Of the three just mentioned, only the consent restriction is occasionally not enforced; the others are quite common. These restrictions can be written into the corporate charter, the bylaws, or the shareholders' agreement. But there are more practical problems:

Repurchase Price. The formula for the purchase price of the stock must be carefully written. *Book value* of the company computed as of the date of the particular event (such as death or bankruptcy) is one of the easiest to apply and is generally legal, but it may prove to be unfair in some cases. For example, it may fail to take into account the earnings potential of a rapidly growing company in a flourishing industry, and some assets (such as patents and trade secrets) are tough to value in this way. A *capitalized earnings* formula is also common. An appropriate capitalization rate will vary with the company's growth potential, its financial condition, and its business risks; it is advisable to obtain advice from an independent banker or other financial consultant if you adopt this method of valuation. Another method is to require that the price be set and periodically revised by the shareholders. Finally, you could provide for an *independent appraisal*, perhaps using the last price set by the shareholders as a benchmark. Whatever the formula, the more complex it is, the greater the room for disagreement and litigation.

Funding the Repurchase. In the event the shareholders' agreement comes into play, the company should be able to pay easily for the stock repurchase. You can buy insurance to fund a redemption in the event of death, but not usually for bankruptcy or a stockholder's desire to sell. In that event, the agreement could provide that the corporation and the remaining shareholders together will make installment payments over time.

Warning: If the company redeems the stock, there may be adverse tax consequences to the shareholders whose interest is redeemed. To the extent the company has accumulated earnings and profits, the shareholder may receive dividend income rather than capital gains for his stock. One way of dealing with this problem is to provide that the company will not redeem the selling shareholder's stock if the redemption would trigger dividend treatment; instead, the remaining shareholders may have the option of buying him out pro rata at a formula. This buy-out may be funded in some cases by loans from the company.

Marking the Stock. If the sale of the stock is restricted, the stock certificates themselves should bear the wording of the restriction or make reference to it and the document that contains it. If this is not done, the representative or creditor of, or purchaser from, the shareholder may successfully contend that he acquired the shares without notice of the restriction. In that event, the stock could be transferred.

Rule 6: The Family Peace:
Understand the Trade-offs of Control

The legal techniques we have discussed are essentially means of allocating power and money. Investors want a return on their funds whether it's psychic, purely financial, or a combination of both. In closely held companies, control is usually the essential goal and the corporate form is peculiarly suited to allocating it in ways that satisfy all investors.

But as you talk with your lawyer and plan ways to satisfy the investors' diverse interests, recognize that even the issue of control—for example, by you as majority shareholder—is not free of trade-offs. Two examples illustrate the balancing process.

Preemptive Rights. We said in the last chapter that one way to attract investors is to offer preemptive rights; that is, the right to buy at a later date a sufficient amount of newly issued stock so that their original interest (say, 15 percent of the outstanding stock) is not diluted. While this technique can attract investors and keep minority stockholders happy, it carries a price: if everyone has preemptive rights in a company with many shareholders, a new offering will be extremely time-consuming and expensive, and a *public* offering may be almost out of the question. There are solutions to this dilemma, but they too involve trade-offs.

Minority Veto. Another technique to keep peace in the corporate family is to give a minority shareholder a veto over certain corporate actions. While this may be necessary to attract an important new investor, it could become a formidable bottleneck to swift corporate decision making.

In short, while some techniques for keeping the family peace are unquestionably sound, such as the observance of corporate formalities, others involve trade-offs that are often difficult to make at any time in a corporation's life.

Rule 7: Anticipate Dissension

Perhaps the most effective way to prevent disputes is to assume they will occur and to plan for them. Disagreement in the corporate family is inevitable; what you want to avoid is corporate paralysis, a deadlock among directors or shareholders. If that happens, consider using some of these techniques to break it:

- A buy-out clause in the shareholders' agreement providing for a purchase by one or more shareholders of a majority of the stock in the event of director or shareholder paralysis for a specified period of time.
- Dissolution of the corporation. (That may be better than paralysis.)
- Mediation, arbitration, or the use of one of the other out-of-court dispute resolution techniques discussed in chapter 2.
- Use of the Provisional Director Statutes. In force in several states, these laws authorize the courts to appoint a temporary director to break a board deadlock.
- Use of the Custodian or Receiver Statutes. Some states also have statutes that allow the courts to appoint a custodian to carry on the company's business if the shareholders can't break the deadlock.

These are extraordinary, last-resort remedies but they are preferable to corporate paralysis.

LIMITING SHAREHOLDER LIABILITY: DON'T ABUSE THE CORPORATE FORM

As we discussed in the previous chapter, a principal advantage of the corporation over the other forms of business enterprise is limited liability—the financial risk of the shareholders is limited to the amount of their investment. But this protection is lost—the corporate veil is pierced—if there is an abuse of the corporate form; that is, if the corporation is used for the primary purpose of escaping liability. If that happens, the officers, directors, *and* principal shareholders of the corporation will be held liable for the firm's acts.

Although shareholders will generally enjoy the protection of the corporate shield, the courts occasionally impose personal liability on them in at least three situations:

- when the corporation is a sham, simply an attempt to avoid personal liability;
- when the shareholders woefully undercapitalize the corporation so it doesn't have adequate financial resources to operate as planned; and

- when the shareholders fail to observe the corporate conventions and formalities.

We have already discussed the third situation, and the second might occur when, for example, the paid-in capital is only a fraction of what the company needs to start business. The first situation is illustrated by a classic case of abuse of the corporate shield.

The founder of a taxicab company made each of his cabs a separate corporation. His theory: if any one of the cabs were involved in an accident, his liability would be limited to the corporation's sole asset—one taxicab. During a lawsuit by a seriously injured patron, the court ruled that the founder and all of the cab corporations and assets were liable for the damages sustained because the multiple corporations were a sham; they were simply an attempt to shield the cab operator from liability.

LIABILITY OF OFFICERS AND DIRECTORS

So far, our recommendations for reducing corporate legal risks have mostly involved shareholders. Now we go down one level in the corporate hierarchy to directors and officers. Both have two sorts of responsibilities and potential liabilities—one to the corporation and shareholders, and the other to the outside world. We will discuss both.

High Legal Duty

Corporate directors and officers are subject to a more demanding legal standard than shareholders generally. As the managers of the business, directors and officers are in a sense trustees for the corporation and stockholders. They must act within the bounds of the law and with utmost good faith; for the benefit of all stockholders, not for a few or for their own personal interest; and with the greatest of care and diligence. If directors and officers fail to live up to this standard, they can be sued by their own stockholders as well as the public.

Danger of Shareholder Suits

Perhaps the lawsuit most commonly brought against officers and directors is one by a shareholder for general misconduct or mismanagement. Termed a "shareholder's derivative suit," it seeks to compel the corporation to sue an officer or director for damage to the corporation. There are countless reasons for bringing such suits including:

- misappropriation of corporate property;
- diverting a corporate business opportunity for personal gain;

- wrongfully representing the corporation in a transaction where the officer or director has a personal interest;
- misuse of corporate funds or property;
- persistent violation of company rules or bylaws;
- acting beyond delegated powers;
- squandering corporate assets; and
- making illegal pay-offs to domestic or foreign government officials.

Occasionally, a stockholder will claim that one or more directors simply failed to run the business efficiently. But a director is ordinarily not liable for the poor performance or even the failure of a company. *Warning:* Any director who pays no attention to the business, fails to attend meetings, or fails to involve himself in the company's affairs does so at his own peril.

Self-Dealing. Suppose you are a director of a company and the company itself sells its products to you, or buys supplies from you, or leases space in one of your office buildings. There is nothing inherently wrong with this, but each officer and director owes a high duty of loyalty to the company and if the company does business with an officer or director, a shareholder may question that loyalty.

The general rule is that an officer or director who does business with the company must fully disclose his conflict of interest and totally absent himself from any decision concerning the commercial transaction. *Warning:* Because of the inherent conflict and the implication of less-than-arms-length dealing, the company and the interested director should be scrupulous in documenting why the self-dealing is in the company's best interest. If this is not done, both the self-interested director *and* the other directors who permitted the transaction to take place can be sued successfully by a shareholder.

Danger of Suits by the Public

Warning: Though you may not have personal liability as a shareholder, if you also serve as an officer or director you can have personal liability for actions you take in that capacity. There are many situations in which this can occur.

For Fraud. Officers and directors of a corporation are personally responsible if they participate in or permit the corporation to participate in fraud. An example is using fraud or misrepresentation of a material fact to induce a third party to sign a corporate contract. An officer or director is not personally liable on ordinary trade contracts, but he is for contracts made fraudulently.

From Creditors. Creditors may try to reach behind the corporate shield to officers and directors if the corporation is experiencing severe financial difficulties. This is another reason why it's essential to observe all corporate formalities so that the shield is preserved.

Contract Liability. An officer may be personally liable on corporate contracts if he fails to observe legal formalities. In the course of a busy day it is easy to sign a letter personally when it contains a business commitment. Example:

Dear Mary:

Can you deliver 10,000 widgets at $1.00 per widget by November 10?

Sincerely,
Bill Jones

Dear Bill:

I guarantee you that we will be able to deliver the widgets you require at the price and date quoted in your recent letter.

Sincerely,
Mary Smith

Based on this letter, Mary Smith (who is President of "Smith Corporation") may have become personally liable for the delivery of the widgets at the quoted price by November 30. *Warning:* Don't risk personal liability by failing to observe legal niceties when signing company documents.

Other Acts and Omissions. An officer or director can be personally liable for torts that he commits even though he is acting for the corporation when he commits them. Furthermore, many states impose liability on corporate *directors* under one or more of the following circumstances:

• For paying dividends when no funds are legally available; and
• For agreeing to have the corporation make a loan to an officer or director.

Of course, neither of these acts is always illegal. A dividend is illegally paid if the company's capital would be impaired; that is, if there is not sufficient earned or capital surplus, as measured by generally accepted accounting principles, to pay the dividend. Loans to officers and directors may be permissible if they are for a corporate purpose; for example, to help shareholders pay for the redemption of stock by a selling shareholder. Other statutes impose special personal liability on corporate *officers* for:

• Failing to file required reports or to pay fees; and
• Failing to properly qualify the corporation to do business in the state.

Qualifying to Do Business. The last officer dereliction deserves special mention. As we said in chapter 3 (page 63), a corporation must register or qualify to do business in all foreign jurisdictions; that is, all states where it transacts business but is not incorporated. This merely involves filing a form, paying a fee, and being subject to the gross receipts or income tax of the state. The company that fails to do this loses important legal rights: unregistered companies cannot sue customers or other trade debtors in the courts of that state, and the officers and directors may lose the protection of the corporate shield and so would be doing business there *personally*. "Doing business" certainly means the opening of a branch office or distribution facility, the purchase of a building, and the establishment of a service center; it does not normally mean casual telephone solicitation or other periodic contacts with residents of the state.

Obtain Indemnification to Reduce Personal Exposure

Clearly an officer or director can be personally liable for illegal acts. In order to minimize the personal risk to those who become corporate officers and directors, most states allow a corporation to "indemnify" or compensate them for any losses sustained while performing their corporate acts. Some also permit indemnification for fraud by the company if the individual had no personal knowledge of it. But indemnification is *not* permitted for criminal acts.

Tip: The company's bylaws should contain a provision permitting the company to indemnify its officers and directors to the extent provided by the laws of the state in which it is incorporated. The following examples illustrate the dimensions of the problem.

Quality. Suppose your company contracts to buy circuits from Circuit Corp. You and the other directors are sued by the shareholders when the circuits prove to be defective and Circuit Corp. goes bankrupt. The indemnity provision in the bylaws should relieve all the directors of personal liability. Similarly, if Circuit's sales vice-president misrepresented the quality and specifications of the circuits without the knowledge of the directors or senior officers, the bylaw provision should relieve them of any liability as well.

Corporate Debts. If your corporation had purchased perfect circuits from Circuit Corp. but was unable to pay because of a short-term cash flow problem, you as a director would not be personally liable to Circuit Corp. because this is an ordinary trade debt. This is true whether or not there is a bylaw provision.

Bribery. Now suppose your corporation, with your full knowledge, bribes a state official to obtain a lucrative new contract. The indemnity provision in the bylaws would provide no relief in any criminal action.

Insurance. Since the corporation will be indemnifying individual directors and officers, it should secure some protection itself. The best way to do this is to purchase what is termed "directors and officers liability" insurance. This should cover the cost of any corporate indemnification as well as lawyers' fees for the personal defense of the directors and officers.

Warning: Insurance will not protect officers or directors from criminal penalities or where they have committed intentional fraud.

CORPORATE RESPONSIBILITY FOR EMPLOYEE ACTIONS

For Harm to People or Property

Most businessmen know that the corporation is generally responsible for the acts of its officers, agents, and employees. If your firm's delivery truck strikes a pedestrian and kills him, the company will be liable for the damages. As we discuss in chapter 6, the company can be liable if it sells defective products that injure persons or damage property.

Of course, there are exceptions to this rule. If the delivery truck struck the pedesterian while the driver was off-duty and on the way to see his girlfriend, the company should not be liable. If the products that caused the personal injury were first mishandled and damaged by the purchaser, and that mishandling and damage was the sole cause of the product failure and personal injury, the company will not be liable.

Buy Insurance. The best way to reduce the company's exposure for personal injuries and property damage is through a well-planned program of insurance worked out with a competent insurance broker. Do not attempt to self-insure; that is a foolish course except for the largest companies. Recoveries in product liability cases can be enormous, and without insurance, management will spend countless hours devising and executing the legal defense. Management time can be spent in more productive endeavors.

For Unauthorized Contracts

A corporation's liability for the actions of its employees in contract matters is more troublesome for two reasons: the law is muddled, and it is generally not possible to purchase insurance to reduce the company's exposure.

Of course, the corporation can only act through its employees even though the corporation itself exists as a legal entity. So when a company makes a contract with its suppliers or customers, it does so only through a contract signed by an employee. But there can be legal exposure to the corporation when the employee who acts for it is not authorized by management to enter into such an agreement. These are "unauthorized" acts of an employee though the executed agreement bears the corporate name.

In these cases, the corporation cannot escape liability (for example, on a contract to buy a new $50,000 computer system) merely by declaring that the company employee was not authorized to sign the contract. *Warning:* Even though the employee does not have the actual authority to bind the corporation, he can still do so if he has *apparent* or *implied* authority.

Apparent Authority. This means that an individual holds himself out to the public in such a way that those who deal with him reasonably believe he is acting for the corporation. If the employee who signed the contract for the computer system was the company's purchasing agent or data processing vice-president with appropriate business cards affirming the position, he had apparent authority and the contract would have to be honored.

Implied Authority. This means that the employee holds a position with the company that usually carries with it the authority to bind the company in certain circumstances. If you enter into negotiations with the president of another company, you can correctly assume that his actions will bind the company.

Tip: Prevention is the best technique for reducing corporate exposure for the unauthorized actions of employees. Adopt a system of internal controls so that top management can review the actions of the company's officers, agents, and employees. Make sure the controls are understood and followed. Require that crucial business decisions be reviewed and approved by the board of directors.

THE SENSIBLE USE OF SUBSIDIARIES AND DIVISIONS

One way of facilitating the expansion of the business is to split company operations into units—either subsidiaries or operating divisions.

Division. A division is merely an internal operational unit of a corporation; it is a way of separating one part of a corporation's operations from another. It is not a separate legal entity. Its main virtue is accountability: it permits the officers and directors to measure more precisely the unit's performance, such as sales for a new product line.

Subsidiary. By contrast, a subsidiary is a separate legal entity; it is a distinct corporation whose stock is usually wholly owned by the parent corporation. It has its own separate board of directors and officers, although some may also serve with the parent corporation. The subsidiary is to be distinguished from the "joint venture corporation" (also called a "jointly owned subsidiary") which is a separate corporation whose stock is owned by two or more parent companies. Today, joint venture corporations are common in the oil and gas and pay-TV/cable television business, both of which require large capital investments.

There are many reasons for creating a corporate subsidiary, the most common being the firm's entry into a new and perhaps experimental line of business. In that event, the subsidiary has several advantages.

Management. A subsidiary fosters a sense of independence from the parent, an important managerial advantage for the officers and directors who should devote all their energies to the success of the new company. A subsidiary also physically concentrates employees rather than having them scattered about.

Liability. If the new business should fail, the subsidiary can be dissolved or liquidated without directly affecting the parent company. Since corporate liability is limited to the size of the shareholder's investment, the parent stands to lose only what it put into the subsidiary. Its capital and credit remain essentially unimpaired, though of course no company wants to develop the reputation of conceiving weak or short-lived subsidiaries.

Taxes. There are also certain federal tax advantages to subsidiaries. On the income side, if the subsidiary makes money, the dividends it might pay to the parent can be excluded from the parent's income if the parent owns at least 80 percent of the stock. If the subsidiary loses money and is at least 80 percent owned by the parent, the parent can consolidate its own net income with the losses of the subsidiary, so it gains the tax advantage of the subsidiary's losses.

Flexibility. The subsidiary gives the parent additional flexibility in satisfying the owner's (stockholder's) goals of money and power—the two interests we discussed in the preceding chapter. For example, suppose an inventor proposes that your firm manufacture and market a new electronic testing instrument. The inventor brings to the negotiating table his patents and know-how, but you bring capital as well as manufacturing and marketing expertise. One way to satisfy both sides is to form a subsidiary and give the inventor 20 percent of the stock. Your company can retain control, extract dividends with no tax penalty, and take advantage of any first-year losses by the subsidiary. The inventor may have the benefit of the minority stockholder's protection we previously discussed.

COMMON SENSE IN CORPORATE OPERATIONS

The use of common sense by shareholders, directors, and officers in all internal corporate affairs will go a long way to reduce personal and corporate legal exposure. Use forethought and learn to anticipate disputes about the allocation of money and power, particularly as the corporation faces new economic challenges. Keep in mind the seven rules for keeping the corporate peace and understand how derelictions by the firm's owners and employees can expose them to personal liability.

5. Business Contracts: How They Can Work for You

by JAY GARY FINKELSTEIN

Contracts are essential to the operation of all businesses. Every purchase from a supplier, every sale to a customer, and every agreement of employment involves a contract. Each of these common commercial arrangements is governed by laws whose traps can be skirted. In this chapter, you will learn:

- Six principles of contract law;
- Everyday rules for buying and selling goods;
- How to avoid the dangers of court-imposed contract terms and warranties;
- The most common sources of contract disputes; and
- Three contracts to keep your options open.

We begin with a primer on contract law and then proceed to a discussion of practical applications.

SIX PRINCIPLES OF CONTRACT LAW

A contract is an *oral* or *written* agreement that creates rights and responsibilities among two or more parties. While it can be simple or complex, the essence of a contract is the expression of agreement—a "meeting of the minds."

Principle 1: Start with an Offer

Every contract begins in the same way, with an *offer*. One side proposes the terms of an agreement, then the other side must agree to them—he must *accept* the offer before there will be a contract.

Offers may be conveyed orally, and in such written forms as letters, orders, and newspaper advertisements. Offers also can be restricted as to time, place, and even the identity of acceptable contract partners.

Example: A father offers his children a dollar if they will wash the family car. This offer is not open to the girl next door. On the other hand, a newspaper advertisement by the local department store is an offer to sell the advertised items to whoever pays the purchase price.

Retail stores often impose time limits on their offers by stating in newspaper ads that sale prices are effective "through Saturday." Without such a restriction, the offer to sell at the lower price could be accepted for a somewhat longer period of time.

Tip: Beware of unintentional contract offers such as through letters or ads, and remember that you can restrict the offer as you wish.

Principle 2: There Must Be an Acceptance

There will not be a contract until someone accepts your offer. An offer may be accepted in one of three ways: (1) by oral or written communication, (2) by conduct indicating acceptance of the offer, or (3) by performing the actions requested by the offer. The offeror (the one who makes the offer) can specify the method of acceptance, but since this is not generally done, the offeree (the one to whom an offer is made) usually makes the choice.

In the example of the father seeking to have his car washed, his children could accept the offer by (1) stating that they will wash the car (communication), (2) assembling the bucket, sponges, hose, and other equipment in preparation for washing the car (conduct), or (3) washing the car and presenting the finished product (performance).

Some offers can only be accepted by one method. For example, if a furrier advertises that it will sell a mink stole for $1 to the first customer to enter the store on Saturday morning, you could not "accept" the offer by phoning the store and announcing that you will pay $1 for the mink stole.[1]

Principle 3: When an Acceptance Becomes an Offer

The law is often perverse: in contract law an acceptance can become an offer. If instead of merely accepting an offer, an acceptance *modifies* the offer by

---

[1]In addition to an offer and acceptance, the law also requires "consideration" for a lawful contract. This is a mystical element that is of great academic interest but less practical concern. In general, it means a change in legal position; if you give up something (money, time, etc.) in a transaction, there is consideration.

including new or different terms, the acceptance becomes a *counteroffer*. This counteroffer replaces the original offer and may now be accepted or rejected by the original offeror. If a counteroffer is rejected, there is no contract; and this rejection does not automatically revive the original offer. There are special rules on counteroffers and the larger problem of adding new terms to an acceptance. These rules apply to certain commercial transactions and are discussed in detail beginning on page 92.

Principle 4: Remember the Mail Box Rule

You may rescind an offer before it is accepted but not after. Because an acceptance and a rescission may occur at approximately the same time, it is often important to determine which one has priority—which occurred "first." Since the Postal Service transmits most offers, acceptances, and notices of rescission, the effective time of each is governed by the Mail Box Rule:

Offer: An offer is effective when it is *received* by the offeree.

Acceptance: An acceptance is effective (and a binding contract formed) when the acceptance is *mailed* to the offeror, regardless of when the offeror actually receives the acceptance.

Rescission: A notice of rescission is effective only when *received* by the offeree.

The effect of the rule is this: if your offer is received on day 1 and the acceptance mailed on day 3, there is a contract even if you mailed a letter on day 2 rescinding the offer. Remember, the rescission has no effect until it is actually received.

Principle 5: Put It in Writing

It is simply common sense to put all agreements in a signed writing. A clearly written document signed by the other party is your only real protection if a dispute arises. Never rely on a verbal commitment for important business transactions.

This axiom has its roots in the "Statute of Frauds," a legal principle that bars the courts from enforcing certain oral contracts, such as those for the sale of goods in excess of $500 and contracts involving land. Consider the following example.

Heavy Equipment Manufacturing (HEM) asks Electric Motor Co. (EMC) to bid on a component HEM needs to manufacture a piece of industrial equipment. EMC asks its supplier for a quote on a part used in manufacturing the component. The supplier replies with the best price of $1,000 per part, but no writing is exchanged. EMC then relies on the oral quote and submits a low bid to HEM. After HEM contracts with EMC for the component, the supplier informs EMC that the price of the part should have been $2,000. Result: EMC has no claim against his supplier since the contract was not in writing; $2,000 is the new price and, even worse, EMC must honor its contract with HEM.

A written contract will generally be enforceable as written, but be certain it contains all the terms of the agreement. The reason is important: a written contract supersedes all prior and contemporaneous understandings. Oral "side agreements" are worthless. If a contract is in writing, a court is not required to enforce any part of the agreement that is not in the document; and it may not allow you to testify about the negotiations or any verbal understandings reached prior to or when the document was signed. Beware of the salesman or supplier who says, "Don't worry, we'll take care of it." Get it in writing or worry.

The rule also means that all contract modifications or amendments should be in writing. This may require additional time and effort but it reduces your legal risks.

Principle 6: Some Contracts Are Unenforceable

The last contract principle is a paradox yet sensible: not all contracts are enforceable. Even if you observe all contract formalities, an agreement will not be binding if there is fraud, a mutual mistake, or an "unconscionable" term or provision. The following examples illustrate the problem and result.

Fraud. Your neighborhood real estate salesman wants to sell you a vacation home on Cape Sunny South. He tells you he has seen the Cape and he shows you a picture of beautiful cabins on white sand beaches with clear ocean waters. You sign a contract for a cabin to be built on Lot 18. On your next trip south you stop by the highly touted Cape and discover that it is an uninhabitable swamp. Even though there was an offer, acceptance, consideration, and a written contract, the contract is unenforceable because it was obtained by fraud.

Unconscionable Terms. Fine Furniture Company offers to sell and finance a sofa that is used as collateral. But Fine Furniture's credit agreement states that the company may repossess *all* its furniture, including that already paid for, if the customer fails to make any payment on the sofa. Mr. Johnson fails to make one payment on the sofa so Fine Furniture repossesses it as well as a lamp and table that Johnson paid for over a year earlier. Johnson sues Fine Furniture. Result: While Fine Furniture can repossess the sofa, it must return Johnson's lamp and table because the language of the credit agreement is unconscionable and against public policy.

Mutual Mistake. You agree to buy a stamping machine for your business based on the representation that it will mechanically interconnect with your present equipment. But both you and the machine's manufacturer discover that the connections cannot be made. Result: You are entitled to a refund because you *and* the manufacturer made a mistake in assuming that the machine would properly interconnect.

EVERYDAY RULES FOR SELLING GOODS:
HOW TO HANDLE THE UCC

The traditional law of contracts was needlessly formalistic and technical. Now there is a body of contract law that is responsive to the needs of the business community and the reality of the modern marketplace. It has been adopted in all states except Louisiana and is known as the Uniform Commercial Code or "UCC." Since most commercial transactions are governed by the UCC, it is vital to understand three ways to reduce your legal risks under it: properly using express contract terms, preventing new terms from being read into your contracts by the courts, and winning the Battle of the Forms.

First, it is important to understand that the UCC only applies to contracts involving the sale of "goods." "Goods" are physical objects including manufactured items, growing crops and other items that may be severed from the land, and the unborn young of animals. Most importantly, the definition of "goods" does *not* include contracts involving land (including leases); contracts for services or securities; or contracts to borrow, lend, or exchange money. These agreements are not governed by the UCC. You will find that much of your business involves the purchase and sale of goods, and the UCC does govern them.

Write Your Own Express Contract Terms

In the world of contracts you as the writer control the script and produce the play. Subject only to the rules prohibiting fraud, duress, and unconscionability, you may include whatever contract provisions you and the other party can agree on. The contract terms contained in the written document are the *express* terms.

The lesson is simple: write your own terms into the contract, be comprehensive and clear. If you fail to do this, the law will read in terms you may find oppressive. (We discuss these terms in the next section.)

If you want to receive deliveries only on Tuesdays between 10:00 and 11:00 A.M., put that condition in the contract. If precise standards of performance are important, write them in too. (Manufacturers routinely buy machinery or parts subject to precise written tolerances, industry standards, and other objective criteria.)

If you contract with someone whose financial condition is uncertain or his performance may take a long time, require him to post a performance bond as insurance that the job will be completed. In some industries, such as construction, it is common to go even further and require the job to be reviewed and accepted by a designated expert such as an engineer.

Other express terms can specify the ways to resolve contract disputes, such as through negotiation, mediation, and arbitration. These and other techniques are described in chapter 3. Finally, you can use contract terms to cover remote contingencies. For example, if you live in a city such as New York, which has a history of power failures, put a term in your office lease permitting access 24 hours a day, 7 days a week. During the next blackout when the elevators do not work, you will have the right to enter your office through emergency stairs.

The Dangers of Implied Terms and How to Avoid Them

If you don't include all essential contract terms, the law will write them in for you. If that happens, you will have lost the opportunity to control the commercial arrangement in the way you wanted, and you run a greater risk of inducing lawsuits and disrupting your business. Consider the following example.

You order goods from one of your suppliers. The acknowledgment provides that the goods will be sold FOB seller's plant. The goods are lost by the trucker in transit. Absent any terms to the contrary, you must still pay the supplier and then go after the trucker since the risk of loss passed to you as soon as the trucker picked up the goods.

If a court must imply or "read-in" contract terms, it will do so based on two factors: the parties' prior business relationship and the business practice in the particular industry.

Example: You order heating oil for your store. Thinking that the oil will be delivered on an "as needed" basis, you fail to specify a quantity. You don't know that it is customary in the heating oil business in your state to sell a minimum amount to commercial customers. In the event of a contract dispute, you would be obliged to accept the minimum quantity of oil whether you wanted it or not.

Absent prior dealings or industry custom, courts will consider "commercial reasonableness" in applying a contract term. This amounts to "common sense."

Warning: The following terms will be read into your contract by a court absent an express provision:

- *Price.* The price is a "reasonable" one at delivery.
- *Time of delivery.* Delivery is called for within a "reasonable" time.
- *Allocation of risk.* As indicated by the trucker example, the UCC governs when the risk of loss shifts from seller to buyer.
- *Place and manner of delivery.* All goods must be delivered in a single lot to the seller's place of business.
- *Buyer's right of inspection.* The buyer may inspect the goods at any reasonable place and time and in any reasonable manner before he pays for them or accepts them. When the seller is required or authorized to send the goods to the buyer, the inspection may be after their arrival.
- *Seller's right to cure imperfect delivery.* If the buyer rejects the goods for not conforming to the contract, the seller may correct the problem and make a conforming or acceptable delivery as long as the time for performance has not expired.

- *Duty of buyer with regard to rejected goods.* If the buyer rejects noncon-forming goods, he must follow any instructions from the seller. If there aren't any, he must make a reasonable effort to sell the goods on the seller's behalf if they are perishable or threaten to decline in value. The buyer is entitled to reimbursement of expenses incurred in selling the goods.

- *Rights of seller in the event of buyer's insolvency.* If the seller discovers that the buyer is insolvent, he may refuse to deliver the goods except for cash and he is entitled as well to demand payment for goods previously delivered under the contract.

- *Warranties.* Among the most important terms that will be implied in any contract are the product warranties which are discussed beginning on page 94.

Know what terms the law will read into your contracts and avoid business disruption by writing your own provisions.

The Battle of the Forms and How to Win It

Most commercial transactions are reflected in order or sales forms. These are the ammunition for the Battle of the Forms.

A business typically orders supplies on a requisition form that specifies the terms of the purchase. The seller then sends to the buyer his own acknowledgment containing his set of conditions. Since it's unlikely the terms are identical, whose terms control, the seller's or the buyer's?

In the Battle of the Forms the party that sends the first form generally wins. By properly drafting and presenting it, you can be reasonably confident that any contract will be only on your terms.

There are two different rules. The right one depends on whether you and the other party are casual buyers and sellers or "merchants," that is, professionals in the business of selling or using the goods ordered or sold.

The Rule for Casual Sales

The first situation is where one of the parties is a casual or inexperienced buyer or seller. Your September purchase of skiing equipment from a mail order catalogue would be an example. In that case, your acceptance of the firm's offer to sell the goods creates a binding contract even though you may have stated new or additional terms. These terms (such as "ship by Tuesday") are treated as *propos-als*, not as binding contract provisions. In this example, the only way they would be binding on the ski manufacturer is if your order (the acceptance) expressly conditioned the sale (the agreement or binding contract) on the seller's accep-tance of your new terms. Without it, there is a contract and the seller need not "ship the skis by Tuesday."

The Rule for Merchant Sales

The UCC has a slightly different rule for transactions between business professionals. Suppose you ordered the same ski equipment, but you were in the business of operating a ski resort and wanted skis for rental purposes. In that event, the law assumes you have specialized knowledge of the goods and the skiing business. For this reason, the new term you add in your September acceptance (such as "ship immediately") *will* be a part of the contract.

There are three exceptions to this rule: (1) if the term materially alters the contract (for example, by giving you until the end of May to reject defective skis); (2) if the other party objects in writing to the proposed terms within a reasonable period of time; or (3) if the original form (in this example the manufacturer's order form) expressly limits acceptance to the terms of the offer.

Tip: If you are the equipment manufacturer you will want to take advantage of this last loophole and state on your order forms that "acceptance is limited to the terms of the offer on this form and in the catalogue." Then orders will create a binding contract only on *your* terms.

If you forego this third loophole and decide that it is inappropriate to limit acceptance of your offers to their terms, there are two other ways to win the Battle of the Forms. But both require a very close reading of the forms exchanged.

You Can't Add Material Terms

While a form that contains additional or different terms operates as an acceptance of an offer, any new term that materially alters the offer will not be included in the contract. Among the provisions that would be considered material additions or alterations of the terms of an offer (and therefore excluded from the contract) would be: (1) the addition of an arbitration clause, (2) the waiver of a warranty provision, (3) waiver of a liquidated damages provision, or (4) the addition of any new term inconsistent with a prior course of dealing between the parties. (Waiting until May to reject the September shipment of skis falls in this category; you would expect them to be rejected before the ski season, not after.) No action on your part is required to take advantage of this exclusion. But there is risk that a provision that you think is material may not be so interpreted by a court.

You Can Object to an Additional Term

Any additional or different term in the acceptance will be excluded from the contract if written objection is given to the other party within a reasonable period of time. In our ski equipment example, the manufacturer could object to the "ship immediately" term and the September–May period to reject skis; that would nullify both proposed terms. *Tip:* If you are suspicious of any new provision added to your form, object immediately in writing; don't assume that it will be material and therefore ineffective.

Why You Should Not Lose the Battle of the Forms

You can sustain severe losses if you lose the Battle of the Forms. Consider this example:

An ambitious seller of electrical equipment, Electroquip, learned of a major construction project and, seeking to be the prime equipment supplier, sent a quotation form to several electrical subcontractors who would be doing the actual project work. The quotation form stated that Electroquip would furnish the equipment for a set price but with an important condition—the equipment "may or may not meet the specifications as written and is subject to engineer's approval." One of the subcontractors, Subcon, received Electroquip's price quotes and used them in its bid for the construction project.

When Subcon's bid was accepted, it sent a purchase order to Electroquip for the equipment described on the original form. Subcon wrote on its own purchase order that the "supplier warrants that he will provide equipment to meet specifications." This language in Subcon's form was a material alteration of the conditions set forth in Electroquip's form. Therefore, the order was an acceptance on the terms and conditions in Electroquip's first form, so Subcon didn't get the warranty it wanted.

Electroquip's equipment failed to meet specifications for the construction project and Subcon suffered substantial damages, yet Electroquip was not liable.

Tip: Your business colleagues may be fighting the Battle of the Forms. Promptly ask your lawyer's advice if you think you are in the cross fire.

PRODUCT WARRANTIES:
THE DANGERS AND HOW TO REDUCE THEM

Products sold by your company carry both "express" and "implied" warranties. If your products don't measure up to these warranties, your company can suffer big financial losses. But buyers and sellers alike should know how the warranties can be legally limited and how the remedies for breaching them can be contained. We discuss elsewhere in this book two related and important aspects of warranties—what sellers must do in order to claim that they offer a "full warranty" on their product (chapter 9), and civil liability for injuries caused by defective products without regard to warranties (chapter 6).

Keep in mind as you read this discussion that warranty protection extends not only to the purchaser of the product but to his family, household members, and guests. This makes for many potential lawsuits, and you can't legally exclude these people from the warranty.

The Dangers of Breaching a Warranty

What happens when a seller's product doesn't measure up, when he "breaches" either an express or implied warranty? Unless the seller has legally limited the remedies in some way (as we discuss later in this chapter), the seller may have to:

- Replace the defective product without charge;
- Refund the purchase price; or
- Pay "consequential" damages; that is, the cost of the business or other losses sustained by the buyer as a result of the breach of warranty.

Even worse, if the buyer suffers personal injury from a defective product, he can rely on these warranties when he sues you for damages. (This aspect of warranties is discussed in the next chapter.) These costs of breaching product warranties should be ample incentive to abide by them or restrict them. But first you must know exactly what they are.

Express Warranties: Beware What You Say and Do

Express warranties are those the seller explicitly and affirmatively makes to a buyer. But express warranties are not limited to oral or written statements or representations about the item, and you need not use the words "warranty" or "guarantee" to create one. For example, an express warranty is created in each of the following situations:

- Where a photo of the product, perhaps in an ad or on the package, depicts it for a particular use or of a particular quality;
- Where a model of the product, often in a store window or at a trade show display, contains the features that supposedly exist on the actual item; and
- Where product samples are distributed.

In each of these cases you have made a warranty—that the product can be used for the use depicted in the photo, that it contains all the features shown on the model, and that it is the same as the free samples.

Puffing. Of course, not all product representations or depictions create a warranty. Sometimes they amount only to "puffing": merely the seller's opinion on something about which the buyer is expected to have some knowledge or to exercise his own independent judgment. By contrast, a warranty is a factual statement or representation of which the buyer ordinarily is ignorant.

Example: Statements that a product has been extensively tested, is "safe," or is "fireproof" are warranties. On the other hand, it is only puffing when an automobile manufacturer proclaims that a new model car has the "smoothest ride ever" or when a coffee manufacturer promises "sealed-in freshness."

Tip: Tell your advertising staff and sales personnel about the difference between factual statements and puffing; hyperbole is only safe with the latter. Without due care, you may later discover that you have offered an express warranty that you can't live up to.

From the buyer's point of view, it is often important to demand specific warranties and not be content with puffing. Suppose your company is about to purchase its first mini-computer and companion software to handle your inventory, payroll, and accounts receivable. You should demand and get an express, written warranty that the hardware and software will be adequate for these purposes. To be doubly certain, get written performance standards, such as turn-around and loading times. That way, you will be protected if the system doesn't perform as promised.

Implied Warranties: Beware of Fitness and Merchantability

In addition to seller-created express warranties, every product sold carries with it other warranties that are implied by law. The two most important are the Fitness and Merchantability warranties. These exist even if a seller says nothing about the performance or qualities of a product.

Merchantability. The Warranty of Merchantability means that the product you sell must meet vague but minimum standards of performance and acceptability—that the product must be suitable for its ordinary purposes. For example, a bottle of soda is merchantable if it contains a properly mixed carbonated drink; it is not merchantable if it also contains decomposed animal matter or polluted water. A hand-held business computer is merchantable if it performs its advertised 48 functions; it is not merchantable if it can only add, subtract, multiply, and divide.

Fitness. A second implied warranty is the Warranty of Fitness for a Particular Purpose. This is created when the seller should know the particular purpose for which the buyer is purchasing the goods and that the buyer is relying on the seller's skill or judgment in furnishing them. Suppose you ask your local hardware store to recommend a product to seal your basement walls from water. The salesman recommends his most reliable product and says "this should do the job." You use the product. During the next heavy rain your basement floods. Assuming you have followed product directions, the hardware store is liable for breaching the implied warranty of Fitness for a Particular Purpose.

The lesson is this: make sure your products do what they are supposed to do, even if you don't make specific performance claims.

How to Limit Warranties, and Whether It Makes
Business Sense to Do So

Express Warranties. The businessman's first step in limiting warranties is not to give them. This is simple with express warranties that must be explicitly and affirmatively made. But this is easier said than done because the competition may force you to offer warranties, and even express warranties can be created by the unwitting seller. Most businessmen today do offer express warranties because of their confidence that the products will perform as advertised or, if they don't, they are prepared to absorb the cost of defective performance by offering refunds or replacements.

Implied Warranties. Implied warranties present a slightly different business calculus. As we have seen, the Merchantability and Fitness warranties are not explicitly offered by sellers so they are less likely to be relied upon by the buyer in making a purchasing decision. Of course, if your product consistently breaches an implied warranty (a basement waterproofing product that is no more effective than paint) consumers will soon know that and sales will fall regardless of express product claims. Where repeat purchases are important, the rational businessman will put a premium on product performance. In this sense, a restriction on an implied warranty should be a secondary technique to reduce legal exposure, certainly not a primary element of the business plan.

If you offer a written warranty for your product, federal law (the Magnuson-Moss Act) prohibits certain restrictions on your implied warranties. You should consult your lawyer before imposing any implied warranty limitations.

If you do *not* offer a written warranty and you opt to exclude or modify either the Merchantability or the Fitness warranty, the statement that does so must be "conspicuous;" you can't put it in small type readable only by sharp-eyed youngsters. The provision limiting the Merchantability warranty must use that term, but the Fitness warranty may be voided by a statement such as, "There are no warranties which extend beyond the description on the face hereof." Language limiting either warranty can appear on the product package or label or in the contract of sale.

Implied warranties (in the absence of written warranties) can also be limited "implicitly," which seems oddly appropriate. These circumstances surrounding product sales can void the implied warranties:

- Where common sense would dictate that there can't be any warranties, such as the sale of a product "as is";
- Where the buyer has examined the goods or samples of them as fully as he desired before the purchase or has refused to do so; and
- Where the course of dealing between the parties or in the industry is such that warranties are not given. (An auto garage regularly sells tire casings to a retreader, but there is no implied warranty that each tire can be retread successfully.)

In sum, both express and implied warranties can be limited to some extent, but give some thought to the commercial risks and benefits of doing so and consult legal counsel when a written warranty is involved.

How to Limit the Remedies: Cutting Your Losses

Instead of limiting the actual warranty (which may be Draconian), many companies prefer to restrict the remedy that is available to the unhappy buyer. This approach is more likely to placate the customer yet it costs the company little. But there are perils in this technique and any attempt should be made in consultation with a lawyer.

A common and permissible approach is this: limit the remedy for breach of an implied warranty to the repair or replacement of the item, or to a refund of the purchase price. This has the effect of preventing the buyer from collecting consequential damages, those business or personal losses that are caused by the warranty breach. Manufacturers of photographic film do this when they state on the film box that the warranty remedy is limited to replacement of the film. This means you can't get money damages for that prize winning shot that was lost because of defective film.

There are three constraints to this approach.

Federal Disclosures

The federal Magnuson-Moss Act requires that certain disclosures be made if the remedy for an implied warranty is limited. A limitation on consequential damages, for example, must declare that some states do not permit such a limitation or exclusion.

Limiting the Damages: Commercial Goods Only

A seller cannot limit his liability for actual losses if to do so would be "unconscionable." While this is one of those infamous legal terms of maddening imprecision, we can confidently say that it applies to bodily injuries sustained using consumer goods. Someone injured by a defective consumer product can get damages even if the package or contract limits recovery to $1. By contrast, a limited consequential damage remedy on commercial goods is not unconscionable. This means that such a limitation would be enforceable between, for example, a manufacturer and his component suppliers.

The theory behind this distinction between commercial and consumer goods is that there is equal bargaining power between a commercial buyer and seller. True or not, as a businessman you should try to take advantage of it. If you are a seller of commercial goods, you may want to limit recoverable damages; if you are a buyer, don't accept such limitations because they won't begin to cover business losses suffered as a result of a warranty breach.

Limiting the Remedy Generally: The Boomerang Effect

Another peril in trying to limit your exposure in the event of a warranty breach is this: you will pay a price for limiting the remedy too much. This boomerang effect can leave you wishing you had never heard of remedy limitations.

The rule is simple: if the exclusive or limited remedy (the one *you* prescribe) does not make the buyer whole, he may resort to *any* remedy available under the law. Suppose you manufacture mini-computers and you provide in the sales agreement and warranty card that repair is the exclusive remedy in the event of equipment malfunction. You then discover that the hardware can't be repaired. Since your exclusive remedy has failed, the buyer has all his original choices left—to get a new machine, or a refund, and perhaps damages for losses to his business. This result could have been avoided by offering the additional warranty options of computer replacement or refund.

Warning: Federal laws prevent you from limiting implied warranties or their remedies if you offer a written warranty in connection with the sale of your product. Consult your lawyer first to avoid a violation of federal law or the boomerang effect.

PERFORMING AND BREACHING CONTRACTS: COMMON SOURCES OF DISPUTE

Agreement on contract terms is only part of the game; now both parties must perform. Although there are endless issues to squabble about, there are a handful of important ones that commonly arise in commercial transactions, particularly under the UCC.

Disputes About the Rules of the Game

If you know how courts interpret contracts—the rules of the game—you can avoid routine contract disputes.

As we have previously discussed, a written agreement supersedes all prior and contemporaneous oral understandings. If the written agreement consists of a printed form, typewritten provisions supersede the provisions printed on the form, and handwritten provisions or modifications supersede both the printed and typewritten terms. Remember this rule as you and your contract partner mark up the "final agreement."

Aside from this hierarchy of format, contract provisions will generally be construed *against* the party responsible for drafting them, such as the person providing the printed contract form.

Tip: If you are relying on a form contract in conducting your business, the provisions should be drafted as clearly as possible.

Courts will attempt to construe a contract to preserve the contractual relationship. If a term is ambiguous, courts will use its plain meaning. But remember that courts will only interpret contractual arrangements; they will not create a new arrangement where none existed before.

Substantial Performance: Is Close Good Enough?

In complex commercial arrangements, actual performance by one side may slightly deviate from the contract specifications. These deviations technically breach the contract, but the cost of correcting them often outweighs the loss suffered by the other side. This accounts for the sensible legal doctrine known as "substantial performance." It says that close is good enough: the damages for the minor breach are limited to the difference in value between the promised and delivered performance.

Example: Your company contracts with a construction firm to build a new factory. The plumbing specification is for grade 2 copper pipe manufactured by a company in Reading, Pennsylvania. The builder inadvertently uses pipe of equivalent grade and quality but manufactured by a different company. Though in technical breach of the contract, the builder would only be liable for any difference between the value of the completed factory building with the wrong pipe and the promised building. That difference is likely to be nominal or zero, and so will the damages. The builder will not have to replace the nonconforming pipe.

Practical Impossibility: When You Can't Perform

Sometimes a seller can't perform after he signs a contract. Suppose a fire destroys a manufacturing facility or a new law prohibits the transaction contemplated by the contract. If the seller gives timely notice to the buyer that he will be unable to perform because of the intervening event, the seller's failure is excused. If the intervening event partially interferes with the seller's ability to perform, as where a fire destroys only part of the seller's manufacturing capability, the seller is obliged to allocate his production capacity and deliveries among his customers in a fair and reasonable manner.

Practical impossibility can be a difficult escape hatch to crawl through because it is subject to abuse. An example illustrates this.

A major electrical manufacturer, desiring to enter the rapidly expanding field of nuclear generation, offered to sell nuclear generating equipment to an electric utility company. Under the contract, the manufacturer agreed to dispose of spent uranium fuel. The manufacturer assumed it would reprocess the fuel and resell it to the utility. At the time of contract signing, reprocessing was not permitted in this country, although it was expected to be permitted shortly. The government later prohibited reprocessing, and the electrical manufacturer notified the utility that it would not be able to remove the spent fuel. The manufacturer then argued that its obligation to remove spent fuel was excused.

The court determined that the contract did not provide that the manufacturer must be able to reprocess the fuel; the manufacturer had merely agreed, at a time when reprocessing was not permitted, to remove the fuel. Accordingly, the subsequent ban on nuclear fuel reprocessing did not render "impossible" the manufacturer's obligation under its contract. Difficult, yes; impossible, no.

Installment Contracts: Problems with One Delivery

An installment contract is one that requires or authorizes goods to be delivered in separate lots that are separately accepted. The rule is that the buyer may reject any installment that doesn't conform to the contract if the particular deficiency substantially impairs the value of that installment; but if the seller gives adequate assurance that he will cure the defect, the buyer must accept the installment.

Of course, worse things could happen: the default with respect to the installment might substantially impair the value of the entire transaction. In that event, the buyer may consider it a breach of the whole contract and pursue his damage remedies. Even if there is a breach of the whole contract, it may be reinstated if the buyer accepts a nonconforming installment without notifying the seller that the contract is cancelled; or if he sues only on a single installment; or if he demands performance as to the balance of the contract.

Anticipatory Breach: Saying You Won't Do It

Suppose you manufacture and sell laboratory testing equipment. An electronics company has agreed to sell you critical circuitry for the testing devices, but several weeks before the components are due, it announces that it won't be able to deliver the circuitry at all. This situation, where one party to a contract announces an intention to breach prior to the time of required performance, is known in contract law as an "anticipatory breach." Since it is common in commercial transactions, the rights and responsibilities of each party are (for the law) quite clear.

Buyer's rights. Upon receiving notice of the seller's repudiation, the buyer may:

- For a commercially reasonable time, wait for the seller to perform (in this case deliver the circuitry); or
- Pursue his legal remedies (sue for damages or performance of the contract); or
- Take steps to secure substitute performance from another seller.

Note that the buyer is *not* required to obtain substitute performance (other sources of circuits) but may elect to pursue damages against the seller. These damages would be the difference between the cost of a substitute performance and the contract price, together with any incidental or consequential damages.

Seller's rights. Until the time of performance, the seller may retract his "repudiation" (that is, his statement that he will not honor his obligation to deliver the circuits) unless the buyer has materially changed his position or has otherwise indicated that he considers the repudiation final. In short, the breaching party has some, but not much, time to withdraw his statement.

Mitigating Damages: It's Your Choice

As we just discussed, the victim of a contract breach may seek substitute performance—another source for the products or goods. That way, he "covers" and thereby reduces or "mitigates" the damages he ordinarily would suffer from the breaching party's failure. While the breaching party is still liable for any additional and incidental costs of the substitute performance, the overall amount of damages paid by the breaching party is likely to be reduced.

Example: Home Builders Inc. contracts with White Paint Company to purchase 100,000 gallons of paint at $6 per gallon to paint its new subdivision. White informs Home that it will not be able to deliver the paint on time. Home has two choices. First, it may calculate its loss due to delay in completing the subdivision and sue White for the total damages incurred. Second, Home may decide to purchase paint from Red Paint Company to complete the subdivision. Home could still sue White for damages, but they would be calculated as the sum of (a) the incremental cost of paint from Red, (b) the cost of the delay in painting the subdivision, and (c) any diminished value of the subdivision because of the use of the substituted paint.

Again, the UCC does not require the victimized party to cover by obtaining a substitute performance; that decision is his alone to make.

The Remedies for a Contract Breach

The most common remedy for breach of contract is a judgment for money damages. The law reasons that if the breaching party pays the losses incurred by the nonbreaching party, the latter is made whole.

But there are circumstances where a court will order a breaching party to perform under its contract—to do what it promised to do—rather than merely pay for its failures. Such an order is one for "specific performance" and it may be obtained under circumstances where the payment of damages will not make the victim whole.

Damages are most likely to fail as a remedy where the contract calls for unique performance. Contracts for customized goods that cannot be made by other manufacturers and contracts involving land are common examples. If a retail store orders a selection of dresses from a popular designer who fails to deliver, a court may require the designer to deliver because there are no other substitutes.

One area in which specific performance will not be ordered is with employment contracts. Example: You own a restaurant and have an exclusive contract with a popular local singer. One day your performer announces that she will leave your restaurant to sing for a competitor. A court will not order the performer to sing in your restaurant, but it may prohibit her from singing for your competitor.

THREE CONTRACTS YOU CAN USE TO KEEP YOUR OPTIONS OPEN

There are many times in a business when the answer is neither yes nor no; it's maybe. Whether you should stock up now on certain crucial supplies depends on whether you expect the price to go up or down. Ideally, you want to preserve the status quo while waiting to see how things will change; you might even be willing to pay a price for this luxury. In this section we will discuss three contracts you can use to keep your options open.

The Option

An option is a contract that buys time. Assume you use corn to manufacture corn oil. The price of corn is currently $4 a bushel but you are not sure if the price will rise or fall. If you knew the price were going to rise, you would buy your inventory now. But instead of buying now only to learn later that the price has fallen, your best choice is to lock in the present price without making a final commitment to the seller. The way you do this is to buy an option on a quantity of corn (say, 100 bushels) for a period of time (30 days) at a specific price ($4 per bushel).

The seller, of course, is not simply going to give you this privilege; you will have to purchase it, perhaps for $25. If the price of corn goes up, you can exercise your option and acquire the corn at the option price. If the price of corn goes down, you would not exercise the option but would purchase the corn at the lower price on the open market.

The Right of First Refusal

A right of first refusal may take either of two forms: It may give you the right to match the terms of an offer from another buyer, or it may give you the right to receive the first offer to buy from the seller. An example of each of these forms is provided below.

First, assume you are interested in leasing a new office for your business. You have looked at several locations and have found one that seems to be the best but is not so perfect that you immediately take it. You may ultimately decide you want it so you try to preserve the right to rent it. You talk to the landlord and he agrees that if another person expresses interest in the space, he will contact you first. You both sign a short agreement and you pay the landlord $25. You have acquired the first type of a right of first refusal to the office space. You may continue to look at other locations knowing that no one can rent the space you have already located unless you pass it up.

Alternatively, you might be comfortable in your current building, but would like the opportunity to consider additional space. You obtain from your landlord an agreement that if additional space in your building becomes available, you will get the first right to rent it. You have acquired a right of first refusal.

A right of first refusal operates in many respects as a form of option, allowing you to buy time while preserving the status quo. It differs from an option in that neither the price nor the period of time for which you have the right needs to be specified. In our first example, you have purchased the opportunity to reconsider your alternatives if someone else expresses interest in your first choice. If someone comes forward the day after you acquire your right of first refusal, you must acquire the property or the right will expire. Furthermore, if the person offers a higher price, you must match it or relinquish any right to the property. In our second example, you have the absolute right to receive the first offer, whenever it may be made, but the price is not specified.

If instead of a right of first refusal, you had acquired an option on the property, you would have locked in a specific price and would have had a definite period of time in which to exercise your option. In short, a right of first refusal leaves more matters open than an option, is more flexible, and still permits you to buy time.

The Contingent Contract

There are times when a businessman wants an ironclad guarantee that one event will occur if another one does first. A contingent contract can provide that assurance.

Example: You want to submit a bid to manufacture a large quantity of office furniture, but you must first get price quotes from your suppliers. How do you commit them to providing the items at the quoted price in the event you get the contract, but not obligate yourself in the event your bid is not accepted?

An option won't work since you are not sure when the bid will be accepted. A right of first refusal is of no help since you do not want your potential supplier to commit the necessary raw materials to another buyer who comes forward before the bid is awarded. What you need is a contract that is binding only if you are awarded the contract to supply the office furniture. This is called a contingent contract. It provides that your supplier will sell you certain quantities of raw materials at established prices *if* your bid is accepted.

A binding contingent contract must be drafted so that the obligations of the parties are dependent only upon objectively determinable events. For example, the contingent contract should state that you will buy the furniture parts and materials if your furniture bid is accepted by XYZ Company. Both parties are in a position to determine if and when the bid is accepted. Compare this to a contract that merely states that you will buy the parts "if you need them." Such a contract is not enforceable.

CHECKLIST OF CONTRACT ISSUES

You can use contract law to your advantage by knowing the principles and perils. Keep these lessons in mind:

- Put all contracts in writing.
- Write your own contract terms to avoid court-imposed "implied" terms.
- Watch out for new terms added to contracts during the Battle of the Forms.
- Your products must measure up to express and implied warranties unless the warranties are prudently and carefully limited.
- Be alert to the common sources of contract disputes.
- Use options, rights of first refusal, and contingent contracts to preserve company business alternatives.

6. Product Liability: How to Reduce and Manage the Risks

by PAUL A. ALLEN

Product liability is a company's legal responsibility for certain injuries sustained by a user of its product. Largely a creature of the twentieth century, it nevertheless had a low profile until the mid-1950s. Since then, product liability cases have mushroomed. For some companies, this litigation has threatened their very survival; for others, it is simply another risk to be managed. But there is no denying that in recent years some cases have graphically illustrated the dimensions of a firm's exposure in dollars and adverse publicity:

- A $126 million damage award against Ford Motor Company in connection with its Pinto car;
- Johns-Manville Corporation's filing of a petition for protection under the Federal Bankruptcy Statute, an action it says it took because of the thousands of cases filed against it in connection with its manufacture of asbestos;
- Lawsuits over Procter & Gamble's Rely tampon; and
- The lawsuits and government investigations in connection with the Firestone 500 automobile tire.

These are extreme examples of a manufacturer's (and seller's) legal exposure for the injuries caused by its products. But the same kinds of problems, perhaps of a lesser magnitude, confront thousands of other manufacturers, many of whom don't make products that most of us would think of as "dangerous." In fact, even the four notorious cases above involved products must people considered benign.

This chapter does not explore the nuances of product liability law; instead, we provide practical suggestions for managing product liability risks. The chapter is divided into three parts: in Part I, "The Basics of Product Liability," we tell you the basic rules and suggest why legal exposure has increased so much in the last quarter century; in Part II we describe a nine-point plan to reduce your legal risks; and in Part III we suggest some preliminary steps you can take to handle any claims that do arise.

PART I
THE BASICS OF PRODUCT LIABILITY

The Risk Has Shifted from Buyer to Seller

If you were a manufacturer 100 years ago, you would never have heard of products liability. Until this century, it was largely the *buyer* who had to be on guard for product hazards and injuries. The old Latin maxim *caveat emptor* (let the buyer beware) essentially meant that the buyer had no remedy for injuries sustained when using the manufacturer's product unless he could prove fraud or blatantly false representations about it. The law has come full circle: now it is largely the manufacturer or the seller who has the duty to protect the buyer from or inform him of the hazards associated with the use of the product. The spotlight is now on the firm that designs, manufactures, and promotes the product. The manufacturer is subject to legal attack under three theories.

The Manufacturer's Legal Responsibility: Three Theories

We will not belabor this subject, but you should understand these three legal theories of product liability because our risk management program described in Part II is designed around them.

Theory 1: The Manufacturer's Negligence

A firm can be *negligent* if it failed to use reasonable care in the design, manufacture, or sale of its product. If that infamous "reasonable" person in the law would recognize an unreasonable risk of harm to others, then there is negligence. Example: Failing to use shields or housing over rotary lawn mowers. Without them, there is an unreasonable risk that a user will be injured; that is, the harm is a "foreseeable" one. Note that a firm can be negligent even if the product was designed and manufactured within the law; but if there was negligence in the sale—such as by failing to warn of hazards associated with its use—the company can still be legally responsible for injuries caused by the hazard.

Of course, a company is not negligent merely because its product is not "idiot proof"; nor is it necessarily obliged to make expensive and radical changes to the product. Courts often use a balancing test: the cost of preventing the harm versus the likelihood of injury and the extent of the loss. If the cost of preventing a harm is nominal, as it would be with a label or warning, it may not take a very likely injury to require the use of the prevention technique.

Theory 2: The Manufacturer's Breach of Warranty

You can also be liable for injuries caused by your products if you have breached a warranty that you made (or that was implied by law) when the product was sold. Under this theory, an injured user does not have to show that you acted unreasonably, as he would under a negligence theory. Instead, he would show only that you made representations about the product ("safe for use with children"), the representations were relied on by the user when purchasing the product, and the statements were false (the child was injured). (As we discuss in chapter 5, some product claims—"the best money can buy"—are harmless "puffing," not warranties. They cannot be the basis for a product liability claim.)

Theory 3: The Manufacturer's Strict Liability

This theory does not require that the buyer prove you acted unreasonably (such as in the design of the product or your failure to warn of its dangers); nor does it require proof that you breached a representation about the product ("safe for home use"). Instead, the buyer must prove that he was injured by your *defective* product and that it was *unreasonably dangerous*. The test is easier to articulate than to define. Essentially it means that the product poses an unreasonable risk of harm to consumers, or that it is more dangerous than one would normally expect. Example: A defective steering wheel in a car will support a strict liability theory.

Of course, no seller is liable under any of these three theories if the product did not *cause* the injury. While it's an obvious point, it's important to keep in mind because a great deal of product liability litigation focuses on this one issue. Did the asbestos exposure *cause* the worker's mesothelioma? Did the Pinto gas tank explosion *cause* the driver's death? Did the Rely tampon *cause* the toxic shock syndrome and was that the cause of death? These questions can be the source of endless legal wrangling, but we will leave them because they are less important to the design of an effective risk management program.

Explosion in Products Liability: The Causes

There has been much publicity about the effect of products liability—the threat to some firms' survival, discouraging the introduction of new products, and the unavailability of insurance for some types of liability. Before we suggest ways in which these risks can be reduced, it's important to understand what has touched off the explosion.

The Expanding Legal Theories. The three legal theories of seller responsibility have been greatly extended in the last few decades. Example: Today an inmate injured in a jail cell fire can sue *all* manufacturers of one type of cell padding even where the manufacturer of that cell's padding may not be known and where the cell had more than one type of padding. Then, each manufacturer has the burden of showing it didn't make the product, that the product was not defective, or that it was not at fault.

The Increase in Punitive Damages. There has been a dramatic increase in the percentage of cases in which an injured user claims and wins punitive damages (damages to "punish" the seller, not to compensate the user for his injuries). Compensatory damage awards of $50,000 or $100,000 often support punitive awards up to $1 million; and $1 million compensatory awards support multimillion dollar punitive awards. The size of these recoveries inevitably encourages more litigation. Since it takes a larger punitive damage award to punish a big company (a billion dollar company will not be "punished" by a small award), the bigger the company, the bigger the punitive award.

Fault Is No Longer an Absolute Defense. It is no longer true, as it once was, that the seller is not responsible if the injured user was partly at fault. Many states have "comparative negligence," which awards damages based on the relative degree of fault. Example: If a worker is injured by a conveyor belt despite his knowledge of the posted warnings to stay clear, he can be awarded an amount equal to the value of his claim reduced by a percent equal to the degree of his fault.

The Consumer Movement. Unlike the last century when the old *caveat emptor* rule prevailed, consumers today can purchase tens of thousands of new products, made with original materials, and designed for novel purposes. While nineteenth century buyers knew they had to look for the product defect and had a fair chance of finding it, today's consumers expect far more. In fact, there are so many products on the market that are so complex in design or composition, it is unreasonable to expect consumers to be able to find the defect or to reasonably anticipate the harm. How would a consumer know about a casing defect in a Firestone tire?

Furthermore, the consumer movement of the 1960s and 1970s may have conditioned people to the proposition that for every injury there must be a recovery: it must be someone's fault so someone will pay. Judges are inclined to believe that product risks must be spread to manufacturers; and jurors (consumers themselves) are equally sympathetic.

The Information Explosion. Each step in the design and manufacturing process is often chronicled by engineers and managers, and these documents generally turn up during litigation. This makes it easier for plaintiffs to prove their case. If they exist, a plaintiff can readily obtain from the company files documents showing how management rejected safety devices that might have rendered the product somewhat less functional and somewhat more expensive.

The Role of Lawyers. A large and capable group of lawyers specializes in representing plaintiffs in product liability matters. This segment of the bar is well-organized: their members exchange data and product claim information, organize into committees, and develop expertise in specific products or industries. Verdicts have increased (million dollar verdicts are quite common today), litigation costs have soared, settlements are more common, and the costs of a manufacturer's legal defense have risen. The burden became so great that a Commerce Department task force recommended the adoption of a Uniform Product Liability Act to make the laws the same around the country. It's doubtful Congress will enact such legislation in the foreseeable future.

In short, claims and lawsuits are being filed against manufacturers on a regular basis; the cost of managing these matters is having a direct effect on productivity and the operation of the business; and "first dollar" product liability insurance is unobtainable or prohibitively expensive.

All this calls for shrewd management of the product liability risks.

PART II
HOW TO MANAGE PRODUCT LIABILITY:
A NINE-POINT RISK MANAGEMENT PLAN

Whether your firm manufactures toys, drugs, tools, electrical products, or any other device, what can it do to effectively manage the product liability risks? The answer is simple, its execution rather complex: establish a program of risk management.

The principal objective is to reduce the number and magnitude of injuries associated with the use of the product. If you do this, you will reduce the number of claims made against you, the number and size of adverse verdicts, and the costs of settlement; you will also increase your chances of winning and the odds of obtaining affordable insurance protection.

Take these nine steps to establish an effective risk management program.

1. Appoint a Risk Management Coordinator

Start by appointing a senior executive with responsibility for coordinating the risk management program. With the strong support of top management, he should look at each aspect of product design, manufacture, and marketing and determine what (if any) modifications must be made to mitigate product liability risks. He would then recommend appropriate changes to senior management.

2. Identify Product Dangers

The risk manager should first examine the product line and determine the *known* and *foreseeable* dangers associated with each product. Note particularly the second test; as we said in explanation of the negligence theory of liability, a seller may be liable where the harm is foreseeable, where it is reasonably likely to occur.

Identify the product hazards, and especially look for injuries that might occur from product misuse; much misuse is predictable. You can collect this information from many sources: company complaint files, company personnel, insurance claims, industry literature, company records of product design and testing, product analysis, and field performance surveys.

Test the Product. Particularly for new products, perform tests so you can identify hazards before marketing. Without adequate testing, you will probably not be able to determine what if any design changes are necessary; and you risk liability under the negligence theory. Consider how you would react as a juror if a manufacturer's president testified that his company failed to conduct any safety tests before marketing a new power tool.

3. Determine What Design Changes Should Be Made

After identifying the known and foreseeable dangers, whether through analysis or testing or both, you are now ready to identify those dangers that can be eliminated by changing the product's design. As would a court, you should use a balancing test when making these judgments: measure the risk of injury against the loss of utility that may result from the design change. Example: you reduce the risk of injury from a pencil by selling them in sheaths or making them mechanically retractable, but the utility of the product would be reduced, few people would buy them, and the risk of injury in the first instance is not that great.

Warning: The way in which you document the company's analysis of the effect of design changes on the cost of the product and its marketability can affect the outcome of lawsuits. These documents can be obtained by your litigation opponents, and if they show a callous disregard for safety or an obsession with profit, a jury may punish you with punitive damages. Example: A firm failed to make product design changes or recall the product even after it had identified the danger of burn injuries. The reason: it was cheaper to pay the claims than to take remedial action. The jury returned with a huge punitive damage award.

4. Eliminate the Design and Manufacturing Defects

Design Defects. Change the product design and eliminate defects or attributes that pose a likely risk of injury. As we discuss in the context of marketing pressures (p. 115), there is often a clash between the interests of the risk managers and the marketers. The latter will resist changes that may have a substantial adverse effect on sales. But the job of the risk manager is to convince senior management that the company has far more to lose by retaining the defect and exposing the company to substantial monetary damage awards.

Manufacturing Defects. Even when the defect has been designed out of the product, you must be sure the previously identified defects, or any others, do not show up in the manufacturing process. Set up a quality control program, appoint a quality control manager, make sure he reports to the risk management coordinator (not the production manager), and give him the authority to stop production when he identifies a manufacturing flaw. Also:

- Randomly sample parts and raw materials;
- Use quality control stations at several stages of the production process; and
- Randomly test the final product to insure compliance with company, industry, or government standards.

5. Prepare Adequate Product Warnings

Even if your product is not negligently designed or manufactured, you can still be liable for injuries if you negligently fail to warn of hazards associated with the use of the product.

Example: It is negligent not to warn users of spray insecticides of the particular dangers associated with the product and the precautions that should be taken to avoid injury. The asbestos, urea formaldehyde, and certain members of the automobile industry have suffered millions of dollars in verdicts, settlements, and litigation costs for failing to warn adequately of known product dangers.

When to Provide a Warning

A manufacturer has a duty to warn of a danger if:

- The product is dangerous;
- That fact is or should be known to the manufacturer or product supplier;
- The danger is not obvious, known, or readily discoverable by the user; and
- The danger does not arise simply because the product is used in some unforeseeable, unexpected way.

Note the last element. As long as the harm is only somewhat predictable, a warning must generally be given. Reason: unlike manufacturing and design changes, it is cheap and easy to provide warnings about product use.

Remote Harms; Obvious Harms. Of course, if the harm is too remote, you don't have to provide a warning. Example: Warning that a television set may cause damage or injury if its antenna is struck by lightning. But what if the danger is open and obvious, such as cutting a finger while using a hand saw? There are many states in which there is no duty to warn of these dangers and common sense tells us that we cannot post warnings on everything that is obviously dangerous; if we did, there would be warnings everywhere. Whether a danger is open and obvious is generally a jury issue, so for many products it's a good idea to provide a warning, even for known and obvious dangers.

Who Must Be Warned

You must warn anyone you reasonably expect to use the product or to be endangered by its use. This includes purchasers, users, consumers, and handlers. Use the "foreseeability" test to determine who might have contact with the product or make use of it.

What Must Be Said

An adequate warning must:

- identify the hazard;
- identify the known means of avoiding it; and
- identify the magnitude of the risk if those means are not adopted.

Example: A warning at pondside that simply says "Danger—No Swimming" is inadequate if the pond is full of alligators. A warning that says "Danger—No Swimming, Alligators" is probably also inadequate, although the danger associated with alligators may be open and obvious. The warning should read, "Danger—No Swimming, This Pond Is Populated with Alligators, Swimming May Result in Severe or Fatal Personal Injury and Indeed Your Consumption."

Consult Government Agencies. The careful risk manager will determine whether there are any warning requirements or design criteria prescribed by government agencies. The Consumer Product Safety Commission (CPSC) suggests, and in some cases requires, specific warnings for certain products. Also check with industry trade associations who may have helpful suggestions.

Adopt Consistent Guidelines. A risk manager should adopt guidelines to be followed by all personnel when they draft warning labels. FMC Corporation of Chicago has a product hazard communication system that uses both symbols and words. The FMC warning label contains three elements:

1. A signal word that identifies the nature and extent of the danger;
2. A symbol or pictogram that conveys the nature of the hazard and the results of a failure to heed the warning; and
3. Words that describe how the hazard can be avoided.

FMC uses different signal words to warn of different levels of hazard:

1. DANGER—immediate hazard that will result in severe personal injury or death;

2. WARNING—hazard or unsafe practice that could result in severe personal injury or death;

3. CAUTION—hazard or unsafe practice that could result in minor personal injury or property damage.

Warnings and Instructions. Your obligation to provide a warning may require more than simply a warning label; it may also require that you provide detailed instructions. For example, if the failure to follow instructions in the assembly or use of the product could be a hazard, you should provide an adequate warning to that effect in the instructions themselves. Of course, the instructions must be sufficiently clear and accurate to avoid a successful claim of negligence in their preparation.

How to Communicate the Warning

Once you know what you should say, where do you say it? It's best to put the warning on all product literature, such as instructions and package inserts, and on the product itself. If it's not feasible to include the warning on the product, as it may not be if the product is small and the warning extensive, put a short but conspicuous warning on the product that directs the user to consult the enclosed literature before use. The product warning should also identify the hazard associated with the use of the product.

Post-Sale Warnings and Recalls

Do you have a duty to warn of hazards that you discover *after* the product has been sold? In some states and under certain federal statutes, the answer is yes. Therefore, it is good practice to warn of hazards even if they are discovered at a later date.

Recalls. A post-sale warning is not the same as a product recall. With the latter, you actually withdraw the product from the market; that is, take it back from retailers and consumers. But this duty to recall is imposed by statute or administrative order (usually from the CPSC); it is not a common law duty. Example: An auto manufacturer has a duty to warn the consumer or recall the product where it discovers, after the sale, an unreasonable risk of harm. The . CPSC jurisdiction extends to consumer products generally. In practice, most recalls are the result of negotiations between the agency and the manufacturer.

6. Consider Limiting Warranties and Remedies

As we discussed in chapter 5, when you sell products you certainly give an *implied* warranty and you probably give an *express* warranty. An express warranty is one the manufacturer or retailer explicitly makes about the product; it can consist of a direct statement, a graphic depiction, or a product sample. In addition, the law automatically implies (reads in) two warranties in product sales—a general guarantee that the products are fit for the ordinary purpose for which they are used ("merchantability"), and a guarantee that the goods are fit for a particular purpose where the seller knows the buyer has a particular purpose in mind and is relying on the seller's superior skill or judgment to furnish the goods ("fitness for a particular purpose").

Since warranties are one of the three theories used to impose liability for defective or hazardous products, is there anything a manufacturer can do or should do to limit the warranties or remedies in order to reduce the legal risks?

Express Warranties. As we said in chapter 5, it is possible to limit express warranties when you sell a product. While this can reduce your legal risk, as a practical matter it is often difficult or impossible to do because your competitors may be offering warranties for similar products. You must balance the benefits in reduced legal risks against the cost in lost product sales. *Warning:* Don't give express warranties of safety. See page 116.

Implied Warranties to Consumers. Generally speaking, you cannot exclude or limit implied warranties (or their remedies) when the warranties are given to consumers. See chapter 5 for an explanation of the special, limited circumstances in which this can be done where the implied warranties are *oral.*

Implied Warranties to Merchants. Although manufacturers have little freedom to limit warranties to consumers, they have substantially more latitude to limit warranties to merchants, such as the retailers or middlemen to whom they sell the product. For example, you may want to insulate your company from liability to a retailer in the event only the retailer is sued. Again, this may be valuable from a legal point of view, but will your retailers buy the product under these circumstances? Indeed, you may have to provide a "vendor's endorsement"; this insures the product against defects existing at the time it left your hands.

Warning: Consult a lawyer before you try to limit an implied warranty. In some cases, it is illegal to do so at all, and in others there are technical requirements for the language that must be used and the manner in which it must be displayed. In any event, there may be good business reasons not to try it.

7. Balance the Legal Risks and the Marketing Benefits

It must be obvious that all but the first and second rules for preventive risk management (appoint a coordinator; identify product hazards) involve a balancing process: how much does a particular action (be it a warning or design change) reduce the company's legal exposure, and what is the adverse effect of the preventive action on product sales? Of course, we hope the analysis goes beyond that: What is the company's public responsibility apart from the legal technicalities?

These are often difficult judgments, and there are inevitable internal tensions: the risk manager wants to reduce risks while the marketing and sales people want to sell more products. Sometimes the action that reduces a risk may make the product less competitive in the marketplace. Three elements of our risk management plan—warnings, safety devices, and warranties—illustrate the dilemma.

Product Warnings: When in Doubt, Warn

As we have seen, a company can be liable if it negligently fails to warn of hazards associated with the use of the product. But marketing managers will resist the use of warnings that speak of serious or fatal personal injuries, particularly if competitors are silent. *Warning:* Management that succumbs to this pressure where there are serious risks of injury subjects the company to charges of conspiracy and concert of action with the competitors. This is particularly true where you and your competitors are members of industry trade associations.

Most lawyers would advise companies to include warnings when there is any doubt.

Safety Devices: Safety in the Product, Not in Marketing of It

To reduce legal risks, the risk manager may recommend safety-related design changes. Again, marketing personnel may resist such changes because the safety device may be unattractive to consumers, too costly, or not used by competitors.

Safety and Image. The dilemma is particularly acute where the safety devices are incompatible with the image of the product. Examples: rollover protection devices arguably destroy the image of convertible vehicles, speed governors reduce the attractiveness of sports cars, and safety equipment on motorcycles may reduce their attractiveness to a large segment of the buying public. The risk manager must be obdurate. He must convince management to take the safer approach, and not to expose the company to undue risk for the lure of immediate short-term profits.

Safety and Marketing. Suppose the risk manager prevails upon management to make safety-related design changes. Should the promotional materials capitalize on these changes, should "safety" be advertised? No. The cardinal rule is: Don't sell safety, sell a safe product. It is a tough but important task to convince management not to seek a promotional advantage from costly design changes that make the product safer. The risk is that injured consumers can rely on these safety representations when they sue the company. If a product is advertised as "the world's safest . . ." the injured person's attorneys and experts will claim that the product was defective and that the defect was a breach of the express warranty.

Express Warranties

The risk manager has a twofold job when it comes to express warranties: to ensure that the sales and marketing people do not say too much about the product (as the previous example illustrates), and to be sure that enough information is conveyed in a product warning. Express warranties are given in advertising, brochures, shop manuals, owners' manuals, and any written material that accompanies the product or is made public in any way. The risk manager must review all this material and persuade management not to succumb to the importunings of the marketing personnel to say too much (such as about product safety) or not enough (such as in warnings).

Here are some other tips for reviewing promotional materials.

- Check graphic depictions for the product; make sure they are consistent with the instructions and label. If the instructions say it must be used with a hardhat and face mask, don't graphically depict its use by a scantily clad youngster.

- If you sell through dealers and distributors, require them to distribute the product warnings and instructions; bar them from making representations that are inconsistent with what you say.

- If you make a "private label" for a distributor, insist that the same warnings and instructions you use under your own name be included on the private label product; the private labeler's literature should contain the same information.

Warning: The only way to prevent publication of legally damaging or inconsistent material is to have it reviewed by the risk manager, in-house attorney or designated outside counsel.

8. Adopt a Sound Document Retention Policy

Documents play a central role in product liability trials, so it's important to have in place a sensible document retention program.

Both the *retention* and the *absence* of documents can be devastating in a lawsuit. Obviously, damaging documents that are still in the company's files can hurt the case; but so can the absence of a document, such as a test report, which a jury would expect the company to have. A company-wide document program should:

- identify the documents to be retained;
- identify the period of time for retaining them;
- require the destruction of documents that are not designated for retention.

9. Buy Insurance

For most companies, financial security from extraordinary product liability claims requires a comprehensive insurance program. If the risk manager has properly done his job—regarding product hazards, designs, defects, warnings, and advertising—then the firm should be able to obtain coverage at the best industry rates. Underwriters consider the safety of the product, the effectiveness of the quality control program, the claims history, and the company's commitment to reducing risks.

Obtain Only Needed Coverage. A risk manager can further reduce the premium by purchasing only necessary coverage and by establishing a proper deductible. Insurance companies will work with you on this, but consider how effective your management program really is, the magnitude of the legal risks, and how much you can safely self-insure.

Don't Cede Total Control. It's not wise to cede total control over litigation and claims investigation to the insurer. To contain your long-term risk, you may want to have the right to investigate claims, select counsel who is familiar with the company and product, and demand that a coordinating lawyer be designated where there are many claims against a single product.

Whether you buy insurance or self-insure, it is essential that you adopt a plan for the management of product claims—their investigation, adjustment, and defense.

PART III
HOW TO MANAGE PRODUCT CLAIMS AND CASES

Put in place as early as possible a system to manage product claims and cases. This should be done before the product is sold: the management of the initial claims of injury frequently determines how burdensome future claims will be. The firm that acts boldly and recalls a potentially defective product, for example, may find that the long-term benefit to the corporate image and full product line offsets the short-term reduction in sales and earnings.

Consider two different types of claims concerning your lawn mowers. In the first, a user files a claim after cutting her hand while reaching under the unit to dislodge a foreign object. In the second, the user is injured when the blade disintegrates after hitting a tree root; or perhaps the mower itself explodes because of a design defect in the carburetor. While a routine investigation might suffice for the first claim, in the other two—where more injuries and claims are likely—you should be prepared to conduct an exhaustive investigation to determine the facts and analyze the defective parts. With cases such as these where the company is clearly exposed to liability, a wrong decision can mean years of expensive litigation.

It is no longer possible for claims that are filed with the company or for cases that are filed in court to be individually settled or tried and then forgotten. There is so much more product liability litigation, the legal fees and damage claims are so high, and similar claims from other users are so likely that a decision on each claim or case must be made with an eye on the larger picture—other potential claims and claimants and what they can do to the company.

For these reasons, it is imperative to have an overall perspective and a systematic approach to claims and case management. Of course, not every manufacturer will have the same approach, but the following four steps are common to any sound management program.

1. Develop a Corporate and Product Defense Philosophy

This is often a difficult task for management because it involves many subjective judgments and objective facts. Together with your lawyers, you should develop an overall strategy for defending the company and its products. Of course, this is a function of many variables including the nature of the product, the industry and your competitive position in it, your financial strength, the corporation's public image, the corporate "culture" (chapter 1), the importance of the product to the company, the product's expected life, the number and value of the likely claims, your zeal for litigation, and your willingness to try other means of resolving the dispute (see chapter 2).

Whatever the facts, it is important to enter the battle with some general strategy or plan. Without it, the particular tactics you adopt may not make sense or, even worse, they may be inconsistent with each other. Of course, you should be prepared to modify the strategy if that's appropriate; don't make the mistake of blindly following a failing strategy.

2. Appoint Coordinating Counsel to Centralize Strategy

To ensure that the corporate strategy is consistently carried out, it's best to appoint a coordinating counsel to manage the claims and cases. The lawyer can be an in-house company attorney or from an outside law firm; the decision depends on the experience and availability of the company's own lawyers, the size of the dollar exposure, the frequency and severity of the claims, and many other facts. If the company's exposure is great, it almost certainly will want to retain experienced outside counsel.

3. Investigate and Evaluate Claims

You should promptly and thoroughly investigate all claims filed against the company, whether directly with the company or in court. Prompt processing of claims often results in early and advantageous settlements. Even if settlement is not possible, the facts uncovered may help in the defense of the lawsuit. Though small claims can be routinely processed, major claims should be handled by coordinating counsel (whether it's an inside or retained lawyer) because the legal exposure is greater. But coordinating counsel should be informed of all claims filed against the company.

4. When the Claim Becomes a Case

When a claim for injury by one of your products becomes a case, the lawyer's role becomes more important. The purpose of this book is not to tell you how to try a case or even how to coordinate a legal defense. But bear in mind that all cases and claims must be coordinated; don't allow several lawyers handling several different product liability cases to set their own strategy and devise their own tactics. This can be fatal.

MANAGE YOUR RISKS

There is today a product liability crisis for manufacturers and retailers. As a function of many forces, it demands that manufacturers implement a risk management system to reduce the bottom-line costs of product claims and litigation. The precise contours of the program will of course depend upon the company, the nature of the product, the risks associated with its use, and many other facts unique to your industry, company, and product. Prevention is the key; if that's not possible, effective management is the next best tool.

7. How to Keep the Labor Peace

by J. ROBERT BRAME, III

Employees are swiftly becoming the most expensive and explosive element in American business. There are historical reasons for this, but courts, government agencies, and state and federal legislatures add to the witches' brew million-dollar verdicts, reinstatement of discharged employees, and new employee rights such as a "sex-free working environment." Consider these astonishing but not unique cases:

- One jury awarded a $300,000 judgment to a $35,000 a year sales manager whom IBM demoted when she continued (after warnings) to date a competitor's sales manager.

- A jury awarded $4.8 million to an employee wrongfully terminated by Kaiser Steel after 21 years.

- An arbitrator reinstated a female tolltaker for the Pennsylvania Turnpike after she was terminated for having sexual relations with a truck driver in her booth during working hours. The reason: "conduct unbecoming a tolltaker" was an insufficient description of her misconduct.

There is no doubt that damage awards are getting bigger, and arbitration decisions are increasingly adverse as well: in 1963–64, arbitrators reinstated 37 percent of employees who contested their discharge, but by 1977–78 they were reinstating over 66 percent.[1] This occurred even though employers were more reluctant to terminate employees and far more likely to take only their better cases to arbitration.

Your company must learn how to cope with these challenges of the mid-1980s. This chapter describes the labor issues that pose the greatest risk to growing companies and the steps you can take to reduce the risk to acceptable levels. The chapter is divided into three parts. Part I is "Hiring, Firing, and Managing Employees;" Part II is "Unions: The Do's and Don'ts"; Part III sums up the chapter with "Tips for Keeping the Labor Peace." In Part I you will learn:

- Four Rules for Employee Selection;
- Eight Rules for Employee Management;
- How to Reward Your Work Force;
- Six Rules for Disciplining Employees;
- Exceptional Worries for Government Contractors; and
- Two New Frontiers in Labor Law

While we recommend specific rules for coping with most of these challenges, there is one general principle for coping with all labor problems: Follow the 3C's—*Use Common Sense*, *Keep Communications Open*, and *Be Consistent*. You will see that these three axioms constantly reappear; if followed, they can prevent labor disputes from ever arising.

PART I
HIRING, FIRING, AND MANAGING EMPLOYEES

There has been a revolution in labor-management relations in this century. The new rules of the game are perhaps distressing, but you must learn them well. The place to start is to understand why your freedom as an employer is being restricted.

THE CURBING OF EMPLOYER DISCRETION:
ANTI-DISCRIMINATION LAWS

The Past: Employment "At Will"

In the last century America was a rural society of independent farmers and small businessmen, and the loss of jobs here and there was socially and economically tolerable. There were three reasons for this. First, the employer and his

---

[1]M. Glendon and E. Lev, "Changes in the Bonding of the Employment Relationship: An Essay on the New Property," 20 *Boston College Law Review*, 457, 462–3 (1979) (based on two six-month surveys of reported decisions).

employee were often neighbors, so even job-related actions occurred on a small scale and in personalized settings. Second, wage income was less important because debt was less common, homes were not encumbered by large, long-term mortgages, family and community ties were strong, and many people raised much of their own food and made their own clothes. Third, in reaction to the European system that bound them to the land or a trade, Americans sought opportunities to better themselves by changing jobs, starting a business or moving west to the frontier; there was excitement and challenge in change.

In this social context, the law of the day made sense: workers without a specific contract or agreement were employed "at will"; they could be terminated any time and for any reason. In the words of a nineteenth century court, an employer could discharge an employee for "good cause, for no cause, or even for cause morally wrong." It worked both ways too; the employee was equally free to quit.

The Trend: Toward Requiring "Good Cause" to Terminate

The nature and importance of employment gradually changed. More and more jobs were created by larger, impersonal corporations characterized by professional management, mass production and specialization. By the turn of the century, the source of middle and working class wealth was no longer farm and family, it was the job: by the 1950s, most people bought homes and cars on credit, and many began to live in apartments and purchase consumer goods "on time." Personal possessions in this new "affluent society" could be obtained only through higher wages paid by growing businesses. As dependency on wages and salaries increased, retaining a job became an essential personal goal and termination became economic "capital punishment."

Local, private solutions were replaced with legal solutions to mitigate personal hardships. First, governments rigged safety nets, such as workmen's compensation plans and publicly financed welfare, social security, and unemployment compensation. Next, they erected umbrellas: minimum wages, overtime premiums, and child labor laws. Unions were legalized, and collective bargaining contracts began to require "just cause" for termination. Courts recognized a "property" right in public employment and required "due process" for termination. Together, these changes spelled the end for the universal right to terminate "at will."

In the 1960s Congress redefined the nature of the employment relationship for millions of people. At first, new protections were created for groups thought to be most victimized by discrimination, such as women, blacks and other racial minorities; later, older workers and handicapped employees were covered too. Although the draftsmen claimed that the laws would not change employment relationships, they did just that.

Beginning in the 1970s, state legislatures began to pass a hodgepodge of laws preventing employee terminations for serving as jurors, claiming workmen's compensation benefits or "whistleblowing." By 1980 almost half of the states had enacted such laws, and each newspaper headline about an "unjust" termination caused the introduction of more bills in state legislatures.

The old "at-will" termination rule has been drastically limited, and its core concept—complete individual freedom to act—no longer applies to promotions or even pay adjustments.

Anti-Discrimination Law Today: Protected Classes

Federal law now prohibits an employer from discriminating against a worker because of race, color, sex, nationality, religion, or age (40–70). It also bars government contractors and subcontractors from discriminating on the basis of physical handicaps. Some state and local laws go further and extend protection to persons of any age; others bar discrimination on the basis of sexual preference or even mental incapacity due to social conditions. Employees who fall within any of these special groups are said to be members of a *Protected Class*, and these Classes have become the focus of government investigations and civil rights litigation.

You should be aware that it is not necessary for a court to find a deliberate act of discrimination directed toward Protected Class members. Such conduct, of course, is discrimination in its crudest form, but courts have found employers guilty of discrimination because of their "disparate treatment" of Protected Class members. Disparate treatment simply means Protected Class members appear to have been treated less favorably than non-class members, and the employer could not offer a "legitimate non-discriminatory reason" for its action. Finally, as discussed on page 125, violations can be based upon "disparate impact." This refers to rules or practices that, though apparently neutral on their face, nevertheless disqualify or penalize a higher percentage of Protected Class members because of some inherent or common characteristic of the class.

Although anti-discrimination laws do not directly state that an employer must have "good cause" to terminate Protected Class members, such as a woman or Catholic, that is the effect of the court decisions. If you are an employer, you should have cause—some objective, nondiscriminatory basis—for terminating an employee who is a member of any Protected Class or union.

There is another reason for these words of caution: today's employees know their legal rights and aggressively assert them. People fight for that which is dearest to them, and the growing importance of a job has made its loss a significant cause of litigation, agency investigations, and hearings. One writer estimated that the number of employee challenges to management increased tenfold between 1970 and 1980.[2] More than ever, it is imperative for employers to have a map of the landmines that make personnel management so dangerous.

---

[2]D. Ewing, "Due Process: Will Business Default?" *Harvard Business Review*, November–December, 1982.

TWO PRINCIPLES FOR MANAGING EMPLOYEES

Two principles should guide all the employee management issues discussed in Part I—from hiring to firing.

Principle 1: Avoid "Adverse Impact"

Do not create an "adverse impact" on Protected Class members, whether it is in the hiring, firing, promoting, or demoting of employees. If you make decisions that affect a disproportionate number of Protected Class members, you may be found guilty of class discrimination. The test is whether there is a "statistically significant" difference in treatment of Protected and non-Protected Classes. The EEOC and OFCCP[3] guidelines define adverse impact as a selection rate for a protected group which is less than four-fifths (or 80 percent) of the rate for nonprotected groups. For example, your criteria may cause you to select men more frequently than women, or whites more frequently than blacks. If a Protected Class is selected at a rate less than 80 percent of the rate of the group with the highest selected rate, you have caused an "adverse impact." Your selection criteria must then be validated as job related, business necessity, a *bona fide* occupational qualification or a *bona fide* seniority system (see pages 126–127).

Remember that even if your system meets the statistical test, you can still be guilty of discriminating against an individual. This means you must consider the possibility of adverse impact both on groups and individuals. Good intentions are not enough: you must be vigilant concerning both the intent *and* effect of each employment practice.

Principle 2: Have a Nondiscriminatory Reason for What You Do

While the "good cause" requirement is technically not the legal standard for most promotions, demotions, or terminations, it is wise to have an objective, legal basis to support your actions. Private lawsuits are common, and government agencies open many investigations. For the employer, the costs of either occurrence can be high.

A defensible reason can save you time, trouble, and money. Without it, an employee can claim that your explanation ("Martha just wasn't 'doing the job' ") is really a lame excuse for the real reason—discrimination. This is why we stress throughout Part I of this chapter the importance of adopting and using objective and legal criteria for hiring, firing, and promoting. Perhaps Martha wasn't punctual, or she wasn't accurate, or she was too slow. Whatever it was, it should be

---

[3]The Equal Employment Opportunity Commission ("EEOC") enforces Title VII of the Civil Rights Act of 1964, the general anti-discrimination law applicable to business, and the Age Discrimination in Employment Act. The Office of Federal Contract Compliance ("OFCCP") enforces nondiscrimination obligations of government contractors through audits and investigations.

reduced to a written, cogent reason. Remember, the old "at will" rule is all but dead.

PENALTIES: THE INCENTIVES TO DO IT RIGHT

What happens if you don't follow the two basic principles or fumble? In general, there are two classes of penalties, and in some cases both may apply.

Government: After hearings or an investigation, some states and the federal government (usually through the EEOC) can obtain court-ordered remedies such as back pay, front pay, reinstatement of employees, a halt to the practice (in the form of an injunction), and loss of government contracts. For large companies, this can reach millions of dollars.

Employee Lawsuits: Many labor laws authorize a private right of action. This permits employees to sue the company for lost pay, attorneys' fees, front pay, injunction, and perhaps even punitive damages. Punitive damages are awarded for the purpose of "punishing" the company, not for reimbursing the employee for his lost wages. As Kaiser discovered in our example on page 121, punitive damages can be very high ($300,000 actual damages and $4.5 million punitive)!

FOUR RULES FOR SELECTING AND PLACING EMPLOYEES

A lawfully selected, productive work force should be an essential company goal. It can be met if you abide by four rules: use lawful, objective hiring criteria; request only essential information when hiring; head off problems with written warnings; and do not discriminate in job assignments and pay.

Rule 1: Use Lawful, Objective Hiring Criteria

When you hire or shift an employee, you should do so only on the basis of *lawful* and *objective* criteria.

To repeat, federal laws forbid employment decisions based on an employee's race, age, sex, religion, color, or nationality. You cannot use the factor that puts a person in the category of a Protected Class—their age, for example—as a criterion for hiring, firing, or promoting. The agency or employee who sues must prove individual discrimination or some "adverse impact" on a Protected Class, but because that's not hard to do, you as an employer should be ready to show that there was some *legal, objective* basis for your action—"good cause." This is why employers should develop and use objective hiring criteria (such as punctuality, accuracy, and speed) and measure applicants against them. If these have an "adverse impact," you must stand ready to show they are "job related."

This general rule has one narrow exception: it is legally possible to use three of those factors—sex, religion, and national origin—when doing so is *"reasonably necessary* to the normal operation of [your] particular business or enterprise." This is called a BFOQ—a "bona fide occupational requirement."

While a BFOQ is lawful in the abstract, it is rarely allowed in practice: do not try it without consulting a lawyer. A lawful BFOQ must be intimately related to the job's particular demands, such as hiring an actress to play a woman.

If this sounds confusing, it is. It's also why companies get into trouble: they may not *intentionally* discriminate, but a melange of muddy legal edicts and sloppy employment practices can lead to the same result as deliberate discrimination. Avoid these by carefully choosing hiring criteria and testing applicants for them.

Use Only Essential Hiring Criteria and Job Skills

Do this when you have a job to fill: identify the required job skills, establish hiring criteria and determine if they are essential and lawful.

If you need a truck driver, a chauffeur's license is a job prerequisite. But is great strength necessary? (Perhaps it is for deliverers of heavy loads but not of UPS packages.) How about a neat, clean appearance? (Yes, for employees who meet the public.) Or quickness and agility? (It may be a useful ability for the folks who stock newspaper vending machines.) The point is that the particular qualifications for your "truck driver" will vary according to his duties. Determine what skills and traits you really need and forget the rest.

Why is this important? Because you must then determine whether each criterion is legal; and the more criteria you use that you have not thought through, the greater the legal risk that one or more will disqualify disproportionate numbers of a Protected Class. The dangers exist even with an apparently neutral criterion, such as a high school diploma; because blacks are less likely to finish school, that requirement may have an adverse impact on them. This is precisely what happened to Duke Power in North Carolina; its high school diploma requirement restricted the movement of black employees into certain company positions and cost the company over $200,000.

To avoid such blunders, ask yourself these questions as you identify job-essential skills and other hiring criteria:

1. Will the criterion or required skill exclude a significant portion of minority applicants? (A six-foot height requirement would exclude most women as well as Oriental or Puerto Rican applicants.)

2. Do your present employees possess these skills or qualifications? (If not, the criteria may not measure job success.)

3. Can you consistently require the skills and still hire all the employees you need? (If not, you will have to waive them for some employees, which suggests that the skills you waived are not essential.)

4. Must *all* applicants possess the skills? (If you would hire someone with compensating qualifications, perhaps the criterion is not essential, or maybe the compensating quality should have been added.)

If you answer "no" to any of these questions but still believe the criteria are essential, check with an experienced labor lawyer. With his assistance, you might be able to justify the criteria in one of three ways. First, you may discover that there is no "adverse impact" on Protected Classes; that is, a disproportionately high number of women or blacks are not affected. Second, you might be able to justify the job skill as job related (good spelling *is* essential for a secretary). Third, you may be able to redefine the criteria to eliminate the adverse impact.

In addition to devising your own hiring standards, you can use "consensus" criteria, such as good attendance and punctuality, honesty, and similar traits. But even these must be job related if they adversely impact a Protected Class.

Tips for Testing Employees

You can administer tests to measure job skills or hiring criteria, but keep these guidelines in mind:

1. Test only job essentials. Physical skills' tests that mirror the work to be performed are lawful when they accurately predict an employee's job success; typing and timed parts assembly are good examples.

2. Do not test for something you do not need; testing for a trait that would adversely affect Protected Class members is dangerous even if you do not use the result; the EEOC assumes you use the results of every test you give.

3. Avoid general written tests. IQ and general knowledge tests are especially dangerous because they often have an adverse impact. Moreover, it is almost impossible to prove that general tests adequately measure the specific skills and abilities required for your job. If you must have a written test, get professional help to tailor it to your business and job. General health tests also create mischief because they frequently have the same effect as IQ tests, and they may not be necessary.

Rule 2: Job Applications Should Request Essential Information Only

This is the logical corollary of Rule 1. There can be serious problems if you do not follow this rule. Do you really need to know an applicant's marital status? If you routinely ask for it and then fail to hire single or divorced women, you may be found guilty of sex discrimination. Inquiries about family size and whether the applicant owns his own home are equally dangerous. The former might be evidence of discrimination on the basis of race or religion, because some racial and religious groups typically have large families; the latter could indicate racial discrimination, because blacks and recent immigrants rent more often than own. In short, be sure the information is necessary before you ask for it; if it is important for administration but not hiring, ask for it *after* an applicant is hired.

Rule 3: Head Off Problems with Written Warnings
and Common Sense

It is not enough to act lawfully; avoid thoughtless actions that create problems.

Every employee should be treated courteously, particularly applicants who are not hired. When you turn someone down, offer general but true reasons. "We do not believe your skills are consistent with our needs" is one of the safest explanations. A disappointed applicant's request for specific reasons should be answered by someone experienced in these matters, not a "soft touch." An answer that avoids hurting an applicant's feelings (but which might not be true) damages the company's legal position. For example, telling an unqualified black applicant there was no opening may save his feelings but it may also cause a lawsuit when his white friend is hired; at best you will be embarrassed when his lawyer asks you if you lie to all black applicants.

Make sure the company's application forms and handouts do not create problems with terminations and turndowns. At a minimum, the application and related materials should communicate the following:

- *The employee is applying for a job that is subject to termination at any time.* (Suggested language: I understand that I or the Company can end my employment by one week's notice with or without cause. I understand that no unit manager or representative of the Company has authority to make any contrary representations.)

- *The benefits may be changed to meet the needs of the work force and the company.* (Suggested language: This handbook does not constitute any part of a contract of employment. Because of rapid changes in the economy and the needs of our employees and Company, it may be necessary to change or depart from these policies and benefits, and the Company may also revise this handbook from time to time.)

- *The application will be kept active for only 30 days.* (This provision is designed to prevent the following situation: (a) you file away the application of a qualified Protected Class applicant because there are no openings; (b) 60 days later an opening occurs; (c) you hire an on-the-doorstep applicant *not* in a Protected Class; and (d) the Protected Class applicant learns of the opening and sues. Your case would be much stronger if the Protected Class applicant had no currently valid application on file.)

Rule 4: Don't Discriminate in Job Assignments and Pay

Anti-discrimination laws also apply to the initial job assignment and compensation level. Some companies hire without discriminating but then illegally place minorities or other Protected Class members in dirtier or lower paying jobs. To avoid this, make assignments according to actual, tested skill levels.

Employee Preferences. Be wary of making job assignments based on your suppositions about employee preferences; you could be behind the times. Failure to assign women to a paint room—because "everyone knows" women don't like to get paint in their hair—could spawn a successful lawsuit. When in doubt, check with an experienced labor lawyer.

Equal Pay. The "equal pay for equal work" issue is sure to create new problems as both the EEOC and women's groups challenge pay systems. Jobs requiring the same skill, effort, and responsibilities should pay the same.

The EEOC is attempting to use this "equal pay" principle to require that comparable (but *different*) effort be rewarded equally. For example, it has been argued that it is illegal to pay secretaries (usually women) less than salesmen (usually men) because the work of the two groups is comparable and equally valuable to the employer. Some states and local governments are adopting this policy for themselves. It is not yet the law, but you should watch the comparable pay trend carefully.

Salary Negotiations. Even individual salary negotiations are dangerous. Negotiations often begin with previous salaries and depend on negotiating skills. If the resulting salary pattern favors white or male employees, the compensation system may be challenged. When paying individually set salaries, identify the required job skills, base job rates or ranges upon these skills, and pay the individual for the predetermined value of his skills.

Wage and Hour Laws. You must also comply with the wage and hour laws. Most requirements are plain, and although compliance is generally not difficult, mistakes can be expensive. The Federal Fair Labor Standards Act requires that non-exempt employees receive the minimum wage for all hours worked and 1-1/2 times his regular rate for work exceeding 40 hours in one week. There are myriad requirements for calculating travel and waiting time, including bonuses in overtime pay and exemptions for "white collar" employees. Talk to your trade association or personnel in the U.S. Labor Department's Wage and Hour Division and your state agency; there may be special provisions for your industry, and these groups can help you comply.

EIGHT RULES FOR MANAGING YOUR EMPLOYEES

Skilled, high quality workers are no guarantee of labor peace; there must be good management as well. With it, workers are capable of greatness; without it, they can be destructive. Two examples illustrate this.

In the battle of the Coral Sea, the aircraft carrier *Yorktown* took several hits, lost power, and limped back to Pearl Harbor. Survey crews estimated that repairs would take two to three months, but the Japanese fleet was menacing our Pacific foothold at Midway and every flattop was vital. With magnificent disregard for human limitations, work crews swarmed aboard the *Yorktown* as she docked on May 27 and for three days worked with no letup for meals or sleep. On May 30, she left Pearl Harbor with work crews still aboard, and on June 4, 1942, four days out of Pearl Harbor, she launched the dive bombers which, together with those from the *Enterprise* and *Hornet*, ended the Japanese naval threat to our Pacific campaign.

By contrast, unchanneled violence more recently caused over $1 million in damages to the Altemose Construction Company's work site in King of Prussia, Pennsylvania. Hundreds of workers ripped apart chain link fences, concrete forms, and trailers; they wrecked the entire project in less than an hour.

Your work force has comparable potential for glory and infamy: the key is good management. We cannot guarantee *Yorktown* results, but following these eight rules will yield a more cooperative, productive, and less litigious work force.

Rule 1: Treat Employees as Human Beings

Ignore this axiom at your peril. Contrary to common belief, low wages are not the primary cause of employee unrest: it is the culprit less than 10 percent of the time. The primary cause is poor management, which is characterized by arbitrariness, favoritism, lack of concern for employees as people, lack of trust, and ignoring or discounting legitimate employee grievances.

The fabric of the employment relationship will become frayed and torn if employees are not treated decently. In his book on leaders and leadership, Dr. Michael Maccoby identified the common traits of successful leaders. One of the most important was a "caring, respectful, and responsible attitude" that caused them to "care about people and identify with their strivings for dignity and self-development."[4] The uniquely human traits of empathy and understanding are not misplaced, even in the competitive business world.

Labor problems arise when management treats employees as irritants to be ignored or productive resources to be tapped and manipulated. Poor managers make decisions without considering employee opinions and emotions. Changes in the method of computing pay and new job assignments are common examples. Mistrust builds until communications become blocked and tardy goodwill efforts are scorned.

Although the problem may be created by top management, it affects everyone. Line supervisors become unwilling to support company policy or unable to delegate; they blame "the boss" for problems they could resolve. More ambitious supervisors play favorites and fail to report employee complaints. All

---

[4]M. Maccoby, *The Leader* (New York: Simon and Schuster, 1981), page 221.

this causes a breakdown in communications, unrest and resentment. The problems often fester untreated until production plummets or management learns from the National Labor Relations Board that its workers have petitioned for a union election. Head off these problems now with humane and sensitive treatment of employees.

Rule 2: Be Consistent and Fair

Inconsistency leads to mistrust, a virulent and invidious labor disease that attacks the core of effective personnel relations—respect for management and confidence in its good faith. Be consistent in all labor matters, whether it be benefits, exceptions to rules, or timing of vacations.

Employees become insecure without recognizable limits and rules, but favoritism may be even worse: favored employees covet the bounty and fear its loss while disfavored employees resent their second-class status. Both problems invite a persuasive union argument: if employees were represented by a union, the rules would be in writing and applicable to all.

Rule 3: Stay in Touch with Your Employees

Superior managers are perceptive and empathetic. They can sense trouble, but not if they secrete themselves in the executive suite and officers' dining room.

If a company is small, the top executive should circulate through the plant and get to know employees by sight and nodding acquaintance. In large plants, the production or personnel manager should do the same. The entire management team should be alert to signs of trouble: employees congregating in groups that vanish when executives approach, sullenness, refusals to make eye contact, harping on employment rights, and regular employee gatherings on the parking lot.

Consider adopting formal listening systems, such as exit interviews and periodic attitude surveys. Surveys can be administered by the company or private consulting firms. It may take such formal techniques as well as sensitivity and a "listening ear" to pick up the sounds of discontent. The cost of not listening, however, is great.

Rule 4: Train Your Supervisors

Many supervisors who perform well as line employees are promoted without further training, and the "Peter Principle" comes into play. This is a common mistake. Supervisors must be competent, trained professionals who are perceived as such by their subordinates. They must know what the company expects of them and how to encourage, cajole, delegate, correct, and reprimand their employees. If you lack supervisory training facilities, enroll your supervisors in courses offered by community colleges, trade associations, or chambers of commerce.

Rule 5: Support Your Supervisors

After you have trained your supervisors, support them. If they just came from the production unit, they are no longer accepted there and may not feel a part of inside management. Recognize this and be supportive. Supervisors are the key to successful day-to-day operations, yet a recent survey disclosed that 60 percent regretted accepting the promotion.

Smart managers encourage line supervisors, make them feel a part of the management team and include them in the information flow. Communications to workers are important, but tell your supervisors first so they can answer questions from their employees. Knowledgeable supervisors are more likely to be respected by their subordinates and that makes them better managers.

Rule 6: Tell Your Employees What Is Going On

It is far better to tell your employees what is going on than to have them waste productive hours in wild speculation. Changes cause disquiet and insecurity, particularly if not explained. Information about important work changes (such as production slow-down, layoffs, new shifts, or additional products) should come from the company, not the rumor mill, the union newsletter, or the local newspaper. Employees have a right to this information because their careers are at stake. Share with them your hopes, expectations, *and* concerns.

Rule 7: Provide a Safety Valve

Every system needs a safety valve for pressures that first-line supervisors cannot handle. Most executives claim they have an "open door," but it is a rare company that allows line employees to walk into the executive suite. A formal grievance system or a complaint box is a more workable early warning system even if it attracts malcontents.

Some companies have elaborate internal grievance procedures that allow employees to appeal decisions to top management or to an independent third party. For example, Control Data Corporation has a complex grievance system and ombudsmen who act as employee counselors and advocates. Whatever the exact design, you must have some way of hearing grievances and correcting mistakes by lower level supervisors before a lawsuit is filed.

Rule 8: Get Rid of Troublemakers

Troublemakers should be identified and eliminated with speed and compassion. Early detection and quick surgery is the only solution. Troublemakers are a diverse group: recalcitrant or hardheaded supervisors who refuse to change, "invaluable" employees (often in the front office) who use gossip and inside information as a source of power, grumbling or petulant employees, and confirmed agitators. The worst are sometimes ones who have been saved from deserved termination. Ingratitude is a well-known human failing, and the more often some are redeemed, the greater their ingratitude and resentment.

HOW TO REWARD YOUR WORK FORCE: RAISES AND PROMOTIONS

As we discussed on p. 125, prohibitions against using illegal factors in hiring (such as race, sex, and age) apply equally to promotions and compensation. The rule is this: management may use any compensation or promotion system as long as it does not have the *purpose* or *effect* of discriminating on the basis of illegal factors.

Note that you can violate the law even if you do not *intend* to discriminate. As a practical matter, any unstructured system that gives supervisors unfettered discretion or sets compensation according to the person and not the job is doomed. The reason: an investigation will inevitably uncover discrepancies between races or sexes that cannot be defended. As we have said before, you must establish a system that consistently applies objective factors.

How to Give Raises

Any reward system that pays different amounts to employees with similar experience or seniority runs the risk of being illegally discriminatory. If you want to reward the better workers, do it as objectively as possible.

Identify in advance the criteria you will use to give raises or bonuses. The safest directly relate rewards to the work, such as piece rate compensation (1 cent per circuit board) or commission (7 percent of net sales by the employee). If the criteria are consistently applied, this kind of scheme will be almost impregnable.

Of course, this method cannot be used for all jobs. But the goal is the same—to develop an objective pay system that identifies and rewards the levels of performance most valuable to you. Your standards should be stated as objectively as possible, and you must work with supervisors to assure uniform application. When you are tempted to shortcut, remember that subjective criteria are hard to apply, and irrelevant criteria are suspect.

Companies depend on supervisors as the Army depends on sergeants; treat them accordingly. Provide them with *written* pay standards, explain the system, and review the program and paper work with them. Make sure they properly fill out the forms and consistently apply the standards. Only then should your supervisor discuss his evaluations privately with each employee and offer each the opportunity to respond with written comments to his evaluation. The complete record should then be reviewed by someone else because it may expose a disgruntled employee or company blunder.

Reducing the Perils of Promotions

Promotions call for tough choices among competing employees. Two rules can reduce your legal risks:

First, establish "minimum" and "preferred" criteria. The minimum, objective criteria perform a safe and valuable screening function. They can include factors such as 95 percent attendance and six months of experience in a certain level job. By contrast, only the rare candidate completely measures up to the "preferred" criteria. These can be more subjective, such as attitude and ability to work with others. Weed out nonperformers by the minimum criteria and select candidates according to the preferred criteria.

Second, select candidates objectively. There are three methods in use:

- Unfettered foreman selection. This is dangerous because supervisors tend to select their own kind: white males may promote white males.

- Self-nomination. It has the advantage of identifying ambitious employees. If they are able, you avoid accidentally overlooking them; if they are not, their self-nomination is a reminder to make sure your decision has been thought through and is supported by the written record.

- Externally created lists. Candidates who meet the "minimum" criteria are included on a list and ranked according to some objective criteria, such as seniority. The hiring supervisor then chooses from the list using the "preferred" criteria. This technique guarantees that all eligible employees are considered, and it requires written justification for passing over higher ranked candidates.

In short, use a promotion and compensation system that includes legal criteria, internal review, written support for decisions, and an opportunity for employee comment.

SIX RULES FOR TERMINATING AND DISCIPLINING EMPLOYEES

The rules for termination and other less severe forms of discipline are essentially the same, so do not naively assume employees will not challenge punishment short of termination: be equally well prepared to defend both actions. Here are six rules and practical tips you should follow.

Rule 1: Don't Create an "Adverse Effect"

As we have repeatedly said, it is illegal to take any employment action that has an adverse effect on members of a Protected Class. Be prepared to show that an employee's membership in such a class was not a factor in the decision to discipline. How? By showing that the employee did not measure up to the objective hiring and performance standards you have devised and applied. Once again, if you act without such objective standards—good cause—you are exposed to charges of illegal discrimination.

Rule 2: Don't Punish Concerted Activity

Activity undertaken by or on behalf of a group of employees is called "concerted activity," and it may be protected even in a nonunion shop. Examples: when several employees leave work at the same time or when one employee acts to protest conditions that adversely affect others. Postpone disciplinary action in such cases until you talk with an experienced labor lawyer.

Rule 3: Don't Retaliate When Workers Assert Their Rights

Beware of disciplining or retaliating against an employee for exercising his rights under federal and state statutes. For example, you must not discipline employees for applying for workmen's compensation, seeking to enforce OSHA standards, exercising ERISA rights, or reporting wage and hour violations.[5] Government agencies are aggressive in investigating employee charges of retaliation, and there are severe penalties if convicted, including fines and imprisonment.

Rule 4: Don't Discipline Workers Acting in the "Public Interest"

This rule is a judicial extension of Rule 3. Many courts are beginning to declare that workers must not be disciplined for acting in the "public interest," even if their acts are not assertions of a particular statutory right. This is difficult to define exhaustively. At a minimum it means that you should not discipline an employee merely because he is a "whistleblower," because he refuses to commit an antitrust violation such as price fixing, or if he insists that your products meet applicable state licensing and labeling standards. If you want to discipline such an employee for other reasons, see your labor lawyer first.

An emerging, broader prohibition is more troublesome: employers can't terminate employees "in bad faith" or for reasons that violate "public policy." One court has said that public policy includes "what is right and just and what affects the citizens of the state collectively." Unfortunately this leaves open the definition of "right and just." Who decides? A jury of six or twelve who may sympathize with the employee and fail to understand your company and its needs.

You should draw two lessons from this evolving "public policy" disciplinary

---

[5]OSHA is the Occupational Safety and Health Act. OSHA imposes safety standards in the work place. ERISA is the Employment Retirement Income Security Act which regulates pensions.

standard. First, the "at will" termination rule is dying. Indeed, in more liberal states, a jury is permitted to decide whether virtually *any* discharge is legal, based on the jury's notion of fairness, and to assess actual and punitive damages if they disagree (remember Kaiser Steel!). Second, it means that you should always have a good reason to support all disciplinary decisions.

Rule 5: Beware of "Implied" Employment Contracts

Workers with union or other employment contracts enjoy more protection in disciplinary matters than do workers without them. Union contracts, for example, generally prevent termination except for "good cause." In short, employers must have sound reasons to terminate employees not employed at will.

Your freedom to terminate may be restricted even if your company never signed a union contract or a formal employment agreement. Courts are beginning to find a contract was made when a company agent made oral promises to a worker or included thoughtless statements in documents, such as employee handbooks or applications. A worker's lawyer might successfully claim that the personnel manager "promised" his client that he would be fired only "for cause" or that language in the employee handbook about the company's "policy" of terminating for cause made that the standard against which *all* terminations must be measured. As a further example, the use of the term "probationary period" in a handbook suggests that *after* the probationary period an employee has more protection from termination, and a vague reference to "progressive discipline" may convince a judge or jury that the employer "contracted" with the employee to use progressive discipline and "just cause."

The outer limits were recently expanded by a California court that declared that an offer of employment carries with it a promise of "good faith and fair dealing" by the employer. This could require good cause for *all* terminations.

In summary, never assume you can freely terminate just because there is no written employment contract or protected class. Avoid risky statements during the hiring process and loose language in your manuals and hiring materials. They might add up to a contract.

Rule 6: Beware of the Meaning of "Cause"

The same forces that are gutting the "at will" rule are causing courts to redefine "cause." Today it generally means repeated on-the-job misconduct, incompetence, or behavior that causes a direct and substantial impact on the economic interest of the employer. Off-the-job misbehavior generally is not "good cause," although there are some exceptions for notorious conduct of employees who deal with the public. Employees in highly visible positions (such as Anita Bryant, the former spokesman for the Florida Citrus Commission) are also subject to tougher standards. There, off-the-job behavior might constitute "cause."

If you are not sure that an employee's behavior gives you good cause, talk to your labor lawyer.

Tips for Disciplining Employees

1. Be fair in your treatment of employees; they will be less likely to complain and you will have less need for discipline.

2. Give employees a second chance and help the employee plan corrective action. Except for flagrant dishonesty or conduct exposing the company or its employees to danger, nonperformers should first be given a written warning and counseled on ways to improve.

3. Counseling and terminations should always be done privately, decently, and courteously; outraged or offended employees are intractable foes.

4. Double-check the basis for severe discipline. A supervisor should first answer the following questions; if satisfied, he should suspend the employee until someone else can review the file and ask them again:

- Are the employee's evaluations consistently bad?

- Has he had similar problems with prior supervisors?

- Have other employees with similar records been disciplined as severely?

- Is his file free of unnecessary or patronizing references to the employee's race, sex, age, or other Protected Class characteristics?

- Has the employee been previously counseled and a contemporaneous written record placed in the file?

- Are the reasons for taking the action clear and important? Were they reasonably known to the employee beforehand?

- Has the responsible supervisor terminated or disciplined a proportionate number of non-Protected Class members? Has the plant?

A "no" answer to any of these questions should trigger a thorough, independent review of the entire matter.

If you follow our rules and tips for discipline, you should be able to avoid serious trouble.

EXCEPTIONAL WORRIES FOR GOVERNMENT CONTRACTORS

Your company has special obligations if it is a primary or secondary contractor for the federal government. The former contracts directly with the federal government; the latter is a subcontractor who works for, or supplies materials to, a primary contractor. You know if you are a primary contractor because of the mass of paper work that you have processed.

Primary Contractors

If you have a written government contract, you will find most labor regulations included within the contracting documents. If you are unsure, details of the requirements are available from the contracting agency or the Office of Federal Contract Compliance Programs. Study these materials carefully because there are severe penalties for not complying and the requirements may change.

The nature of the requirements generally depend upon the level and type of contract; here are four:

Handicaps. Firms with contracts of $2,500 or more are required to "take affirmative action to employ and advance in employment" handicapped individuals. This requires you to make a "reasonable accommodation" to their handicap.

Wage Rates. Certain construction and service contracts require payment of "area wage rates," which may be above your present scale, and daily overtime after eight hours to employees performing the government contract.

Discrimination. Firms with contracts of $10,000 or more may not discriminate on the basis of race, color, sex, religion, national origin, or age. These requirements are similar to those applicable to most employers, but these contractors must also take "affirmative action" to avoid discrimination. Similarly, they must take affirmative action to employ and advance in employment "qualified disabled veterans" and Vietnam era veterans.

AAPs. Companies with contracts valued in excess of $50,000 must prepare written "Affirmative Action Plans" ("AAPs") that include a self-analysis of their utilization of Protected Class employees as well as compliance goals and timetables; and employers then must take "affirmative steps" to eliminate underutilization or discrimination.

Subcontractors

Companies that supply materials to, or do work for, government contractors may be subject to the same requirements. For example, subcontractors that satisfy the various threshold requirements of contract dollar amount and number of employees are subject to the nondiscrimination provisions as if they were prime contractors.

Evaluate the Costs and Benefits of Government Work

Whether you are a subcontractor or prime contractor, you should understand how an AAP or other contract requirement might change your company's employment practices and thereby increase labor costs. Be sure to include these costs in your projections before you accept a government contract or subcontract.

You should also consider whether the benefits of government work are outweighed by the cost of complying with the special requirements. Particularly

for smaller companies, the answer may be "yes." Consider the hotel that contracted to house military inductees. As required by government regulations, the
hotel charged the lowest rate applicable to its commercial customers. Later, a
government auditor backcharged the hotel for thousands of dollars in overtime
pay for laundry employees and higher hourly rates for maintenance and cleaning
employees. The government had insisted on the lowest commercial room rate,
but under the obscure Service Contract Act it substantially increased the hotel's
labor costs. This could happen to you.

TWO NEW FRONTIERS IN LABOR LAW

Harassment and the "Neutral" Working Environment

One recent development in the definition of sex discrimination offers clues
to future challenges. If it becomes accepted and applied to race, national origin,
and age discrimination, it will pose even greater challenges to management.

By the late 1970s, a supervisor's demands for sexual favors were treated as
sex discrimination; this "sexual harassment" was then expanded to include co-
worker demands known to management. Now the EEOC is attempting to
broaden sex harassment to include crude jokes or sexual remarks by supervisors
and co-workers, even where no sexual demands are made on the employee. The
test, according to one court, is whether the working conditions affect the employee's "psychological well-being." A harassed employee need not show any loss
of job or salary, only an intangible psychological detriment.

You will recall that we began Part I of this chapter by noting that the
discrimination laws require that an illegal practice have an "adverse impact" on
members of a Protected Class. Employees who assert the existence of such an
effect will have a far easier time making their case if they can win by showing only
psychological harm.

Your company's employment practices must change according to the law; if
the EEOC prevails, you must tighten your rules. The best defense is to include
in employee handbooks and personnel materials clear, flat prohibitions against all
forms of sexual, ethnic, or racial harassment. You should also establish a complaint mechanism that includes direct access to a top-notch personnel office.
Complaints give employers an early opportunity to investigate and take remedial
steps; an employee who went to court before he visited the personnel office
would have more difficulty convincing a jury that he suffered real injury.

Age Discrimination

A second frontier is age discrimination. In response to growing pressures
from an aging population, Congress prohibited age discrimination, which includes mandatory retirement or demotions prior to age 70, and there is now

increasing pressure to apply these protections to workers who are over 70. This means management must show good cause each time it lays off, demotes, or passes over any older worker. With a shaky social security system, older employees fear retirement, and the elimination of mandatory retirement could create very real problems for your company, such as:

Jury Trial. Unlike most civil rights violations, age discrimination cases can be tried to a jury. Most jurors can identify with an older employee, for we all face the prospect of growing older (the alternatives are worse). Consequently, a jury is likely to sympathize with an older, long-term employee who was fired or demoted and replaced by a younger employee he trained.

A Hobson's Choice. The need to reward middle level, aggressive managers creates a Hobson's Choice—leave older employees in place and lose or disillusion your younger "hopes for the future," or bite the bullet and risk high damages from an impassioned jury. If you opt for promoting, follow the Tips for Disciplining Employees (p. 135).

In the next few years, there will be further (and, for management, possibly frightening) developments in the areas of harassment, required working environment, comparable pay, and age discrimination. Someone in your company must follow these developments and seek innovative solutions. The future will belong to the creative.

PART II
UNIONS: THE DO'S AND DON'TS

Most firms resist unionization, often because they don't want to share management authority. This anti-union sentiment is particularly strong in small and mid-size companies, but curiously many employees as well are becoming apprehensive about unionization. Between 1965 and 1980, for example, there was a fourfold increase in the number of bargaining units that voted to end their union representation, and the unionized percentage of the U.S. work force fell from over 33 percent to less than 25 percent. Whatever the trend, management usually feels strongly about unions one way or the other, and we assume you do not welcome unionization attempts.

If you do your job well, employees will resist covert solicitation and force the unions to show themselves by engaging in public handbilling or other high visibility tactics. On the other hand, if the first hint of union activity is a notice from the NLRB, you or your supervisors have fumbled the ball and allowed the union to successfully solicit enough "cards" to obtain an election.

Whether you are fortunate enough to have advance notice of a unionization attempt or are taken by surprise, the game is not lost. There are certain steps you must take immediately and there are others that you must shun.

What You Must Do

1. Immediately hire a labor lawyer experienced in NLRB elections. The rules of this game are complex and the stakes are high.

2. Streamline your decision-making apparatus. The NLRB may schedule an election within 30–45 days, so you cannot waste time. The executive with final responsibility must take charge. His staff should include an attorney as well as a production supervisor and a personnel representative. They should meet daily and be available on short notice.

3. Announce formally the company's position: "We do not believe the union will be in the best interest of the employees or the company and we intend to fight it by every legal means."

4. Keep supervisors informed and involved. Show them the importance of a team effort, tell them what they can do, and give them advance notice of all company announcements and actions affecting the employees.

5. Identify the union's source of strength (by age, sex, race and department), issues (such as pay, fringes, and working conditions) and its record (such as for corruption or violence).

6. Open lines of communication with employees; use fact sheets, handouts, department meetings, and question boxes. Explain why you believe a union would not be good for them or the company.

7. Maintain even-handed discipline. Union organizing is protected activity if it does not interfere with company operations. Termination of an employee for union activity can lead to an NLRB investigation, an order requiring reinstatement with back pay, and a public notice that the employer has been found guilty of an Unfair Labor Practice. Discipline must be continued, but it must be consistent and fair.

8. After identifying the issues, address them through group talks, department meetings, posters, and speeches. With proper advice, there is much you can tell your employees.

What You Must Not Do

When you think about what you must not do, think of TIPS. This will steer you away from most legal pitfalls.

- *"T" means THREATEN.* You cannot threaten workers with reprisals, such as reduced benefits or termination, or take any other retaliatory action.

- *"I" means INTERROGATE.* You cannot ask employees whether they signed a union representation card, whether they are supporting the organizing activity, how they intend to vote, or what they think about union representation.

- *"P" means PROMISE.* You cannot promise (as a reward for a "no" vote on the union) wage or benefit increases, promotions, or fringes.

- *"S" means SURVEILLANCE.* You cannot "spy" on union activities or employees to determine who is attending union meetings. This is true for both working and nonworking hours and on or off the company premises.

Above All, Don't Be Paralyzed

Remember, inaction means a union victory. Don't temporize; act decisively. It is better to act than lose by default.

Use common sense when confronted by a union challenge. Give your personal opinion or comment on your actual experience with unions, warn employees to read carefully anything the union asks them to sign, caution that a union may force an employee to strike even if he personally would accept the employer's wage offer, and state that union organizers will not know how an employee votes in the secret ballot election.

PART III
FINAL TIPS FOR KEEPING THE LABOR PEACE

The labor laws are equal part peril and potential: though the risks are great, the opportunities for decisive preventive action are equally so. We have discussed as many problems as solutions, but whichever problem you have or solution you devise, keep the following principles in mind:

1. *Use common sense, courtesy, and consistency.* The 3C's should be the templet for all decisions. Consider the effects of your actions from the employees' point of view, communicate your goals and hopes, and prompt the workers to speak of "us" and "our company," not "them" and "they."

2. *Provide employees with a safety valve.* Give employees an opportunity to respond to evaluations and voice their concern about other matters that directly affect them, including job changes, promotions, favoritism, and managerial callousness.

3. *Do your paper work.* More and more business decisions become jury matters, and juries are more impressed by what was written at the time of the incident than your after-the-fact, witness-stand explanations. If your written records reflect persistent, inferior employee performance after counseling, a jury will be impressed. If there is no written record, the trial becomes a swearing contest, and a jury is likely to be more sympathetic to the pleas of a terminated employee than the company. Written records also alert upper management to latent problems.

4. *Avoid adverse impacts.* Avoid employment practices that disqualify or adversely affect a disproportionate number of Protected Class members.

5. *Have a defensible reason for what you do.* For employment practices generally, this means having objective, legal criteria as the foundation of each personnel decision.

6. *Provide internal checks on every important decision.* Supervisors and executives should have the benefit of other views. A strong personnel officer is a valuable second voice. He should understand the employee perspective; screen reviews, promotions, and discipline; keep and review necessary records; and act as a listening post and early warning system.

When applied with sensitivity and common sense, these guides are tools to shape your work force. It is now in your hands—will you have an Altemos construction blowup or *Yorktown* heroism?

8. How to Protect Your Products, Innovations, and Secrets

by ALAN J. KASPER

Your ability to make a superior product is no guarantee of success in the marketplace. More is required: you must protect the product's integrity, maintain secrecy about marketing strategies, use efficient production techniques, and devise an effective promotion program. You can increase your company's chances for long-term success by adopting legal strategies that promote each of these business goals. At a time of rapid technological change and increased competition, the survival of many companies may depend upon the creative use of that area of the law known as "intellectual property"—patents, trade secrets, copyrights, and trademarks.

Companies and individuals alike go to great lengths to protect their "tangible" property against theft, misuse, or damage: they install automatic security systems, hire guards, and purchase insurance. Different but equally effective techniques should be adopted to protect your "intangible" property—inventions, confidential information, expressions of ideas, and distinctive names or symbols. Who would question the importance of protecting an exclusive right to the *Star Wars* screenplay, an integrated circuit design, or the Xerox® trademark?

This chapter will tell you what intangible property you should protect, which techniques to use, and how to use them properly. We discuss four legal fields, each identified by the subject matter they primarily cover:

- *Patents*—used to protect *inventions*. (Part I)
- *Trade Secrets*—used to protect *information*. (Part II)
- *Copyright*—used to protect the tangible *expression* of an *idea*. (Part III)
- *Trademark*—used to protect a *name* or *symbol*. (Part IV)

While we will separately describe the protection available in all four fields, remember that each is related to the other. For example, more than one form of protection may be used for most commercial property: computer software can be used in a patentable product, can be identified with a trademark, and can be the subject of a copyright. But there are other times when the forms are mutually exclusive: a patent requires full public disclosure of an idea, while trade secret protection depends on secrecy.

When attempting to protect intellectual property, carefully evaluate which form of protection is best under the circumstances. As you will see, each one has features that make it appropriate in some cases but not others. But this generalization may be a helpful guide:

- *Hardware products* (such as electronics equipment, mechanical devices, and chemical compounds) may utilize patent, trademark, and occasionally trade secret protection.
- *Software products* (such as computer programs, advertising, manuals, films, and artwork) typically utilize copyright, trademark and, to a limited extent, trade secret protection.
- *Service industries* (such as communications, entertainment, repair, and construction) typically rely on trademark and trade secret protection to provide the competitive edge.

We first look at patent protection: what it is, five criteria for patent protection, a checklist of key points to use in deciding whether to patent, how to patent, an eight-point patent management plan, and how to avoid patent infringement. After discussing trade secrets, copyrights, and trademarks, we conclude the chapter with an Intellectual Property Scorecard that permits you to see quickly the pros and cons of each technique.

PART I
PATENTS: HOW TO PROTECT AN INVENTION

Suppose you or one of your employees has just developed a revolutionary product that is certain to make millions for all concerned: a lightweight automobile battery using nickel and hydrogen gas as the active materials. You have been reading the technical literature, you are familiar with the rechargeable batteries marketed by the competition, and you are confident that your new materials provide a quantum leap forward in battery cost, performance, and lifetime. How do you market it while also protecting it? While your first thought may be "the patent laws," we will show in this chapter how that choice involves important trade-offs.

Patent Protection: The Right to Exclude

In the United States, federal patent laws give the inventor or the company to which he assigns the patent ("the patentee") a right to exclude others from commercializing (specifically, making, using, and selling) *the invention* for a period of 17 years.

This "right to exclude" is in fact a limited monopoly. Its value is threefold: (1) to prevent the competition from making, using, or selling the invention; (2) as a source of royalty income from licensees whom you allow to manufacture the invention; and (3) as a legal defense to rights that may be asserted by others.

As valuable as it is, the patent does not guarantee you the right to commercialize the invention; that is, to market it generally and reap the profits. The reason is that another inventor may have previously secured patent rights to the components or basic concept of your invention. For example, you could be prevented from making and selling your automobile battery, even with its new components and designs, if there is an earlier and unexpired patent on the basic concept of a nickel electrode in a battery. But all is not lost: perhaps you can make a deal with the inventor who has the rights to the basic concept whereby the two of you exchange rights. That way, both can commercialize the battery.

Worldwide Patent Protection

Since there is a large overseas market for your new automobile battery, you want to know if you can prevent its manufacture in France, its sale by the Japanese, or its use in Brazil.

The United States patent right is enforceable against anyone whose activities are subject to the laws of the United States, including the United States Government. However, in the absence of competitor activity in the United States, it is not enforceable against commercialization in other countries. You must look to protection under the patent laws of each country of concern—clearly, at a substantial overhead cost for your new product.

The good news is that the process of obtaining international protection has been simplified. Today, most industrialized nations are signatories to international treaties that standardize the criteria, streamline the procedures, and reduce the costs for obtaining patent protection.

Who Owns Patent Rights?

A U.S. patent is granted to the person (or persons if it's a joint activity) who first makes the invention. The patent right, like other property, may be transferred or "assigned" to someone else by contract.

The vast majority of patent applications are filed by companies whose employees work under agreements requiring them to assign the invention to the company. These employee agreements are generally valid but some states restrict them to inventions that are products of a task specifically assigned by the employer, that are directly related to the employer's business, or that result from the use of the employer's time, materials, facilities, or information. Absent such an agreement, most states permit the employee to retain ownership of the patent but grant the employer a "shop right" to practice the invention—to use, manufacture, and sell it without paying a royalty.

Tip: Your production employees, as well as those in research and development, should be required to sign an assignment agreement. This will assure that you have patent ownership, which means you alone have rights to license and enforce all patents on ideas relating to your business.

Deciding Whether to Patent:
A Checklist of Key Issues

Despite the allure of a national right to exclude others from using, selling, or making the invention, before proceeding to apply for a patent it is prudent to first analyze the costs and benefits of patent protection. There are eight important issues to consider.

1. Dollar Cost

Patent protection is valuable but it's also expensive. There are two sets of costs. First, the U.S. Patent and Trademark Office levies fees for filing patent applications and for issuing and maintaining the patent over the course of its 17-year life. Although the fees are lower for individuals and small businesses, they have recently gone up and are likely to do so again. Second, you will need the assistance of a patent lawyer—someone with knowledge of the technology, statutory requirements, and government procedures. Expect to spend $5,000–$10,000 over the life of the patent for lawyers' and government fees combined.

2. Time Delays

Patent protection is available only after lengthy government processing. This review often takes two years or more, and during that time you have no statutory right to prevent someone else from using the invention. This delay is the reason some companies will not bother to patent an invention that uses rapidly changing technology; by the time the patent is granted, the invention has lost its commercial advantage to a second generation product.

3. Dangers of Disclosure

You must make a detailed public disclosure of the invention in the patent. Consider that this act alone may extinguish your competitive advantage; the published details may enable others to design around your protection. Also, improvements of your product by your competition may be made easier with those details in hand—and they may patent those improvements as well. Carefully weigh the benefits of the patent monopoly against the dangers of disclosure for each product. If the latter are excessive, consider trade secret protection, which is discussed beginning on page 155.

4. Patents Are Pregnable

More than one patent holder has belatedly discovered that even though issued by an expert federal agency, patents are only presumed to be valid; they are still subject to attack in a court of law. Suppose you get your battery patent and some years later sue a competitor for infringing it when he too makes a nickel–hydrogen car battery. He is certain to claim your patent is invalid, and you may have to prove validity before a court will give you any relief. You may be surprised to learn that many patent holders lose such cases. *Tip:* Be certain to have the validity of your patent confirmed in an opinion by a patent attorney before even threatening enforcement or litigation.

5. Patent Protection Is Finite

As we said, the term of the U.S. patent grant is 17 years; it exists for comparable periods under the laws of other countries. It can't be extended; when the term is up, the protection ends. By contrast, trade secret protection runs for as long as the secret can be maintained.

6. Commercial Value

The decision to apply for a patent should also turn on an objective assessment of the commercial potential of the invention and the role of a government patent grant in developing it. Is there a market for products that might embody the patented item? Will the product sell on its own? Is there a reasonable expected return in license royalties? What kind of market share can you expect?

7. Is It a Basic Invention?

Commercial value may be significant if your invention is basic and covers several possible embodiments; that is, various combinations of elements or process steps. But if the patent covers only one process for making your new battery and there are two more comparable processes known to your competitors, there may be little commercial benefit in securing a patent.

8. Consider the Alternatives to Patent Protection

Patents often are sought on inventions that are not basic or do not have a significant commercial value. While the patenting of such inventions may serve certain defensive purposes—by publishing them and thereby preventing the patenting by others—this may not be an effective use of government resources, to say nothing of the patentee's money. An assessment of the goals for seeking a patent should be made early on, and again during the course of patent examination and maintenance. Consider whether these goals can be served in other ways—such as defensive publication in trade journals. Evaluate patent protection with an eye on trade secret protection as well; each is best under different circumstances and trade secret protection is cheaper.

Do You Have a Patentable Item?

Patent protection is available only if the following five criteria are satisfied.

1. Proper Subject Matter

Patents are granted for inventions and their improvements within these categories of "subject matter":

- Machines—such as an electric motor or manufacturing device.
- Processes—the steps or ways a particular product or chemical is manufactured or functions, such as the steps in making the rechargeable nickel–hydrogen car battery.
- Articles of manufacture—such as the parts of the electric motor: its coils, resistors, and armature.
- Compositions of matter—such as chemicals.

Your new product may be protectable by patents covering inventions in more than one category. Our nickel–hydrogen battery, for example, might be patentable as an "article of manufacture" and its manufacturing steps as a "process."

Patents are also available for designs and asexually reproduced plants but they will not be granted for abstract ideas, formulas, mathematical equations, algorithms, or products of nature. But the rules are mutable: patents have been granted where the mathematical equation or algorithm is part of a process or device invention, and the U.S. Supreme Court has affirmed that man-made microorganism inventions are also patentable.

2. Utility

The patentable invention must be useful, not frivolous or contrary to public policy, health, or welfare. A stretching machine is "useful" when it is designed to limber an athlete's muscle; a similar one may not be "useful" if it is designed for torture.

3. Novelty

The invention must be "novel." This means it must be new or different. Something as subtle as a color change can be novel, although the invention probably would not pass the fourth test of "obviousness." In patent law jargon, if information about the item has already been publicly disclosed, then "prior art" is said to exist. Prior art, often the biggest hurdle to patentability, is most likely to surface in two ways.

First, the inventor–applicant can destroy patentability in the U.S. by publishing articles about the item, by selling it, or by commercially using it in some other way more than one year before the application is filed. In most foreign countries, no "grace period" is given and any unrestricted use, disclosure, or sale will immediately destroy novelty. There are exceptions to this rule in the U.S., such as where the use is experimental or the disclosures are oral. But a safe general rule is this: preserve novelty by maintaining secrecy until the application is filed.

Prior art arises in a second way: other inventors may develop and sell a similar product and publish articles about it, or they may apply before you for patent protection. These and similar acts that give the public information about the invention may destroy its novelty.

4. Not Obvious

If the differences between one or more items of prior art and the invention are "obvious," the invention is not patentable. Example: where telephones and radio volume controls are known as the "prior art," an invention comprising volume controls on telephones would be obvious. The test is to evaluate the differences at the time the invention was made and decide whether they would have been obvious to someone of "ordinary skill in the art" to which the invention pertains; that is, obvious to makers of telephones or radios.

5. Full Disclosure

This is technically not a test of patentability, but if you don't make the required full disclosure in your application, you will not be granted a patent. The patent application must contain a sufficiently detailed description of the invention to enable someone of ordinary skill in the art to make it or practice it. Furthermore, the description must reveal the best or preferred embodiment of the invention and its operations—often the design you intend to market and not one of lesser quality. Clearly, competitively valuable information may be placed on the public record in order to comply with this requirement.

A secondary requirement is to disclose all prior art you know about; this allows the Patent Office to test for novelty and obviousness. The failure to make this disclosure can be a fraud that would later invalidate the patent. *Tip:* Tell your patent attorney about all prior disclosures, sales, and public uses as well as any publications pertaining to the technology directly related to your invention.

Patent Pointers: The Decision to Patent

We have identified key issues to address before you file a patent application and the criteria for patentability. At this stage—before you file an application—keep these pointers in mind:

- Once you have the invention, perform a cost-benefit analysis to determine if a patent is a sound investment.
- Identify all prior art that pertains to the novelty and obviousness criteria; a preliminary search of the Patent Office files can be helpful.
- Avoid public use, sale, or publication of the invention before an application is filed.
- Seek patent protection promptly; maintain records of the invention's development from concept to prototype, as well as records of the decision to seek patent protection.

How to Obtain a Patent: Procedures

You have an invention, it satisfies the five criteria for patentability, and your analysis of the key-issue checklist comes down in favor of patent protection. What next?

First, gather all pertinent items of prior art, including information on its use and sale. You also should review appropriate professional journals and search the public files in the U.S. Patent and Trademark Office to see if any U.S. or foreign patents have been issued for similar items. These files are open to the public and the government staff is available to help you. Patent attorneys also can perform this task and advise you on the scope of available protection. Counsel fees for this preliminary work should be no more than a few hundred dollars.

If adequate protection appears to be available, a patent application should be prepared and filed, but only by a patent attorney or someone who is familiar with the technology as well as the knotty rules of the application process. *Warning:* Rights can be lost and high costs incurred by failing to follow these rules and requirements; a cost-effective business strategy demands that the application be handled by patent experts. In addition to certain formal documents and the fee, an application itself usually contains drawings, a detailed technical specification, and claims.

The Scope of a Patent

Claims. "Claims" define the protected invention and limit its scope. After filing, a Patent Examiner who specializes in the invention's technology will examine the application and compare your claims to the invention—the particular description of the subject matter you want to patent—to any prior art he discovers during his research. Using formal procedures, the Examiner will attempt to reach an agreement with you on the allowable scope of patent claims that satisfy the criteria for patentability. Unresolved issues can be appealed to a Board of Appeals and then to the new Court of Appeals for the Federal Circuit that adjudicates all issues involving patentability and infringement.

Note that your "patent claims"—what you say should be protected—are vital in this process. The claims can be very broad (a battery using nickel and hydrogen as the reactive materials) or very narrow (the special chemical process for producing a nickel–hydrogen battery comprising detailed steps A, B, C . . .). If your claims are allowed and a patent is granted, they mark the boundary of the protected invention and become the standard against which an infringement is measured.

Reexamination. As further evidence that patents are pregnable, even after a patent is granted it can be "reexamined" by the Patent Office to determine if it's still valid. You can initiate such a proceeding for both offensive or defensive purposes. Defensive: You can use it to assert that your competitor's existing patent is no longer valid because, unknown to the Patent Office at the time of initial review, there was prior art that precluded registration. Offensive: You can ask for a reexamination of your own patent to strengthen it in anticipation of infringement litigation; for example, where new prior art has been found that would be asserted by an infringer as a defense of invalidity.

How to Protect Your Patent from Infringement

Infringement. Your patent is "infringed" when someone makes, uses, or sells the patented item in a way that you have not previously authorized. The direct infringement of a patent claim requires that each element expressly stated in the claim (or its functional equivalent) be present in the offending device. Liability can also be found for actions leading to an infringement, such as the sale of an item that is a unique and essential element of the patented invention (a "contributory infringement") or for inducing someone else to infringe. The tests for direct, contributory, and inducement infringement are set out in the patent statute and have been interpreted extensively by the courts.

Remedies. The damage caused by an infringement of patent rights is most often remedied in one of two ways. Most commonly, the patent holder grants a license to the infringer in return for which the latter pays royalties for each item sold. Where the patentee and infringer are competitors, the rates may be high enough to maintain the patent holder's competitive advantage. A "cross license" also can be used; here each side licenses the other to produce or use the items subject to its particular patents.

Second, the patent statute authorizes the courts to grant orders ("injunctions") halting the infringement, but these are given only if other remedies do not adequately compensate the patent holder. You also may be able to recover triple damages, but this is an extraordinary remedy available only when there is intentional infringement.

An Eight-Point Patent Management Plan

To protect your patent rights, you must be both vigilant and aggressive—vigilant to those acts that can dilute or destroy your rights and aggressive in defending your patent rights against infringing acts of others. Execute an eight-point patent management plan:

1. Carefully monitor all your agreements including licenses, purchase orders, sales contracts, and joint venture arrangements for terms that dilute your right to exclude others from making, using, or selling the patented item. *Warning:* Pay particular attention to government procurement contracts that often grant the government actual title to the item or a royalty-free license to use it.

2. Don't make oral representations or take actions that can create an "implied" license right in others. Some examples are: Saying to an infringer, "You know I won't sue you for that"; ignoring a known infringer's actions entirely; or failing to enforce rights after making a claim of infringement.

3. Don't abuse your patent rights through licenses that fix prices, tie products to unpatented goods, allocate markets among your competitors, or foster other antitrust violations. (See the next chapter for a discussion of these problems.)

4. Establish a system to ensure payment of U.S. government patent maintenance fees (in years 4, 8, and 12 of the 17-year grant).

5. Be careful when treating members of a group of licensees differently, since discriminatory licensing could be a patent misuse that destroys your rights.

6. Mark patented goods with the official numbers of the applicable patents (in order to take advantage of statutory notice requirements); conversely, don't identify patents that are not relevant to the product. The use of "patent pending" has no legal significance, but it does serve as a warning to potential infringers.

7. If you suspect an infringement, don't prematurely threaten litigation because that may cause the infringer to sue you first for a "declaratory judgment"—a court order—that your patent is invalid.

8. If you suspect an infringement, obtain an opinion of legal counsel on the validity and infringement of your patent; do it before attempting to enforce your legal rights.

How to Avoid Infringing Someone Else's Patent

Just as you should aggressively defend your patent rights, so your competitors will defend theirs. Don't invest in a new business or penetrate new product markets without first determining whether you might infringe someone's patents. Such a thoughtless action can spawn costly litigation that can lead to royalty payments to the patent holder and even a court order halting production of the infringing product. Adopt a plan to reduce the risk of patent infringement:

1. Subject new products to an "infringement audit"—a review of all potentially applicable and unexpired patents. This will identify likely litigants, companies to which you may have to pay a royalty.

2. Be aware that you can infringe a patent even if one of the elements of the claim is an equivalent. In our battery example, a firm might infringe even if its battery used nickel cadmium, rather than nickel hydrogen as claimed, assuming all other elements are present and the batteries are substantially similar.

3. If you analyze or "reverse engineer" a competitor's product (buy it and then develop each component by working backward), you should identify and carefully examine each patent owned by the competitor.

4. Study the patents listed on your competitor's products; you may unwittingly be infringing them.

5. Don't intentionally infringe; damages are tripled in such cases and you may have to pay attorneys' fees and costs as well.

6. If you think you may be infringing a patent, consider asking the Patent Office to reexamine it; if you have discovered prior art that was not reviewed at the time of the application, the Patent Office may declare the patent invalid.

The Sensible Use of Patents

Before you invest time and money in patent protection, weigh it against the benefits and costs of trade secret protection we discuss next. If you already have patents, adopt a patent management plan that defends them from infringement; with or without patents, be alert to inadvertent infringement of another company's patent claims.

PART II
TRADE SECRETS: HOW TO PROTECT INFORMATION

Whether a "secret" is whispered across the backyard fence or a boardroom table, its security is primarily dependent on the soundness of the speaker's judgment and the integrity of the listener. Each of us has learned the hard way that the best kept secret is the one that is never disclosed; yet in the commercial world, the secrets that produce company success often must be disclosed to others. The question is, how are they protected? As you will see, the answer to that question involves as much common sense as law.

What Is a Trade Secret?

The short answer is that it is secret business or technical information that is valuable, not generally known by others, and protected against disclosure. As we will repeat throughout Part II, the essential nature of the concept and the protection is secrecy: information must be secret even though it is shared with others, and it is protectable only if secrecy is maintained by all those with access to the information, including employees, contractors, and customers.

Definitions aside, there is a broad spectrum of information that is protectable as a trade secret: formulas, manufacturing know-how, customer lists, financial information, and business strategies. In short, virtually any confidential information that provides a commercial advantage over competitors may be protectable.

What Protection Do You Get?

Trade secret protection is a matter of state and common law; in contrast to other intellectual property, there are no applicable federal statutes on which you can rely. The theory of protection can be based either on the breach of an express or implied agreement to protect the secret or on the "misappropriation" of the secret—its illegal use. To confound matters further, this fluid and mushrooming area of law is rooted more in the public policies of "fairness" and "equity" than on precise legal principles. State courts differ on the scope of available trade secret protection and the nature of available remedies.

In applying a standard of "fairness," courts will try to do "what is just" under the circumstances of each case. If a court finds that one of your employees has misappropriated a trade secret, your remedy depends on the "equities" of the situation—your efforts to protect the secret, what you lost, what the employee gained, why he did it, and the importance or value of the secret.

Two basic remedies are available:

Damages. A company whose trade secrets have been misappropriated may be able to recover the profits gained by the infringer or lost by the owner, royalties, and even punitive damages.

Injunctions. A court will often order the guilty party to cease his misappropriation, but the length of time covered by the order can vary from perpetuity to only a few months.

Warning: In contrast to patent protection, you have no remedy at all if someone independently develops a technology that is the subject of trade secret protection. You have a remedy only if someone wrongfully appropriates, uses, or discloses your secret information, an action that is often difficult to detect.

Legal Requirements for Protecting a Trade Secret

Most trade secret lawsuits arise out of situations that are or should have been governed by contracts. The agreements may be *express*, as in the case of written employee and confidential disclosure agreements, or they may be *implied* by a course of conduct that indicates to a prudent businessman either that something of value is to be protected or that there is no permission for free use. The written contract generally does two things: it tries to identify the information you want kept secret (such as a customer list, a business plan, or a circuit design) and it extracts from the other party an obligation not to disclose or use the information in an unauthorized way.

The clarity of the notice, the particularity of the identification, and the scope of the commitment often are the subject of dispute. In resolving the dispute, there is a tension between your right to protect your confidential business information and the freedom of the other party (often a present or former employee) to engage in his own business or profession.

Example: Suppose one of your valued technical employees leaves the company, but without taking blueprints or drawings of any kind. Sometime later he designs *from memory* and begins to market a nickel–hydrogen battery that is virtually identical to one you sell. Your ability to recover damages or to prevent the sale of the competitive product will depend on many factors including the language of any written employee agreement, the notice you gave him of the secrecy of your design, the availability of the design by product analyses or "reverse engineering," and the origin of the design from the general skills and knowledge he gained while working for you for the past ten years.

In deciding on the basis of all relevant facts, a court is likely to see if at least the following elements are present:

1. *Secrecy.* This is the essential element; the information must be sufficiently secret that it is not generally known to others in your industry. You can communicate the information to some employees and even third parties but they must be pledged to secrecy. Of course, if you tell too many people, it's no longer secret.

2. *Value.* Your secret must have some intrinsic value so that its loss will cause you damage. Value may reside in its novelty or cost of development; even the simple fact that the secret is not known to others supports its value.

3. *No Access.* You must limit access to the information. Conversely, an infringer must have illegal access to the secret; that is, without your authorization. Note that access to information by independent development, reverse engineering, or analysis of public information *is* permitted.

4. *Identification.* The secret must be identifiable and determinable; clear boundaries must separate the secret from other similar information. In our battery example, you must be able to show a court which part of it or its manufacturing process was a trade secret.

5. *Notice.* There must be proper and specific notice to the holders of your secret that they have an obligation to protect it. A general admonition of "secrecy" may not be sufficient.

Steps You Can Take to Protect Your Trade Secrets

Though the perfect secret is the one only you know, there are five practical steps you can take when confidential business information must be released. Precisely what you do will be a function of the information's value to your competitors.

1. Maintain Tight Security

Maintain tight security to preclude easy access to secrets by unauthorized individuals. Whether in documentation or in visible designs or processes, the secrets should be retained in secure areas that are guarded, locked, and accessible only by authorized personnel. Establish procedures to regulate access by employees and visitors to the areas where the secrets are kept, the devices containing them, and of course the documents themselves. Mark the documents with a "proprietary" legend (owned by you). A brief statement of the restrictions on access, use, and disclosure will help the legend speak for itself.

It is imperative that these policies and procedures be unambiguous and strictly enforced. Senior executives must observe them too: the weak link will be discovered in litigation and the failure to adhere uniformly to secrecy requirements can be fatal to trade secret protection.

Periodically review security arrangements to see if they have kept pace with the number and value of secrets. But recognize that sometimes you have to compromise: to close an important business deal you may have to disclose confidential information to the other side.

2. Educate Your Employees

Employees at every level must be given a formal education in trade secrets. Explain the five elements of trade secret protection, demand absolute secrecy, and tell them how to avoid infringing someone else's trade secrets. Hold seminars, post notices, and use entrance and exit interviews to demonstrate your commitment to security.

3. Use Employee Trade Secret Agreements

You need not have a written contract with an employee to prove that he misappropriated your trade secrets, but it surely helps: you can clearly define the protected information as well as the rights of the company and employee. A written contract is also strong evidence that the employee has notice that you consider your information valuable and secret, essential elements in trade secret law.

Most lawsuits about trade secret misappropriation involve contracts of one sort or another. There are several issues to consider.

When to Sign the Contract. The best time to have your employees sign a trade secret agreement is when they are hired. This puts them on notice from day one that they have access to confidential business information that should not be disclosed, and it makes their hiring conditioned on their consent to the agreement's terms. Even if such an agreement was not initially signed, you can use them after the employee has been hired, but consult your lawyer first in such cases.

Describe the Secrets. The trade secret agreement should identify the information you want the employee to protect: "the retail customer list of Electric Car Battery Company," or "the engineering drawings, specifications, and manufacturing processes for a 12 volt, 32 ampere nickel–hydrogen electric car battery design. . . . " You should also include a dragnet provision that broadly covers other confidential information associated with battery design, production, and sale. Ideally, new secrets should be periodically identified in modifications to the agreement or in employee briefings or memos.

In-Term Covenants. The trade secret agreement should bar the employee from disclosing the information to unauthorized persons (anyone other than those you identify as "authorized") while still a company employee. You don't want an engineer working part-time for someone else or leaking the information to a competitor; you may not want him disclosing details of the secret even to other company employees who do not have a "need to know."

Post-Term Covenants. The most important provision, and the most likely to be challenged by a former employee in the event you claim misappropriation, is one that tries to regulate the employee's behavior *after* he leaves the company. The restrictions are of two types: preventing him from competing against his former employer ("noncompete clause"), or preventing him from merely using or disclosing the confidential information ("disclosure clause"). Use both provisions subject to the following guidelines:

- Some states, such as California, have statutes that essentially bar the enforcement of a noncompete clause. Check with a lawyer to see what the rule is in your state.

- Most courts say a noncompete clause must serve a legitimate business need of the employer, such as preventing our electric car battery designer from leaving and immediately competing with his employer. If the clause doesn't serve any purpose or is merely designed to stifle competiton, it won't be enforced.

- The noncompete and disclosure clauses must be "reasonable" in their geographic scope, time limit, and definition of prohibited activities. You may not be able to prevent a former employee from engaging in a similar business everywhere in the country if your business is limited to Washington. Similarly, the post-term noncompete restrictions must be reasonably limited in time (generally to no more than two years); and the disclosure prohibition usually can't exceed the useful life of the trade secret. Finally, you can restrain the employee only from the activity in which he was engaged; you can't prevent the electric car battery designer from going to another company and designing solar collectors.

- You probably can't enforce a post-term covenant if you have breached the trade secret agreement yourself or if you have acted illegally, such as by firing the employee in violation of his employment contract.

Each state determines the legality of trade secret agreements enforced within its boundaries. For this reason, it is essential that you consult a lawyer familiar with trade secret protection in your state. The cost of not doing so is high: some states have an "all or nothing" rule that denies enforcement to the entire agreement if any part of it (such as the geographic boundary term) is found to be unreasonable.

4. Use Third-Party Trade Secret Agreements

Use a written contract when dealing with customers, suppliers, subcontractors, or business partners to protect confidential information that must be disclosed.

The agreement should identify the restricted information; describe its permitted uses (such as "for evaluation and review, but not manufacture"); and specify the time period of confidentiality that reasonably and fairly reflects its "period of obsolescence." Don't make the restrictions so broad that they are unreasonable and unenforceable.

5. Carefully Evaluate Enforcement Options

Be cautious and deliberative before releasing confidential information to third parties or your employees. Even with a written trade secret agreement, a company is placing its secrets at risk since detection of misappropriation is often difficult and litigation can be costly with no assurance of success. Litigation also raises the risk of public disclosure of the secret during court proceedings, but judges can issue a "protective order" that restricts such disclosure. To get damages or an injunction, you must show that the information is a trade secret, the steps you took to protect it, the reasonableness of the restrictions, and the harm you have suffered. Consider whether you can prove your case, and the present competitive importance of the information. Also consider whether you have *received* information that could be the basis for a legal counterclaim.

Tip: Often you can get 80 percent of what you want—and all you reasonably can expect—with the threat of litigation and a quickly negotiated settlement.

Tips for Protecting Trade Secrets

Keep these tips in mind as you try to protect confidential information:

- Establish a high security business environment; carelessness in document control, visitor access, or marketing practices can destroy secrecy.

- Use trade secret agreements for employees and third parties in order to protect proprietary and confidential information.

- When an employee leaves the company, require him to return all proprietary documents. Warn him against disclosing or using your trade secrets, and remind him of his obligations under the trade secret agreement.

- Be prepared to pass up a business opportunity if its price includes the disclosure of valuable trade secrets; remember, even a trade secret agreement with your business partner is not ironclad protection.

- Beware of making disclosures in proposals, speeches, and trade publications; have a company executive screen public remarks by employees with access to secrets.

- Take advantage of government procurement regulations that allow contract proposals to be considered proprietary; follow the prescribed steps carefully.

- Be selective: a practice of calling everything proprietary and confidential may defeat trade secret protection.

- Make sure you have kept the information secret before you try to enforce your rights; if the person gained independent access to the information (such as by reverse engineering) he may not be guilty of misappropriation.

- Avoid license arrangements that may violate the antitrust laws by disclosing the secret only if certain goods are purchased, prices fixed, or markets divided.

- Absent a written agreement, disclose only what you are willing to lose to your competition.

How to Avoid Infringing Someone Else's Trade Secrets

In addition to protecting your own secrets, avoid infringing someone else's. Although it's a less pressing commercial priority, prudent yet inexpensive steps can keep you out of court:

- Use a standard visitor form that prohibits visitors from disclosing their own secrets during meetings with you without first signing a confidential disclosure agreement.

- Promptly return unsolicited ideas or suggestions. If you want to examine the information, have the proposer sign an agreement stating that a confidential relationship has not been established and that no compensation except under patent and copyright laws is expected.

- When you solicit ideas in correspondence or conversation, make clear that the initial disclosure will not be in confidence and request a written confirmation of this understanding. If you remain interested in the idea, the subsequent disclosures should be made after carefully negotiating and signing a confidential disclosure agreement.

- Instruct employees not to accept another company's written or oral proprietary information, such as at meetings or during visits, without a written agreement.

Trade Secrets Today

Trade secret protection is extensively relied on in this age of technological sophistication: it offers the broadest protection, demands little paper work and no government fees, does not require the disclosure of any aspect of the protected information, can be swiftly invoked, and may be a basis for damages, royalties, and injunctions. But there are some disadvantages: state laws vary greatly, you can't prevent independent development of the protected technology, infringement is hard to detect, extensive licensing may be difficult, and there is some risk that the secrets can be disclosed during a lawsuit to enforce trade secret rights. For each technology or innovation, carefully weigh and compare the risks and benefits of trade secret, patent, and copyright protection.

PART III
COPYRIGHTS: HOW TO PROTECT THE
EXPRESSION OF AN IDEA

The familiar copyright symbol "©" has appeared on almost every art form, although you are most likely to think of it as the "stop sign" on the title page of a book or the masthead of a magazine. Most people understand it as the warning "don't copy me without permission and credit," but it really means much more. A copyright holder also has the right to exclude others from adopting, distributing, publicly performing, or publicly displaying the work, and each right can be separately owned and enforced. But like trade secret protection, a copyright does not shield you from the independent development of the work by someone else.

Copyright protection extends to such disparate works as literary and artistic products and technological innovations. Examples: plays, books, advertising copy, packaging, records, sculpture, computer software, codes, printed circuit designs, and video games. You can enjoy commercial advantages by copyrighting these items and then licensing others to reproduce or use them.

Copyrights: The Basic Rules

If you are considering copyright protection, read this part of the chapter and then write to the Copyright Office, Library of Congress, Washington, D.C. 20559. The office is the depository for works that are published with a copyright notice and it has many free publications that explain the copyright rules. Ask for the circular, "Publications of the Copyright Office."

National Protection. Unlike the law of trade secrets, copyright offers uniform legal standards throughout the United States; in fact, the federal Copyright Act of 1976 precludes the states from granting similar rights. Protection for material already copyrighted in the U.S. is also available in foreign countries that are parties to U.S. bilateral agreements or the multilateral Copyright Conventions. Most industrialized nations are signatories of one or more of these agreements.

Ownership. The copyright is owned by the author because it is an "incident of authorship"; that is, the copyright is automatically secured as soon as the work is created. (More about this in a moment.)

Broadly speaking, there are two exceptions to this rule of ownership. First, if the work was made for the author's employer, it is said to be a "work for hire" and the copyright is the employer's property. Example: computer software written by your engineer; you hold the copyright, not the employee. The same is true for a specially commissioned work that is part of a larger work (such as articles for a textbook) if all parties agree in writing that it is a "work made for hire." The second situation where the author is not the copyright holder is an obvious one—when the copyright is assigned in writing to someone else.

Definition. Copyright is a form of protection extended to the authors of "original works of authorship." It is available for the categories of works we identified in the opening paragraph. The work must be "original"—independently created—but it need not be novel; your photograph of the Washington Monument is copyrightable as is the picture taken by the person standing next to you. The work does *not* have to be published to enjoy copyright protection.

Duration. For works copyrighted after January 1, 1978 the term of protection is the author's life plus 50 years; for works made for hire, the duration of the copyright is 75 years from publication or 100 years from creation, whichever is shorter. Works copyrighted before January 1, 1978 are protected for various periods of time expressly stated in the statute.

What's Not Protectable

As most people know, a bare idea cannot be protected; the copyright laws protect only the *expression* of it in some tangible form. Computer software codes can be protected but the underlying algorithm cannot be. Similarly, you cannot get copyright protection for:

- Procedures, processes, systems, concepts, discoveries, principles, or methods of business (but you can for a *description* or an explanation of them);
- Titles, slogans, phrases, or names;
- Content or ingredient listings;

- Works of no original authorship such as standard calendars, tables from public documents, or height and weight charts; and

- Works that are not tangible, such as improvised speeches that have not been recorded or written.

How to Get Copyright Protection

Copyright protection is inexpensive and easy to obtain, but you may lose the right to stop others from infringing your copyright if you fail to follow these simple rules.

Fix the Work in Tangible Form

There is widespread misunderstanding about the way to secure copyright protection. Under the 1976 Copyright Act, protection is automatically secured when the original work is fixed in some tangible medium. Publication is not necessary and you need not immediately register the work in the Copyright Office. You have copyright protection with the stroke of the brush, the typing of the manuscript, or the writing of the software code. This is true for all drafts and works preliminary to the final product no matter how sloppy or incomplete they may be.

Use the Copyright Notice if the Work Is Published

Although your work automatically enjoys copyright protection at the moment it is created, one additional step should be taken if the work is published: apply the copyright notice. By "publish," we mean "distribute" whether it be by sale, rental, or gift. Publication certainly occurs when the work is widely distributed, but it may also occur when the work is distributed only to a few others.

The proper copyright notice is the symbol "©" (or the word "Copyright" or "Copr."), the year of first publication of the work, and the name of the owner of the copyright. Example: © 1982 Electric Battery Corporation. The notice should appear in a place that gives "reasonable notice" that you claim copyright protection; where practical, avoid burying it at the back or printing it in tiny typeface. When the work is published, all published copies must bear the proper notice. Under certain circumstances, failure to properly place the notice on published works may be excused, but in other cases it would result in a loss of rights.

The Advantages of Registration

For a $10 fee, you can "register" a published or unpublished work with the Library of Congress. In general, registration is *not* a condition of copyright protection, but there are some advantages in doing so:

- There is a public record of your claim; and

- It is generally necessary to register the work before you can sue someone for infringing the copyright. (You could also wait until the right is infringed, register, and then sue.)

There are other advantages as well, but you should still be selective when choosing works for registration: even a small company has hundreds of copyrighted items but it's not worth the time and cost to file applications for all of them.

The registration procedure is simple: you must file a completed application, pay the fee, and deposit the work.

The Benefits of Copyright Protection

A copyright holder can get a court order ("injunction") halting any infringement of the right as well as damages. Actual damages and profits are always available, or damages specified in the statute (up to $10,000) are available if the work was registered within three months of publication or before infringement. There are also special remedies. For example, a court can order that the offending goods be impounded or destroyed, a valuable remedy where your work is being diluted in the eyes of the public. In some cases attorneys fees are awarded and criminal penalties imposed.

Infringement. A copyright is infringed when your rights—to distribute, reproduce, prepare derivative works, perform, and display the work—are violated. This can occur overtly, for example when your pamphlets or printed circuit designs are copied or your packaging is imitated. The violation can also be more subtle: one can illegally induce someone else to infringe or contribute to an infringement.

Fair Use. Despite these benefits of copyright protection, there are several statutory exclusions or limitations to copyright protection; in these cases, no remedies are available. The best known example is the permitted right of the "fair use" of a copyrighted work. This permits the use or copying of the work for the limited purposes of "criticism, comment, news reporting, teaching, . . . scholarship or research." The Act identifies the elements to be weighed in determining what is fair use. *Warning:* This provision is narrowly construed by the courts. For example, there may be copyright infringement when song lyrics are copied for classroom use. Companies that routinely copy journal articles in connection with their research should not rely on the fair use exception.

Copyright Tips

There are a number of practical steps you can take to preserve your rights and avoid infringing another copyright.

Tips to Preserve Your Rights

- Put a proper copyright notice on copyrightable material before it is published.

- You need not register the work until you want to enforce your rights.
- Remember that deposit of the copyrighted item exposes it to the world, and this destroys trade secret protection.
- Although copyrighted material is published with a copyright notice, the idea is not protected, just the way it is expressed.
- Consider copyright protection for clever advertising, service manuals, and other unique business materials; the real value may be in the way the information is presented.

Tips to Avoid Infringing Copyrights

- Look for the copyright notice in books, magazines, advertising, and other promotional materials. Don't excerpt, imitate style, or copy content without permission.
- Before you try to reverse engineer, look for the copyright notice on printed circuits and software.
- If you routinely copy materials, such as articles in professional journals, join the Copyright Clearance Center (CCC). This avoids the need to secure a license each time you copy; you pay CCC and it pays royalties to publishers who subscribe to the CCC service.
- When you buy software or software-based products from vendors, get a copyright infringement indemnity; this way, you won't financially suffer if there is a copyright violation.
- Avoid intentional infringement; it can be a criminal violation.

PART IV
TRADEMARKS: HOW TO PROTECT A TERM OR SYMBOL

Have you ever felt the disappointment of having your name called only to find that the comment was directed elsewhere? Sharing a personal name with others is frustrating but confusion among commercial names can be financially disastrous. That's why trademark law protects names and symbols that are applied to goods, services, and organizations. These are names that identify your favorite automobile, toothpaste, computer, or football team.

Marks and Names

This is not an inherently complex area of the law if you understand what's in a name.

Marks. A "mark" is a word, name, or symbol used alone or in combination with others to identify particular goods or services and to distinguish them from the goods or services of someone else. When a mark is applied to *goods* it is called a *trademark*. A mark generally is an adjective to a common noun, although that is not always the case. Examples: Xerox® copying machines, Scotch® tape, and TRS-80® microcomputers. A commercial symbol may be a trademark. Examples: famous logos such as the CBS eye, the General Electric circular design, and the Weyerhaeuser tree.

A mark can also be applied to the sale or advertising of *services*, and when it is, we call it a *servicemark*. Examples: "Citi of Tomorrow" (a servicemark of Citibank, N.A.) and "Avis."

Names. A name is not a mark. A name that identifies an individual firm, corporation, or business is a *trade name*. But unless it is also applied to goods or services, it is not considered to be a "mark." A trade name is usually just a company's name, such as "Electric Car Battery Company." By contrast, sometimes a company name is also a trademark. Example: Exxon.

Two Ways to Protect Marks

This is the one area of intellectual property where there is some overlap of state and federal protection. There are basically two ways to seek protection.

Marks: Federal Statutes

Federal trademark law provides comprehensive protection throughout the United States for marks that are registered with the United States Patent and Trademark Office. Federal registration, whose requirements are discussed below, should be obtained in order to fully enjoy the benefits of federal protection: access to the federal courts and such federal infringement sanctions as injunctive relief, damages, destruction of infringing labels and advertisements, and attorneys' fees. Federal registration is essential for companies that do business in more than one state. (Federal protection has been granted for unregistered marks where the offending mark creates a false designation of origin.)

Marks: State Statutes and Common Law

Most states have statutes that provide some sort of protection for trademarks; some require formal registration while others merely have a broad prohibition against "unfair competition," which can include misappropriating the mark or causing it to be confused with the offending mark. Many states also have "Anti-Dilution" laws that are usually applied where a distinct, well-known mark is being "diluted" or weakened by someone else's use of a similar mark, even though the two marks are not applied to competing products or services. Such uses are prohibited because they injure the goodwill or reputation of the well-known mark and may cause the public to be misled or deceived. Many states also have a body of court-created law that prohibits the misuse or misappropriation of marks or business goodwill.

Although state law can be a valuable source of protection, it's best to look to the federal law for uniform protection nationwide.

How to Choose a Mark

As with the name of a child, the mark of your product or service should be a choice for life. Choose carefully because your reputation and goodwill will go with it. A strong mark can vastly increase product sales, so keep these principles in mind:

- Make your mark distinctive, something that will set apart your goods and services from the marks of your competitors. Make it something your customers will remember.

- Coined (Exxon gasoline) or arbitrary marks (Camel cigarettes) are strongest. Suggestive marks (Drizzler jackets) have obvious marketing advantages. Avoid descriptive terms such as "Easy Pour Salt"; they are hard to protect and are too easily diluted by similar marks.

- Marks that are primarily surnames, geographical names, or obscene or immoral cannot be registered.

- Avoid marks that are similar to existing marks or likely to be confused with them; registration may be denied or a claim of infringement made.

- Select several candidates for trademark protection and perform for each one a complete trademark search of the current federal and state registrations. Computerized "trademark searches" are conducted by professional search firms for a few hundred dollars and the results can usually be obtained within a week. On your own, check telephone books, trade directories, and journals to see if a competitor is already using a similar mark.

- If time and money permit, conduct market research before registration to gauge the public's response to the names you select.

- If you think your choice is catchy because it reminds you of another mark, it may not be registrable and the owner of the existing mark may object.

You will probably spend a great deal of money developing goodwill in the name through advertising and labeling. This will not be a good investment if you select an inherently weak mark—one that is plain, easily mimicked, or merely descriptive of the business. A weak mark may retard product growth and, in the long run, may be more expensive than a strong mark; generally, costs will be greater to establish your exclusive right to use it and to defend it later against infringement.

How to Register a Mark

You should federally register a mark even though states permit registration as well. Federal registration gives you uniform, national protection and, except in unusual cases, means that you will prevail over subsequent users of a confusingly similar mark.

Use the Mark

You must use a mark before you can register it because federal rights are established and maintained only by actual use. In certain cases the first use can be for such purposes as advertising or promotion. If you fail to use the mark after registration you may legally "abandon" the mark; in fact, in order to maintain federal protection you must affirm six years after registration that you are still using it. As long as you continue to use it, the mark is protected. *Tip:* If you later use the mark on new products or for new purposes, you should file another trademark application so that the protection is co-extensive with the use.

File an Application

Federal registration is routine and inexpensive: file an application on designated forms, include a sample of the mark, identify the date of first use, and specify the classes of goods that the mark will be used on. *Warning:* Though the procedure is simple, a layman should not attempt to register a mark. If errors are made, the application may not be accepted and you may not find this out for some time.

If the application is approved, the mark will be published in a federal journal called "The Official Gazette." This publication gives other trademark holders the opportunity to object to proposed registrations. If someone does object, the Patent and Trademark Office holds a hearing to resolve the matter. Otherwise, the mark is formally registered.

Look for Infringers

Once you have a registered mark, it is imperative that you aggressively defend it; otherwise, you will lose your trademark rights.

Rights are most often eroded when someone uses another word, phrase, or symbol that is "confusingly similar" to yours; that is, when the public is not sure whether the mark signifies your product or someone else's; or when the word is used generically. Example: Communications Satellite Corporation has an aggressive campaign to defend its COMSAT trademark against infringement and misuse. The company has prevented use of COMSAT by high technology equipment manufacturers as well as rock groups, firecracker manufacturers and watchmakers; it also vigorously polices generic use of the word "comsat" as a shorthand version of "communications satellite."

Of course, infringement actions are not always successful. Not long ago, the Amstar Corporation of New York, owner of the "Domino" sugar trademark, lost its effort to prevent Domino's Inc. of Michigan from using its "Domino's" pizza trademark in connection with its restaurants. The court found the public was unlikely to be confused because the business and products were different (sugar and pizza).

How do you know if one word or phrase is confusingly similar to another? The courts use these criteria:

- The visual appearance of the marks.
- How they sound.
- The goods or services to which they are applied (pizza and sugar *are* different; but sugar and flour are so alike that similar marks probably would not have been allowed).
- The respective channels of commerce—are they coincident?
- The sophistication of the purchasers.
- The uniqueness of the marks.
- The existence of actual confusion.

There is one other situation where trademark rights can be lost, though the company that must worry about it can surely afford the associated legal expenses. This is when a mark becomes so well known that it is said to be "generic": the public identifies it with the product, not just a brand of the product. Example: cellophane and thermos were marks but are now words for generic products. It is for this reason that Xerox Corporation proclaims that "Xerox" is a brand of photocopying machine (and other office equipment); it is not synonymous with photocopying machines generally. Similarly, General Foods advertises that "Sanka" is a brand of decaffeinated coffee; it does not describe all such coffees.

If There Is an Infringement

The best remedy against infringement is an injunction, a court order halting the use of the mark or requiring the destruction or withdrawal of the offending packages or labels. Damages are also available, but only where there is proof of lost sales and profits.

Trademark Tips

The mark is a dynamic, living asset that must be nurtured with proper care and attention; otherwise rights may be lost. Follow these tips:

- Choose the mark carefully. Don't scrimp in market testing or trademark searches.
- Once you use the mark in commerce, register it under federal law and state law as well; register only under state law if your business will be restricted to one state.
- Properly identify the mark. Use superscript "®" only if federally registered; use "TM" in all other cases.
- File all pertinent papers and pay fees to avoid losing trademark rights.

- Monitor marks that are pending for registration. Use a lawyer or a commercial trademark watching service so that you can oppose registration of similar marks.

- Review joint venture, sales, franchise, or distributorship agreements to ensure they contain restrictions on the use of your trademark.

- Maintain adequate control over the use of your mark by others.

- A trademark does not insulate you from the antitrust laws; read the next chapter for a discussion of these prohibitions.

INTELLECTUAL PROPERTY SCORECARD

Patents

Use: Protection of an invention

Examples: Hardware such as electrical, mechanical, and optical devices; chemicals; manufacturing processes

Advantages	Disadvantages
—protects against independent development	—only 17 years of protection
—right to license for royalties	—full public disclosure
—presumption that patent is valid	—only for limited subject matter
—access to federal courts and clear federal law	—time delay in registration
—court orders halting infringement; damages	—high cost
	—many patents held invalid
	—narrow protection—for the patent claims only

Trade Secrets

Use: Protection of information

Examples: Any confidential information such as formulas, circuit designs, customer lists, and business strategies

Advantages	Disadvantages
—broadest protection	—does not protect against independent development
—few statutory requirements	—hard to detect infringement
—right to license for royalties	—state laws and policies are diverse
—right to prevent use of misappropriated information	—difficult in practice to license extensively
—low cost	—no presumption that information is a trade secret
—procedures are owner-controlled	

Copyrights

Use: Protection of the tangible expression of an idea

Examples: Advertising, manuals, films, recordings, computer software, packaging

Advantages	Disadvantages
—presumption that copyright is valid —quick, simple procedures —low cost —a right to license for royalties —access to federal courts and clear federal law —court orders halting infringement; damages	—does not protect against independent development —public disclosure if published —inconsistent with trade secret —does not protect the idea, just the expression of it —hard to detect infringement —some limits on exclusive rights of owner (fair use exception)

Trademarks

Use: Protection of a name or symbol

Examples: Company names, advertising symbols, product names and slogans

Advantages	Disadvantages
—low cost —quick, simple procedures —court orders halting infringement; damages —uniform federal law	—hard to detect infringement —must aggressively defend mark —different state laws (not applicable if mark is federally registered)

9. Doing Business with Your Competitors and Customers: A Practical Guide to the Antitrust Laws

by ARTHUR WINEBURG
and PAUL A. ALLEN

Few legal subjects bewilder businessmen more than the antitrust and trade regulation laws, for it often seems there are no precise rules or regulations to govern commercial conduct. But there are some general principles that affect all businesses, from the smallest retailer to the largest conglomerate. These norms apply to such disparate practices as price fixing, full stocking requirements, sales quotas, and cooperative advertising.

We would waste your time by exploring the nuances of antitrust law; instead, we will discuss only those business practices (the law calls them "restraints") that either pose the greatest legal risk to you or are the most common. Part I shows you how to deal safely with your competitors; Part II describes the many restraints you can legally impose on your customers and suppliers; and Part III offers a grab bag of antitrust issues. In this chapter you will learn:

- Tips for managing the antitrust laws;
- The perils of arrangements with your competitors;
- The risks of trade association activities;
- How to legally restrict a dealer's sales territory;

- How to legally restrict a dealer from selling to certain kinds of customers; and
- How to select and terminate distributors and dealers.

The incentive for learning the antitrust lessons is twofold. First, the informed executive knows there are many business practices he *can* engage in—practices that further the company's business strategy but that he previously thought were forbidden. Example: Imposing tough marketing restrictions on dealers and distributors. Second, the dollar cost of violating the antitrust laws—the financial "exposure" of a company—is greater than in any other area of law. Example: In 1980 Hartz Mountain Corp. paid $42 million to A.H. Robbins Co., the maker of Sergeant's pet products, to settle claims that Hartz' marketing practices violated the antitrust laws.

TIPS FOR MANAGING THE ANTITRUST LAWS

Keep these tips in mind as you read this chapter:

1. Don't resort to illegal means to accomplish a business end; the costs are too high and you can probably achieve the same goal legally.

2. Someone—a competitor, a customer, or a state or federal prosecutor—sooner or later will uncover your antitrust violations.

3. Don't automatically assume that a restrictive business practice is illegal. A few are, but the law in other areas (such as the "vertical" restrictions you impose on dealers) is fluid and at the present time becoming more liberal. You may be able to do today what you could not do two years ago.

4. Conversely, the absence of hard and fast rules for all contingencies means you have to think ahead: determine what is legal today and anticipate what will be illegal tomorrow.

5. Carefully balance the risks and benefits before imposing trade restraints. As you will see in Part II particularly, many restrictions that firms want to impose on their dealers (such as limits on the customers to whom the product can be sold) may ultimately be legal, but if they give birth to litigation, there will be a high cost in money and lost management time.

6. The antitrust laws can be a sword as well as a shield. Government regulators and private parties alike can attack you for committing illegal acts; conversely, if you know your rights, you can use the law as a shield to protect yourself against the illegal practices of your competitors.

A LOOK AT THE ANTITRUST LAWS

The antitrust laws have been analogized to a constitution and termed a "charter of freedom" for businessmen. The purpose of the laws is to promote and maintain free and fair competition in the marketplace. This chapter primarily deals with illegal "restraints of trade"; these are unreasonable restrictions on commercial behavior.

The Statutes. We rarely refer to the antitrust statutes but you should know what they are. At the federal level there is the Sherman Act (enacted in 1890), the Clayton Act, Federal Trade Commission Act, and Robinson–Patman Act. Taken together, they prohibit the artificial manipulation of the free market including tampering with prices, unfair competitive practices, and some forms of price discrimination. While these laws do not *require* that you compete in the marketplace, they do bar you from agreeing with your competitors *not* to compete or from competing unfairly. Most states also have their own antitrust laws, typically a version of the Sherman Act.

The Enforcers. One reason for prudence in the antitrust arena is the number of marketplace observers and law enforcers. At the federal level, the U.S. Department of Justice and the Federal Trade Commission enforce the federal statutes; each has a central Washington, D.C. office and field offices around the country. State Attorneys General enforce state laws and can enforce federal laws on behalf of the citizens in their state. Finally, the antitrust laws permit "private enforcement," that is, lawsuits by individual victims of illegal trade restraints. In summary, there are many enforcers, and while federal activity has recently declined, the states and private parties are increasingly active.

The Penalties. Antitrust laws pose great risk because the penalties are so high: for some federal violations, fines (up to $1 million) for the company, and fines (up to $100,000) and imprisonment (up to 3 years) for the individual. More commercially harmful, private parties can recover triple damages and attorneys' fees from violators in amounts that can be staggering. Robbins' recovery from Hartz is only one example. Finally, a violator is also subject to a court order ("injunction") halting the illegal practice.

The Legal Standards. For our purposes, there are essentially two standards for judging the legality of a trade restraint.

(1) *Per Se.* Some practices have such a pernicious effect on competition and are so lacking in any legitimate business purpose that they are automatically unlawful; in lawyers' jargon, they are *per se* illegal. Examples: fixing prices with competitors, group boycotts, and competitor agreements to divide up geographic markets.

(2) *Rule of Reason.* Many less invidious practices restrict competition but are nevertheless legal if they are "reasonable"; that is, if the main purpose of the agreement is not to restrain trade but to attain a legitimate business goal. Examples: restricting a distributor to a defined sales territory and reserving "house accounts" to the manufacturer. In these cases, the "rule of reason" is applied.

Part I deals with certain agreements with your competitors; these are governed by the first test and are automatically or *per se* illegal. You won't be allowed to defend the practice with a business justification. Part II discusses a variety of commercial relationships with your customers and suppliers. Since these are governed by the second test of "reasonableness," you can structure them to stay on the safe side of the law.

PART I
HOW TO DEAL SAFELY WITH YOUR COMPETITORS

Learn to recognize the practices discussed here: each one is automatically illegal, so its commercial benefits to the company are irrelevant. In short, there are no excuses.

Do Not Fix Prices

Surely every merchant knows it is illegal for competitors to conspire to fix prices. Yet price fixing remains the most common antitrust violation uncovered, and it accounts for most criminal cases under the Sherman Act. There is no defense for price fixing, either commercially or legally. A company's insignificant market share in the industry is no excuse, nor is the "reasonableness" of the chosen price a moral or legal justification. There is harsh treatment for price fixing agreements because their aim and likely effect is the elimination of marketplace competition.

Even obvious price fixing agreements are still common. The U.S. Justice Department recently secured hundreds of indictments of companies and individuals in the road-paving business. The companies allegedly rigged bids on government asphalt contracts. Even the legal profession is not immune; in a civil action a few years ago, the Supreme Court prohibited the use of minimum fee schedules by bar associations because their use amounted to illegal price fixing.

While bid rigging and agreements on written fee schedules are obvious examples of price fixing, there are other commercial practices whose price effects are more subtle. But the result is the same.

Maximum price fixing. It is just as illegal to agree on a maximum price as a minimum price. Example: An agreement among manufacturers not to sell to any distributor who resells above the maximum price of $10 per unit.

Price exchanges. It is illegal to exchange information on prices where the intended or actual effect is to stabilize prices. Example: It was illegal for corrugated box manufacturers to exchange detailed price data on past sales.

Tip: It's best not to exchange price sheets with your competitors, even though such an exchange by itself is not always illegal. It is safer to learn of market conditions through suppliers and customers.

Third party price lists. If you cannot safely exchange price lists directly with your competitors, don't expect to use an intermediary to accomplish legally the same thing. Example: It was illegal for a local trade association of Plymouth dealers to publish a uniform price list for Plymouth cars. Of course, the trade association acted at the behest of its member–dealers.

Behavior that affects prices. Even if an agreement among competitors is more subtle, it can be automatically illegal if it has a substantial effect on price. Example: The trade association of radio and television broadcasters until recently had a voluntary standard that prohibited advertising more than one product in a TV commercial that was less than 60 seconds long. This was *per se* illegal because it had the effect of artificially increasing the demand for commercial time which, in turn, affected the price. Agreements among retailers not to offer trading stamps or to close on Sundays have been held illegal for the same reason.

Warning: Any agreement among competitors that artificially increases the demand for a product, restricts its supply, or substantially affects price is probably illegal. Do not assume an agreement with a competitor is legal just because you have not explicitly agreed on a price.

Coercive Behavior. It is illegal to conspire with your competitors to coerce others on prices. Example: It was illegal for Los Angeles area Chevrolet dealers to work with General Motors to eliminate the discounting of Chevrolets by other dealers. Again, there was no explicit agreement on what the price should be, but the actions affected prices.

Joint Advertising. Of course, it would be illegal for you and your competitors to jointly advertise prices of the same products. But the problem is trickier when you jointly advertise with someone who is part competitor, part customer. Example: A joint advertising program between Hamburger King Franchisor and its franchisees when the franchisor *also* has nearby company owned stores. The particular facts will determine whether this is legal. If Hamburger King uses this program together with its nearby owned stores to coerce its franchisees to charge certain prices, the practice is illegal; otherwise it probably isn't.

Some safe activities. Not all joint activity is illegal. Example: It's legal to have an industry-wide credit bureau where company representatives exchange credit reports on individual customers. It would not be legal to go further and have the credit bureau limit a company's freedom to extend credit.

Warning: The practical lesson of these price cases is clear: don't agree with your competitors, directly or indirectly, on commercial restrictions that will affect prices.

Do Not Engage in a Group Boycott

A boycott is an illegal combination of companies to refuse to deal with another company. It can arise as an agreement among competitors (say, two manufacturers) or noncompetitors (a manufacturer and wholesaler). Usually the purpose of a boycott is to enforce a price. These boycotts or "concerted refusals to deal" are *per se* illegal.

The case of General Motors and its L.A. dealers is an example. There, General Motors and most of the 85 area Chevrolet dealers combined to refuse to sell cars to the few dealers who were reselling their cars to discounters. This was an illegal group boycott.

Two other examples: Several manufacturers agreed, at the behest of a large dealer, not to sell appliances to a competing retailer. That's illegal. Also, several dress manufacturers agreed through their trade association not to sell designer dresses to retailers who also handle dresses that were "pirated" from the originals. The joint activity is illegal, though each manufacturer could have individually and unilaterally decided on such a policy.

Tip: If you no longer want to do business with someone, or you don't want to start in the first place, make that decision on your own. Do not even appear to consult about it with a competitor.

Do Not Divide Up Markets

It is automatically illegal to engage in a "market allocation" scheme with your competitors; that is, to carve up geographic territories, customers, or products. For example, it would be illegal for you to agree with your competitor that you will serve the east side of town and he the west; or that you will sell only to retail stores and he only to discounters.

Several independent mattress manufacturers were guilty of this kind of practice when they geographically allocated the entire U.S. market. Bid rigging, such as that allegedly committed by the asphalt contractors mentioned earlier and certainly committed by electrical equipment manufacturers in the 1960s, is a form of market allocation. In these cases, the conspirators agree to take turns submitting the "low" bid; that way, everybody is guaranteed a profitable contract.

Be Wary of Trade Associations

As we have illustrated with the examples of boycotts and price list exchanges, illegal commercial practices are not immunized from antitrust laws when laundered through a trade association. In fact, many government prosecutors believe in "guilt by trade association." Prosecutors and judges alike often remind businessmen of Adam Smith's cynical observation two hundred years ago:

> People of the same trade seldom meet together, even for merriment and diversion, but the conversation ends in a conspiracy against the public or in some contrivance to raise prices.[1]

Cynicism is not limited to the great minds of history. In a veiled reference to the many meetings of executives at trade association social outings, one contemporary defense lawyer remarked that his client could not be guilty of price fixing because "he doesn't even play golf!"

---

[1] Adam Smith, *Wealth of Nations*, Canon Edition, Volume 1, page 130.

While you can gain much from trade associations, be on notice that they are fertile ground for government prosecutors and private litigants: the meetings provide ready documentation that competitors met, and a temporal link to price changes can be enough evidence to get to a jury.

Even written association materials pose risks. The dissemination of such industry-wide data as costs, prices, and sales volume is particularly suspect because it may affect members' pricing decisions. If the data are of an aggregate nature, such as average prices and costs, distribution is probably legal unless the members agree to abide by the average price.

Balance the risks and benefits of association membership. If the benefits are few, pass up the meetings or withdraw entirely. Some big companies have done just that.

Beware of the Wink or Nod: An Agreement

We have said throughout this part of the chapter that you and your competitors must not "agree" on prices or other actions that affect prices. What do we mean by "agree"?

An illegal agreement—the law calls it a "contract, combination, or conspiracy"—can be far more subtle than a handshake deal. Yet executives accustomed to doing business their own way find this concept hard to accept. In truth, an illegal antitrust agreement can be tacit—silent, understood, unvoiced. It requires only that each knows of a proposed common course of action and goes along with it. Example: One Realtor announced to other Realtors at a country club dinner that he was raising his commission rate from 5 percent to 6 percent. There was no further comment, yet each Realtor subsequently raised the rate to 6 percent. All were found guilty of a criminal conspiracy to fix prices. There were no papers, handshakes, or even oral statements; but they all knew, they all understood.

This actual case illustrates the truth of the legal maxim, "There is no such thing as an unwitting conspirator." This is why contacts with competitors, at trade association meetings or elsewhere, are so suspect.

- Illegal agreements can be tacit and implied from a course of conduct; express agreements, oral or otherwise, are not necessary.

- Illegal agreements do not require direct communication among competitors; if each one knows the others were asked (for example by a third party) to participate in the activity, a judge or jury can infer a conspiracy.

- Contemporaneous notes of contacts with competitors are helpful when they clearly demonstrate the contact was innocent. But some notes can be twisted against you, and it can be dangerous for unsophisticated employees to make notes of their communications with competitors.

Remember, an unwritten or unspoken understanding can be just as illegal as a signed contract to restrain trade.

PART II
HOW TO DEAL SAFELY WITH
YOUR CUSTOMERS AND SUPPLIERS

Now we discuss a host of trade restrictions that commonly arise in dealings between a company and its customers or suppliers. In legal jargon, these are "vertical" restrictions because they are imposed from the top down—from manufacturer to distributor or from distributor to dealer. (The legal rules for dealers and distributors are the same, though their marketing roles are different. We will use the terms dealer and distributor interchangeably.) The names of the actors are not important; the point is that these are not competitor–competitor or "horizontal" restrictions.

Reasonable Restrictions. None of the nonprice restrictions in this part of the chapter is *per se* illegal; in fact, many are quite permissible. But they all share one thing in common—they are legal *only* if they are found to be "reasonable" under the circumstances. The "rule of reason" test means a court will look at many facts: the nature of the restraint, its purpose and history, how much it benefits or hurts competition, the nature of the business and industry where it's used, and the evil it remedies. Distilled to essentials, the question is, how much does the restraint promote or suppress competition?

Warning: Since the legality of nonprice restrictions depends on many industry and company-specific facts, all measured against the ill-defined and fluid "reasonableness" standard, companies must often spend tens of thousands of dollars defending their restrictions in court. Though the restraint may ultimately be declared legal and the commercial purpose is achieved, the price of vindication is high. Moreover, firms are particularly vulnerable to a successful lawsuit if the restraint was selectively enforced or imposed in the first instance as a means of enforcing price recommendations. Before you use such restrictions, obtain antitrust counsel, and together carefully weigh the pros and cons.

Price Restraints. Note that we said the "nonprice" restrictions are tested by the reasonableness standard. For example, the legality of manufacturer-imposed sales quotas for dealers will be judged by weighing all the facts just identified. In most cases the quotas will be legal. If the manufacturer goes further and seeks to *force* the dealer to post lower prices to accomplish the same end—sell more units of the product—the action will automatically be illegal. *Warning:* Restrictions on prices are still *per se* illegal even if they are imposed in the vertical relationship of manufacturer to dealer.

Except for these price restraints, vertical arrangements are more favorably treated than their horizontal cousins because they often promote competition; that is, they help to make the market more efficient or productive. You enter into these arrangements (for example, by setting up an exclusive distributorship) to strengthen your forces for the marketplace wars. You make an agreement, not with a competitor, but with someone else in your chain of distribution. These agreements typically *reduce* the competition among your dealers on the theory that they will devote more time, energy, and money to promoting your product. That should *increase* the competition with other manufacturers. In short, with a vertical agreement the battle is sharper than ever; with a horizontal one the opposing armies have called a truce.

While the theory and logic are correct, the following restraints illustrate that it's still possible to go too far. That happens when the competitive benefits are slim.

Do Not Use Legal Restraints Illegally

At the end of this part of the chapter, we will give you practical legal and business rules for selecting and terminating dealers. But the issue comes up throughout the discussion of specific restraints. The reason is this: an otherwise legal restraint can be illegal if it is used to coerce dealers. As we discuss next, a manufacturer can suggest resale prices to dealers, but if it terminates them for not sticking to the price, that's an antitrust violation. Similarly, you can impose sales quotas on your dealers, but if the quotas are unreasonably high and selectively applied to terminate a dealer, that too may be illegal. Don't use a sensible restraint for an illegal purpose.

Do Not Impose Price Restraints

You cannot dictate to a dealer or distributor the resale price he must charge for your product. Though in a vertical context, this amounts to price tampering, and all price restraints are *per se* illegal. Like naked price fixing among competitors, this prohibition on "resale price maintenance" is well known. But there are some things you *can* do.

Suggested prices. Although you cannot dictate prices, you may "suggest" them. Do this with price lists or by "pre-ticketing" the item—putting stickers or tags on the product before it leaves the factory. If you issue price lists or pre-ticket, be sure to use the word "suggested." As long as the retailer is free to vary the price, sending out price lists and pre-ticketing are legal.

For most companies, the real question is, how much further can I go? Clearly, you can't coerce a retailer to charge the suggested price, nor can you threaten to terminate the dealership for failing to do so. In fact, the Federal Trade Commission recently went so far as to declare Russell Stover Candies guilty of a *per se* violation when it announced in advance that it would refuse to deal with retailers who sold below suggested prices and then terminated some who did just that.

Warning: Don't go beyond suggesting a price. Anything that can be construed as forcing a dealer to abide by a price can be an antitrust violation. A threat of actual termination would be illegal, but so would more subtle actions that accomplish the same result. Example: It would be illegal for the Hamburger King Franchisor to set low prices in its owned restaurants as a way of forcing its nearby independent franchisees to charge the same suggested price. Even if in particular instances these actions are legal, they are invitations to a courtroom battle, and judges are reluctant to dismiss these cases without a trial.

Do not try to immunize your actions through third parties. For example, don't induce middlemen to stop dealing with discounting retailers, or ask customers to police other retailers for you. This is the kind of activity that caused problems for GM and the L.A. Chevrolet dealers.

How to Restrict a Dealer's Territory

Manufacturers often protect their dealers from excessive competition with each other by imposing restrictions on the territory in which the dealer can sell. This increases dealer loyalty and usually promotes more aggressive competition with the products of other manufacturers. These restraints, which are often combined with customer restrictions discussed next, come in many forms and are generally legal.

The Location Clause. This requires the dealer to sell only from the location approved by the manufacturer. In the early 1960s GTE Sylvania imposed such clauses on its few retailers in an attempt to increase its small market share in television sets. The result was that each dealer had, in effect, a protected market area where no competitor sold Sylvania. The retailers then aggressively promoted Sylvania and the company's market share increased to 6 percent. Then it cut off a retailer who was selling at an unapproved location, but both the clause and the cut-off were approved by the Supreme Court. Reason: the restriction increased competition in the sale of television sets generally, even though it obviously reduced competition in the sale of Sylvania sets alone.

Location clauses are now used for many consumer products, frequently for those that require some sales expertise. Example: A large manufacturer of personal computers requires its dealers to sell only from their designated stores; they may not sell the units by mail. The manufacturer wants the units promptly serviced where they are purchased, and it knows that a computer sale requires a good deal of time and technical expertise. None of these is available through the mails. The restriction is probably lawful because the mail-order restriction is reasonably related to the manufacturer's legitimate business purpose. In general, the greater the skill, expertise, or point-of-sale service that is required, the tougher the restriction that can be imposed.

The Closed Territory. A manufacturer imposes a closed or "airtight" territorial restriction when it prohibits a distributor or dealer from selling outside a defined territory (such as "the state of Missouri"). Some of these restrictions have been held illegal (including some in the soft drink industry), but others have been upheld. Their legality depends on the particular facts in the industry, so you should consult an antitrust lawyer for advice. But a closed territory is probably legal if the manufacturer can provide a good business justification for it and show that it will increase competition with other manufacturers. This is likely to be true for companies with a small market share, or in connection with the distribution of new products. *Warning:* A company with a dominant market share probably cannot use closed territories (because they may be "anticompetitive"); and a firm cannot impose them for price-related reasons.

The Open Territory. This defines the sales territory ("the state of Missouri"), but permits the dealer to sell outside of it. Usually legal, it is often coupled with one of the restrictions discussed immediately below. Example: It is legal for a windmill manufacturer to require that the units be stocked by the Arizona distributor before selling them outside the statewide territory (in, say, Colorado).

Area of Primary Responsibility. When coupled with an open territory, a primary responsibility clause designates a sales area that must receive special attention by the dealer. The clause should describe the area (such as, "Cook County, Illinois"); state that it is the dealer's area of primary responsibility; state that the dealer must use its "best efforts" to exploit fully all sales opportunities; and require prior notice to the manufacturer before selling outside the territory. These clauses are lawful as long as they are not combined with illegal practices such as resale price maintenance.

The Profit "Passover." This clause might require a dealer whose territory is Dallas but who makes a sale in Fort Worth to turn over 6 percent of his gross receipts on the sale to the Fort Worth dealer. The theory is that the Fort Worth dealer's promotional efforts were partly responsible for the sale; true or not, the clause discourages out-of-territory sales. These are permissible restrictions as long as, in this case, the 6 percent "passover" bears some reasonable relationship to the cost of the promotional efforts of the nonselling dealer. The restrictions can also be applied in other ways, for example to warranty work performed out of the territory. But as always, if the restrictions are part of a scheme to force dealers to post certain prices, they are not legal.

Warning: Although these territorial restrictions are generally legal, there are two traps; one is fatal and the other potentially so:

- As we said in Part I of this chapter, territorial agreements hatched among your *competitors* (horizontal) are automatically illegal; this is true even if the restrictions are imposed on your own dealers.

- Because the territorial restrictions you unilaterally impose on dealers are judged for "reasonableness," the particular facts of your business and industry are vital. With a small share of the market, you have great flexibility; with 50 percent of it, your freedom is much more limited. Of course, you must have a good business reason for your action.

How to Restrict a Dealer's Customers

Manufacturers often combine a "territorial" restriction with a "customer" restriction to focus the dealer's marketing efforts; sometimes it is hard to distinguish one restriction from the other.

Special Accounts. Sometimes a manufacturer will reserve to itself national, government, or other large accounts and restrict or prevent dealers and distributors from making these sales. There have been few cases directly addressing this issue, so it is somewhat more risky than territorial restrictions. But the test is of "reasonableness" and some courts have approved of the practice. Again, for products that require special service or training, such as the sale of 1,000 personal computers to a school system, the restriction should be easy to justify: only the manufacturer, not the small dealer, has the capability to provide the necessary product training and support.

Special Customers. Apart from discouraging or preventing sales to a few large accounts, can a manufacturer prevent dealers from reselling the product to certain classes of customers? Yes. Clairol, for example, prohibits the resale of its "salon" or "professional only" hair dyes to the general public. This is legal as long as there are no price restrictions and it can be justified with a good business reason. Similarly, newspaper publishers can bar their home delivery dealers from competing with street vendors.

Two other examples illustrate how overtones of price fixing can affect the result. In a case resolved by the FTC, Amway was allowed to continue its practice of preventing distributors from selling Amway products to retail stores. There were good business reasons for the restriction (it furthers the home-sale philosophy of Amway) and there were no price overtones. On the other hand, the FTC prevented Levi's from continuing to bar its retailers from selling jeans to nonfranchised stores or discounters. Presumably, this tended to stabilize prices and was therefore suspect.

Limiting Quantities. A "back door" way of limiting the customers to whom a dealer can sell is to curtail the quantity of product delivered; that is, to limit deliveries to the amount needed to serve the designated territory or class of customers. This is permissible, but don't taint the practice with price restrictions or do it for price-motivated reasons.

Requiring a Full Line of Products

This is another obligation commonly imposed on dealers: requiring each one to stock the full line of the manufacturer's products or to stock all parts necessary for repairs. Except for automobile dealerships (which are protected by a special federal statute), such restrictions are usually legal. Be alert to one situation that could present a problem—overreaching. You could not reasonably require small hardware stores, for example, to stock all 30 of your electric hand tools; only the biggest stores would be capable of that. But this is rare and for the most part full line forcing goes unchallenged; when it is, it's generally approved.

Requiring Only Your Products

Perhaps you don't care if your distributors carry *all* your products, but you do want them to carry *only* your products. What then? These are "exclusive dealing" arrangements and two are common.

Exclusive Fixtures. Suppose you sell ice cream and in connection with the sale provide a special cooler with your stamped logo. You want to prevent the retailer from putting any other brands of ice cream in the cooler. You can do that.

Exclusive Products. Now suppose you also want to prevent the retailer from carrying any other brand of ice cream; it's your brand or nothing. Can you? As lawyers are wont to say, maybe. Like other nonprice vertical restrictions, the test is one of reasonableness. If you are a new company with a small market share and you face entrenched national brands with many other sales outlets, the "exclusive" is probably legal. But if you are the number one brand in your market with a 40 percent share, it's very risky and probably illegal. As with all restraints tested by the reasonableness standard, what is legal for an also-ran may be illegal for a market leader. Before you adopt a strategy of exclusivity, have an antitrust lawyer give you a written opinion on the risks involved.

Imposing Sales Quotas

A common technique to maintain dealer performance is to impose yearly sales quotas for the product. These objective standards are generally legal unless, as we mentioned earlier, they are patently unreasonable and selectively applied. If the dealer doesn't meet the quota, he can be terminated. Quotas can be imposed even if the dealer must lower prices in order to meet them. If that's the way the quota will have to be met, make sure you are pristine; a prior hint of coercion on resale prices will spawn a lawsuit.

Don't Illegally Tie Products

You probably won't encounter this arcane aspect of the law. But know enough to identify the problem: You can't use product number one, for which the customer has no practical alternative, as the means to force the customer to buy product number two. For example, in the early days of computers, the courts said that IBM could not lease its machines on the condition that the users purchase IBM punch cards. After that, the rules became tricky. There is much litigation on this "tying" issue, including about such academic matters as the meaning of the word "product," so be sure to talk to an antitrust lawyer for advice.

How to Select and Terminate Distributors

Manufacturer errors in dealing with retailers and distributors are the primary cause of antitrust lawsuits. Few companies conspire with their competitors, but thousands of companies have tacit and express agreements with their distributors, and most invoke some of the vertical restrictions we have described. These restrictions are usually legal, but even if some are not, often there is neither complaint nor lawsuit until one of three things happens: the dealer's profits fall, he gets greedy, or he is terminated. We can't forestall the first two events, but we can help you adopt a prudent strategy for selecting and terminating dealers. That alone can douse most antitrust fires.

Select a Distributor for Life[2]

It's much easier to turn down an applicant for a distributorship than to terminate later. Avoid future problems by selecting carefully and spelling out the terms of the relationship:

- Conduct interviews and get references; determine sales history and financial status; make sure the applicant accepts your marketing strategy.
- Spell out the terms of the relationship in a contract: who sets quotas, who is responsible for service, how often the territory can be changed, whether you can reserve accounts to yourself, whether you insist on a full line of your products.
- You can reject an applicant for no reason at all, but you risk an antitrust lawsuit if you first check with existing dealers. They have no right to veto the decision, and if they oppose the newcomer for price reasons (such as a fear of being undercut) and you decide on that basis, the turndown is illegal.
- Make distributors a part of the team; they can be invaluable when you are introducing a new product.

Terminate with Caution

Don't impulsively terminate a distributor; a small investment in time can spare you from legal fees and litigation:

- If a dealer doesn't perform, try persuasion first, but don't coerce, discuss prices, or threaten termination.
- Look again at your termination rights under the contract.
- Ask your lawyer if any special state laws apply. Many states have laws that give special protection to dealers in autos, farm machinery, gasoline, and liquor.

---

[2]This and the following subsection are based on an article Mr. Allen wrote for *Inc.* magazine, November 1981.

- If you are changing your entire distribution system so that all distributors will be terminated, be ready for a unified response. Your action is legal, unless it's part of a price fixing scheme, but it may still be challenged.

- Don't terminate to enforce your suggested resale prices.

- Don't terminate one dealer at the behest of several others. It's illegal if it is in direct response to their complaints that the dealer is a discounter; otherwise, it's just risky.

- Are you in direct competition with the dealer, for example, do you have "company stores" that compete with him or do you sell to the same accounts? Terminations in this context are harder to defend because some courts apply the test of *per se* illegality: they say the dealer and manufacturers are competitors, the restraint is horizontal, and the termination is illegal.

- Do your records document the dealer's poor performance? Is there anything in the files that could damage your case, such as memos of the dealer's excellence, records of uneven evaluation of dealers, or selective enforcement of company restrictions?

- Have your own employees, such as the district or regional manager, done anything to jeopardize your legal position? Have they ever threatened, coerced, or dealt unfairly with the dealer?

By answering these questions beforehand, you will reduce the risk of a dealer lawsuit.

PART III
A GRAB BAG OF OTHER ANTITRUST WORRIES

Most day-to-day antitrust problems for you will involve restrictions or activities discussed in parts I and II of this chapter. But there are several other topics that deserve passing comments.

Monopolies and Monopolization

You probably will not need to worry about the prohibition on monopolies and acts in furtherance of monopolies—monopolization. These bans are well known, but what is not so well known is that the acts need not be national in scope. A company can run afoul of these laws by monopolistic behavior in small geographic regions or "submarkets," a metropolitan area, for example.

The Antitrust–Patent Link

As the preceding chapter indicated, though a patent grant is a limited monopoly, it does not immunize a patent holder from the antitrust laws. If a patent holder violates the antitrust laws or commits other unlawful acts, the patent itself is in jeopardy:

- If a patent is "misused" by the patent holder (for example, by imposing improper license restrictions), the patent is not enforceable.

- If in addition to misuse, the patent holder commits an antitrust violation (for example, by a boycott—agreeing with the licensees not to grant another license without checking with them first) the patent holder is subject to an antitrust suit.

- Fraudulent procurement and enforcement of a patent can also give rise to an antitrust claim.

Companies with patents should have patent lawyers; check with them to avoid jeopardizing your patents.

The Federal Trade Commission

The FTC is an independent regulatory agency with broad authority to enforce the antitrust laws. The procedures and operations of the agency are not our concern here, but be aware of the enforcement activities that can affect you the most.

Prohibiting Deceptive Practices

The FTC prohibits a variety of unfair and deceptive business practices, but if you conduct your business in a responsible, sensible manner, you should not have to worry. Deceptive practices include "passing off" products as those of a competitor, making false or highly misleading claims in advertising, and making false claims of price reductions. FTC enforcement tends to shift with the political winds, so you or your lawyer should stay alert to recent agency initiatives.

Prohibiting Unfair Methods of Competition

The FTC's broad authority to prohibit "unfair methods of competition" encompasses the antitrust violations discussed in parts I and II of this chapter as well as other practices that may not technically violate the Sherman or Clayton Acts. In practice, the FTC does not often try to so extend its authority.

Business Guides and Rules

Over the years the FTC has published many "Guides" and "Rules" regulating conduct in specific industries—everything from furs to tires to credit. Your lawyer or the regional FTC office can advise you whether any pertain to your business.

Franchising

The FTC now requires lengthy public disclosures (in an "offering circular") in connection with the sale of a franchise. The FTC's definition of a franchise is broad and many companies have discovered to their astonishment that they are "franchisors."

Warning: More than a dozen states require that franchises be registered before sale, a second layer of regulation. Consult with a lawyer as you develop your business strategy; that way, you can either structure the commercial relationship so you do not offer franchises or develop a franchise agreement and offering circular that will pass FTC and state muster.

Warranties

The FTC administers a federal statute (the Magnuson–Moss Warranty Act) that sets forth standards for offering written warranties on consumer goods. The Act applies only if a manufacturer gives warranties; there is no requirement that a consumer product be protected by a warranty. A warranty that falls under the Act must be clearly and conspicuously disclosed, it must be designated a "full" or "limited" warranty, and both the full and limited warranty must meet certain statutory standards.

Warning: Check with your lawyer or the FTC's regional office before offering a warranty.

International Trade Commission

If you happen to be facing and fearing competition from abroad, you should be aware of the special "unfair competition" statute enforced by the International Trade Commission (ITC). Modeled after the FTC's statute, it prohibits any unfair method of competition or unfair act in connection with foreign articles: their importation into, or sale in, the United States where the effect may be to injure a domestic industry. Unfair methods of competition include infringement of patents and trademarks, as well as antitrust violations and false advertising.

What makes the ITC an attractive forum to prosecute complaints is its unique authority to direct that the offending articles be excluded from entry into the U.S. It also promises speedy resolution of any complaint: the ITC must decide on any permanent relief within 12 months.

Discrimination in Prices and Services

Discrimination in prices charged and services offered to customers may be unlawful, but there are probably more instances when such practices do not violate the law. The pertinent federal statute (the Robinson–Patman Act) suffers from imprecise language and it is presently in considerable disfavor with government enforcers. But the law may still be invoked by your competitors, your customers, and customers of your customers; and since it exposes you to triple damages, you should be aware of its general terms.

The law prohibits the sale of goods "of like grade and quality" to different purchasers at different prices where such sales may substantially lessen competition. Like most trade statutes, it does not force you to offer all prospective purchasers the same price, but in some cases it prohibits discrimination in actual sales. The law's particular requirements can be gleaned only from court opinions, but the following guidelines should be helpful:

1. The law applies only to actual sales; *offers* to sell at different prices are not illegal.

2. The price difference between the actual sales is legal if you set the lower price to meet an equally low price of one of your competitors.

3. The difference in price between the actual sales must be significant; if it is not, there is no violation of the law.

4. The purchasers of the product must be competitors or their customers must be competitors; if not, there is no violation.

Although there is now relatively little litigation under the Robinson–Patman Act, there is still the threat of triple damages, and government enforcement may someday increase. For this reason, you should review your legal position if you charge significantly different prices for the same product or service.

THE RISKS OF THE ANTITRUST LAWS

Unlike other fields, the antitrust laws cannot easily be summarized with a list of do's and don'ts. Understand that your legal exposure may be great— because of the threat of triple damages and criminal penalties—and that the federal and state governments as well as private individuals can bring a lawsuit. Remember that trade restraints with your competitors are usually automatically illegal, but that nonprice restrictions imposed in a vertical setting (for example, by a manufacturer on a dealer) are legal if they are reasonable. Before you impose a vertical restriction, carefully balance the commercial benefits of the restraint against the costs of litigation and the probability that you will ultimately prevail.

10. Financing: How to Obtain It and Avoid the Traps

*by JON F. HARTUNG and
MICHELE D. STRATTON*

Obtaining affordable financing is the number one business problem for many growing companies. Gone are the halcyon days of steady economic growth with low inflation and interest rates. Now there is economic volatility and uncertainty, persistently tight credit, and the enervating mix of inflation and recession. In this climate, there remains at least one economic imperative: companies must raise money with the least expense and the greatest safety. How should they do it?

This chapter will explain the basics of business financing and its most common perils. You will learn:

- The basic rules of borrowing;
- The meaning of the Banker's Lingo;
- The most common types of bank financing;
- How to make a proper loan request;
- The most common borrowing mistakes;
- Nonbank sources of financing; and
- Some tips on money management.

In this chapter we discuss the many forms, sources, and problems associated with *debt* financing—loans, lines of credit, and similar arrangements that obligate the borrower to repay an exact sum at a specific time. We refer only briefly to *equity* financing—raising money by issuing stock and similar instruments. For an understanding of the legal problems in the equity or securities field, read chapter 12.

KNOW THE FIRST RULE OF BORROWING

Bankers, lawyers, and businessmen alike agree on the first rule of borrowing: always borrow enough. Its corollary—don't borrow too much—is less often violated. The timid businessman fears a rejected loan application, so he asks for less (in dollars and time) than he really needs. This is a mistake: the borrowed amount is inadequate and the company will need more cash later. By then new money will be even harder to get because the company's balance sheet will look worse. Perhaps the borrower can stumble along without another loan, though working capital will be desperately low.

Leverage. The more sophisticated businessman understands the concept and benefits of leverage: loan proceeds can produce profits exceeding the costs of the loan. Not timid, he aggressively seeks all the financing he needs and can justify; some seek as much as they can get. This way the loan proceeds are put to productive use and the business grows and prospers. If you go in with a solid business plan and supporting documents, you'll get the loan. After all, banks want to make money too, and they make more on big loans than they do on small ones.

UNDERSTAND INTEREST RATES

Fixed or Variable?

You must know about interest rates to negotiate an attractive loan package. A *fixed* interest rate stays the same throughout the term of the loan. A *variable* or *floating* rate fluctuates over the life of the loan, typically according to movements in the lender's prime rate; if the rate goes up, so do your payments. ("Prime" usually is the rate charged to the bank's largest and best customers.) Not all variable rate loans are based on the lender's prime rate. Some float on the basis of the Federal Reserve discount rate while others, such as very large loans, vary according to the Euro-dollar rate.

Be alert for variable rate "kickers." For example, your interest might increase faster than the prime rate. Example: If the prime rate goes up 1/2 percent, your interest might increase by 5/8 percent. If you are lucky in negotiating your variable rate loan, you might get a cap on the rate increase (for example, no more than 1 percent in any six-month period), or even an upper limit on the maximum rate that can be charged.

There is even a fixed-variable hybrid: the fixed payment, variable-maturity loan. Under this instrument, the amount of each payment is fixed but the maturity of the loan (when it must be paid off) increases if the interest rate increases.

When you compare lenders' interest rates, determine whether they will be calculated on the basis of a 360-day year or a 365-day year. If it's the former, the annual rate will be slightly (5/360) higher than if it were quoted on a 365-day year. To compare quotes you must use comparable standards.

Warning: Know what interest rate is charged, how it can change, and how it affects your payments. Evaluate the cost of borrowing and determine whether you can afford the payments over the life of the loan.

Usury Laws Won't Help

You should be aware of federal and state usury laws that limit the amount of interest that can be charged on certain loans. If the interest rate exceeds these limits, the lender can be barred from collecting any interest on the loan and may have to pay a severe penalty as well. But these laws have largely been swallowed by their exceptions: many states exempt loans made to corporations or from commercial banks. In short, the usury laws probably won't shelter a company from high interest rates.

On the other hand, if you are borrowing for personal purposes or from a private source the usury laws may apply.

Warning: Before your business lends money to its employees or others, determine whether your state has these laws and the maximum interest rate you can impose. If the highest rate you can legally charge is lower than your cost of obtaining the funds, don't make a direct loan; instead, offer to guarantee a bank loan taken by the employee.

LEARN THE BANKER'S LINGO

There are many technical terms that are used in loan negotiations and documents. You should know what they mean.

Compensating Balance

As a condition for obtaining a loan, a bank may require you to maintain with it a noninterest bearing or low interest account in an amount equal to 10 percent to 20 percent of the loan. Banks often require a deposit or *compensating balance*, not just because it's profitable (the banks make money on the deposit as well as the loan), but also because it permits lenders to monitor your cash flow. A compensating balance also increases the cost of obtaining credit. If you must deposit $5,000 with the bank to obtain a $50,000 loan, the effect will be this: you will pay interest on $50,000 but you will have only $45,000 of new cash in hand. Of course, you must have a bank account somewhere, and you might elect on your own to maintain it with the lender in order to strengthen the business ties.

Guaranty

The lender may ask you to *guaranty* your company's loan. As a *guarantor*, you are responsible for repayment of the loan on the terms described in the guaranty in the event your company is unable to repay. This means that the lender can tap your personal assets if the company defaults. In the alternative, a lender may ask you to sign for the loan as a *co-maker* on a promissory note, the document containing the loan terms. A co-maker is a borrower who has the same obligation as the primary borrower—to repay the loan to the bank. Although the reasons aren't important, a co-maker is legally more vulnerable than a guarantor.

Security Interest

The lender may take a *security interest* in your company's assets, such as its equipment, crops, accounts receivable, or inventory. That means the assets are the collateral for the loan and can be taken by the lender if the loan isn't repaid. Such an arrangement is called a *secured loan*. The term "security interest" is usually used in connection with personal property in the same manner as "mortgage" is used in connection with real estate.

Subordination

The lender may request that some of your company's creditors, typically shareholders who have loaned it money, *subordinate* their loans to the lender's. In other words, the creditors agree that the lender is entitled to be repaid first. The terms of such an arrangement are put in a *subordination agreement* which must be signed by the bank and the creditors.

Term Loan

This is a loan for any precise period of time, such as 60 days, 2 years, or 20 years. The full amount of the loan is advanced at the beginning of the term. The borrower must repay the principal throughout the term of the loan in partial payments called *installments* (an amortizing loan) or in a lump sum at the end of the term. Interest is usually paid monthly or quarterly over the term of the loan.

Recourse and Non-Recourse Loans

A loan is *non-recourse* when the lender agrees in the event of a default to satisfy the debt only from the collateral for the loan and not from the borrower's other assets. In many states, home mortgage loans must be non-recourse. Other types of secured loans may be non-recourse by agreement, but count yourself lucky if you can get such a deal. Usually secured loans are *recourse*: the lender can require the borrower to make up any difference between the value of the collateral and the loan balance.

Understand the Types of Standard Bank Financing

There are many types of bank financing and you should be familiar with each one. Of course, there are other loan sources that you may want to consider and these are discussed beginning on page 204.

Despite the great variety of bank loans, growing companies are frequently mere window shoppers. Commercial banks are conservative lenders subject to many regulations, and they will not often finance new ventures or loan money to businesses with an uneven credit history. Also, banks may not offer the type of financing you need, some may not loan at all to certain types of businesses, and many demand tangible collateral such as equipment. These factors make it almost impossible for some businesses, such as high technology consulting and research firms, to obtain bank loans.

If it's available, commercial bank financing has advantages: it is generally cheaper than other sources and it can be tailored to your business needs.

Short-Term Unsecured Loans

These are loans with 30, 60, or 90 day maturities. Interest only, at a fixed or variable rate, is payable monthly or quarterly. If variable, the interest rate is usually based on the lender's prime—for example, three points over prime or "prime plus three."

A short-term bank loan permits a seasonal retail business to build up inventory before the selling season, and it can help a manufacturer's cash flow until a major customer pays its bills. In either case, the bank will want to know the source of the cash that will be used to repay the loan. Banks view short-term loans as less risky than other types of financing because the borrower's financial picture is not likely to deteriorate significantly during the relatively short life of the loan. That is why short-term loans are easier to obtain than long-term loans, such as those for three or more years.

Revolving Credit Line

If your cash needs fluctuate from month to month, a revolving line of credit will allow you to draw, repay, and redraw funds again throughout the term of the loan according to your needs. Interest is periodically paid, but only on the outstanding balance, not on the funds you aren't using. There is a charge in the form of a "commitment fee" on the unused portion of the loan. The outstanding balance is repayable at the end of the loan period unless the credit line can be converted to an amortizing term loan with installment payments. You should try to get this conversion feature because it will help your cash flow.

Credit lines may be secured or unsecured. They are usually offered for a period of one year or less but are frequently renewable. Some banks require that the credit line be fully repaid or "cleaned up" for a period of time each year, perhaps for as long as three months.

Ordinary Credit Line

Most banks also offer credit lines without the revolving feature. The bank commits funds to you in advance of your actual needs and charges a commitment fee for doing so. When you need the funds, you can borrow any amount up to the maximum available on the credit line. Once drawn and repaid, the funds are not automatically available to you again as they would be in a revolving credit line.

Receivables Financing

If you do not want to wait 30 to 45 days for your customers to pay their bills, ask a bank to lend you cash secured by your accounts receivable. Receivables financing may take the form of a revolving credit line or a short-term loan. Depending on the credit and payment record of your customers, a bank may lend 75 percent to 85 percent of the value of your nondelinquent receivables. The bank's security interest in the accounts receivable generally includes the right to collect directly from your customers if you default on the bank loan.

Be aware that since the bank does not make an outright purchase of the accounts, you still bear the cost and risk of collection. If your customers don't pay, you are still responsible for repaying the loan. (Some banks will purchase your accounts receivable, but that is really the business of "factors." See our discussion of factors on page 205.)

Equipment Financing

If your business wants to finance the purchase of new equipment, bank financing secured by the equipment itself may be available in an amount up to 80 percent of the purchase price. The term of the loan will be related to the useful life of the equipment. Equipment loans are usually repayable in equal installments over the life of the loan. Equipment financing is also available through nonbank sources as well, and this is discussed on page 205.

Real Estate Loans

Banks with real estate lending departments can finance the acquisition, construction, or remodeling of your plant or warehouse. Such a loan is secured by a mortgage on the property (called a deed of trust in some states) and it can be for a term of 15 years or more. Real estate loans are usually repayable in equal installments of principal and interest.

Letter of Credit

The next time one of your suppliers wants cash before starting on a special order, see if he will accept a bank's letter of credit instead. This will obligate the bank to pay the supplier the specified credit amount at a stated time or on presentation of evidence that payment is due. Payment of the letter of credit by the bank then becomes a loan from the bank to you. The bank charges a fee or commission for this service.

Letters of credit were once used almost exclusively in international sales transactions, but they are now common in domestic commercial arrangements as well.

HOW TO PRESENT YOUR LOAN REQUEST

You will never get the loan you need, no matter what kind you want, if you make a sloppy presentation. You must thoroughly document the company's financial position as well as your plans for using the money and paying it back. It's wise to hire an accountant to help prepare the materials and to participate in the meeting with the loan officer.

In addition to having the basic financial facts at your fingertips, be prepared to sell yourself and the company's business potential. Paint a positive picture of the future but do not misrepresent the facts; willful misrepresentation may be fraud.

Good timing is essential. Ask for a loan when your business is healthy; don't wait until it's critically ill with survival uncertain.

When you meet with the loan officer, you should have:

- Current financial statements, including an income statement and a balance sheet certified by a company officer or preferably by your accountant.
- Documents with a specific request for an exact sum, acceptable alternative amounts or ranges, and a description of how you will use the money.
- Realistic financial projections incorporating the loan proceeds.
- A clear description of the amount and source of repayment funds based on alternative borrowing plans.
- A projected repayment schedule.
- A description of available collateral and its value; and the identity and net worth of potential guarantors.
- A description and history of the business, its markets, customers, and short- and long-term plans.

- Records of prior banking experience and credit references.
- A description of key management personnel, their role in the business, and their previous experience.

With this information, you will make a professional presentation and inspire confidence in your company's capabilities and financial strength.

HOW TO CHOOSE AMONG LOANS AND BANKS

As you think about the loan request and recall the many types of bank financing, ask yourself two questions: Which loan is best under the circumstances? Which bank should I do business with?

The first question assumes you will have a choice of loans which, as we have said, may not always be the case. Given your financial position and the condition of the credit markets, you may be eligible only for a small short-term loan. If you have a choice, think about the following questions as you evaluate your options:

- Is the loan amount adequate?
- Will it be available when you need it?
- What are the payment terms?
- Will your cash flow be adequate to make payments comfortably?
- What assets will the lender require as collateral?
- Does the bank want to impose restrictions on your business activities, uses of cash, sales of company stock, hiring and firing of management personnel, or borrowing from other sources? Are you giving up too much control?
- What is the total cost of borrowing? In addition to the interest rate, look for commitment fees or the cost of maintaining a compensating balance.

Just as the lender evaluates the risks and returns before it makes a loan, you as borrower should figure the cost of borrowing and weigh the burden on the business of any bank-imposed restrictions. Some managers will pay more for borrowed funds in order to retain control of their business activities; others accept even onerous restrictions as the price of obtaining attractive financing.

The answer to the second question—which bank to go to—calls for a more subjective judgment. Shop around and compare prices. Consider your future needs as well; the bank that eagerly gives you a real estate loan today might not be willing to finance your inventory tomorrow. Look to the other services the bank offers:

- Does it handle lease financing?
- Is it experienced in international commercial transactions?

- Does it offer financial or general business planning assistance?
- Will the bank support you in good times and bad?

Consider these factors; they can have a substantial though indirect economic effect.

WHAT TO LOOK FOR WHEN YOU SIGN

Now that you have the promise of a loan, should you go ahead and sign the papers? A commercial loan can be a complex transaction pitted with traps concealed in many legal documents. On the next few pages we describe both the traps and the documents, but you can usually avoid the snare simply by following three common-sense rules:

Read Them. If the documents differ in any way from your understanding of the lending arrangement, do not sign them! Carefully read the papers and ask the loan officer about any provision you don't understand. If he previously agreed to provisions you suggested, such as a release of the guarantor if the business performs well, ask him to point them out to you. If you are not satisfied with his assurances, do not sign the documents. Instead, propose your own written modifications.

Negotiate. Although the loan documents will often be on the bank's standard, printed forms, assume that the documents are negotiable. Feel free to ask the loan officer to delete unacceptable provisions and to add attractive new ones. At worst, he will say no.

Get Advice. When in doubt you should consult your attorney before signing any loan papers. You may want him to draft important provisions, to take an active role in negotiating the deal, or simply to assure you that the loan papers match your understanding of the deal. Of course, if the financing is simple, such as a short-term loan evidenced only by a promissory note, it may not be necessary to get professional advice. This is particularly true if you have enjoyed a satisfactory long-term relationship with the bank.

As you look through the loan papers, be alert for the loan documents described next—the note, the security agreement, the stock pledge agreement, the guarantee, and mortgages or deeds of trust.

The Loan Agreement

Unless you obtain a simple term loan or a small credit line, most banks will use a *loan agreement* or a letter of understanding to describe the financial arrangement. The loan agreement should be tailored to your business needs and it should accurately reflect the terms to which you and the loan officer have agreed. Look for many of the following provisions:

1. Funding and Repayment Terms

These are the essential issues. When will the loan proceeds be available? Will they be deposited in your account? What are the commitment fees? When is interest payable? How is it calculated? When and how is repayment to be made? Can you elect to prepay the loan, extend the term, renew it, or convert it to another type of loan? The answers to these questions should be in the loan agreement and the terms should be consistent with the parallel provisions in the promissory note (see *The Note*).

2. Covenants

The loan agreement will normally contain a list of obligations and restrictions called *covenants*. These affect the conduct of your business in two ways: they will force you to take some affirmative steps you might not otherwise have taken, and they will prevent you from operating in ways that may have become routine. Look for any of the following covenants in your loan agreement:

- Minimum financial standards—net worth, cash flow, income, debt-equity ratios, and similar financial standards required during the loan's term.
- Reporting requirements—The bank will require quarterly and annual financial reports, and perhaps monthly statements of income, sales, and receivables.
- Restrictions on your use of the loan proceeds.
- Restrictions on paying dividends, increasing salaries, buying company stock, and making other payments or disbursements that reduce the company's available cash.
- Restrictions on incurring other debts, selling major assets, or changing business lines.

If your company fails to comply with the covenants, the bank can declare the loan in default and demand immediate repayment.

Warning: Make sure *before* you sign the loan agreement that you can abide by the covenants and that they won't snarl company operations or stifle innovations.

3. Representations and Warranties

The loan agreement normally contains a description of your company and its financial condition. You must "warrant and represent" that your financial statements accurately reflect the real facts, that there are no pending and undisclosed lawsuits, and that your business is conducted in accordance with the law. When you sign, you represent that the statements are true; and for many loan agreements you also represent that the statements continue to be true each time you draw any of the loan proceeds. If any statement is materially false, the bank can call in the loan; and if you signed *knowing* there were false statements, you might be liable for other damages for fraud.

4. Events of Default

The loan agreement identifies the events that trigger a default and permit the bank to call in the loan; that is, to demand full repayment. Typically, these events include failure to make payments on time, a decline in the company's net worth or cash position, and a fall in the collateral's value. If you have several borrowings from the same bank, you may find a *cross-default* provision in the loan agreement. This permits the bank to call in all loans if you default on any one of them.

Because default can be so disastrous, you should request a "cure" provision. This entitles you to a period of time, usually 10 to 30 days, to correct the problem that led to the default. There should also be a notice provision that requires the bank to inform you perhaps a week before it intends to call in the loan. If the bank demands payments that you cannot make, it can foreclose on the collateral and collect any deficiency from the guarantors.

Many banks will stand behind their borrowers during brief periods of financial stress and agree to a postponement of payments. The key to obtaining a postponement is twofold: give early warning to your loan officer and convince him that this is a transitory cash crunch that you can survive.

The Note

If a loan agreement is not used, a *promissory note* will be the principal loan document. The note shows the amount you are borrowing, the interest rate, and the repayment schedule. If there is a loan agreement, the note and the loan agreement should be consistent.

Principal

The principal stated in the note will be the amount you are borrowing. If you are obtaining a revolving line of credit, the note will often be written for the maximum amount available and then annotated later on the reverse side to show the monies borrowed and repaid.

Interest

We have already discussed the different types of interest provisions. Carefully read the note to make sure the interest terms are clearly stated.

Repayment

Unsatisfactory repayment terms can destroy your cash flow. Many standard form bank loans declare that the note is payable "on demand" or "on demand, and if no demand is made, on August 1, 198X." This means that the note can be called in *any time* even if you have made timely payments and your business is healthy. If you must agree to a "demand loan," ask that the note be payable "30 days after demand" so you have time to refinance the debt.

Prepayment

Can you prepay the note—that is, pay it off early? In days of rising interest rates, you would expect banks to be delighted to see you repay your note before it is due. Unfortunately, a note is *not* prepayable unless there is a specific provision permitting it. Always ask for such a provision in a long-term note (over 24 months). This way, you won't be locked into one source of borrowing if you find lower interest rates later from another source.

Sign the note when you are satisfied that it accurately reflects the terms of the financial agreement, but sign only one note or set of notes. When you pay off your loan, obtain the original note from the bank and void it.

The Security Agreement

You will be asked to sign a *security agreement* and a Uniform Commercial Code *financing statement* if the loan is "secured" with collateral. The security agreement describes the bank's interest in and rights to the collateral (your assets, such as equipment), and the financing statement (a form the bank files in the public records) gives legal notice to other potential lenders that the bank has a "security interest" in the collateral.

This means that the bank as a secured creditor has the right to take these assets without going to court in order to satisfy the debt in the event you default on the loan. For example, if the security interest is in your new mini-computer, the bank would be able to take it, sell it, and keep the proceeds up to the amount of the unpaid loan balance. Make sure the security agreement gives you the right to use and replace in the ordinary course of your business any assets you have pledged as collateral.

If you also plan to seek secured financing from other sources, plan your bank financing with their requirements in mind. For example, the inventory supplier who extends you credit will want the inventory and related accounts receivable as security. Offer the bank your other assets and a second security position in the inventory and receivables.

Stock Pledge Agreements

In connection with a loan to a closely held business, a bank may ask for a "pledge" of the company's corporate stock. If so, the owners of a majority of the stock, or perhaps all stockholders, must sign a "stock pledge agreement" and deliver to the bank their stock certificates and a signed stock assignment form. The bank holds these items in escrow.

As long as the loan is not in default, the shareholders have the right to vote the stock and receive dividends. If they sell the stock, it is still subject to the bank's security interest; and if the company defaults on the loan, the bank has the right to manage the company as the sole or majority shareholder until the loan is repaid. The bank may even have the right to sell the company's assets to repay the loan.

Guaranty

If your company's assets are too low to support the amount of money you want to borrow, the bank may require the principal shareholders to execute a separate "guaranty" of the loan. This means the bank can collect the guaranteed amount (which may be all or part of the amount borrowed) from any of the guarantors.

If you are one of the shareholders who signs a guaranty, be aware of two dangers. First, as soon as there is a default the bank can demand payment from you without ever trying to collect from the actual borrower, the company. Second, the bank can collect the total loan amount from you alone, even if there are other guarantors. It would then be your job to get your co-guarantors to pay you their fair share.

Mortgages and Deeds of Trust

When a bank finances real estate or takes real property as collateral it has the borrower sign a *mortgage* or *deed of trust*. Be alert for the recourse (page 195) and cross default provisions (page 201) that we have discussed. Also watch out for the following:

- Impound provisions. These require you to post enough money to pay the annual taxes and insurance on the property.

- Insurance provisions. These require you to carry certain insurance and they may provide that casualty proceeds be paid directly to the bank in repayment of the loan rather than to you to repair the damaged property.

- "Due on sale" provisions. These require, in the event of a property sale, that the mortgage loan be repaid rather than assumed. The legality of these provisions depends on state and federal law and the type of institution providing the financing.

- Default clauses. Certain provisions put the mortgage into default if any other loan secured by the same property goes into default or if the borrower defaults on other major obligations.

Like all other loan documents, mortgage agreements are subject to negotiation; try to eliminate offensive terms.

THE MOST COMMON MISTAKES OF BORROWING

Before we turn to nonbank sources of financing, let us review the most common errors small firms make when they attempt to secure bank financing:

Not Borrowing Enough. Businesses grow on borrowed money. Don't limp along with inadequate financing. Ask for as much as you need and can comfortably pay back.

Poor Internal Accounting. No lender will strike a deal with a firm that cannot show the source of its profits, the amount of its expenses, and how the loan will be repaid. Set up good accounting systems *before* you ask for your loan so both you and the loan officer can evaluate how much you should borrow.

Not Putting a Request in Writing. Make a professional looking loan request: write a persuasive letter explaining who you are, the company's financial and managerial strengths, and why you need the funds. Deliver the letter in person at a scheduled meeting.

Not Talking to the Bank. If you have a bad season, immediately tell the loan officer about it; conversely, when times are good, tell him about that too. Bankers are conservative: they hate surprises. If the banker took a good risk, you might be able to arrange more favorable financing the next time you need it.

Failing to Read the Loan Documents. Merely scanning and then signing the paper work can lead to trouble later. There are many do's and don'ts in the financing process and loan documents themselves have subtle provisions that can trigger a default. Example: letting the value of the bank's collateral erode.

Excessive Loyalty. Loyalty is a virtue but not if it comes at the expense of corporate profits; the bank you have used for years may not offer the creative financing you need today. Shop around for other sources of funds. Another bank may be more impressed with your credit history and more responsive to your present needs.

OTHER SOURCES OF FUNDS

The financial markets are increasingly competitive and banks are no longer the only source of business financing.

SBA Guaranteed Loans

The Small Business Administration is the U.S. government agency that guarantees bank loans made to qualifying small businesses. SBA programs are designed to provide financing to firms that traditionally have had difficulty obtaining it. SBA details are beyond the scope of this chapter; your local SBA office can give you up-to-date, helpful information about its programs.

When you visit the SBA, pay particular attention to their qualifying standards; only small companies are eligible for SBA assistance. Also, because of the SBA's procedures and paper work, it's a good idea to deal with a bank that has made SBA-guaranteed loans before.

Look carefully at both the advantages and disadvantages of SBA programs; they are a mixed blessing. On the plus side, you can get a loan for a fairly long term (six to ten years), at a low interest rate (perhaps two percentage points below bank rates), and in circumstances where you may not otherwise qualify for a loan. On the minus side, the application process may take several months, collateral and personal guaranties are usually required, and other secured financing may then be difficult to obtain.

Commercial Finance Companies

Look to commercial finance companies if you don't qualify for a bank loan. They extend secured credit based primarily on the value of your collateral (75 percent to 85 percent for accounts receivable; 30 percent to 50 percent for inventory) rather than on the strength of your cash flow. Since the lender's risks are greater, its interest rates are higher (usually three to five percentage points over bank rates). The higher cost may be offset by the later maturity date in many of these loans and the fewer restrictions imposed on your company's business operations.

Factors

Factors don't *loan* you money; they *buy* your accounts receivable, usually for 80 percent to 90 percent of the gross dollar value of the acceptable receivables. The factor assumes the responsibility and risk of collection, and the debtor (your customer) usually pays the factor directly. If the debtor does not pay, the factor has no recourse against your business.

The cost of this financing is high but it might provide you with cash when other methods won't and it relieves you of the administrative burdens associated with collections.

Equipment Leasing

You can lease almost any type of equipment—from office machines to forklifts. Leasing becomes a form of financing when it is used in lieu of an outright purchase. Here is how it works.

A leasing company can be independent, affiliated with your bank, or the actual manufacturer of the equipment. The leasing company buys the equipment you need and then leases it to you. It makes a profit on the difference between the cost of the funds used to acquire the equipment and your lease payments. Money you would have used as the down payment in connection with an equipment loan remains available for your other business needs.

As in other forms of financing, the costs and terms of equipment leasing vary widely so it's wise to shop around and do some bargaining. Leasing is generally more expensive than other financing unless you can take advantage of the tax benefits it offers. Ask an accountant or lawyer to determine exactly how leasing would affect your company's financial picture. This review should be conducted as part of a more comprehensive analysis of all your financing alternatives.

Company Pension Plan

Do not be tempted by that pile of money you and your employees have contributed to the company pension or profit sharing plan. Except under narrow circumstances and only when an exemption has been obtained from the U.S. Department of Labor, loans between companies and their plans are illegal. Exemptions are available, but you should see a qualified lawyer for advice and assistance in preparing the application materials.

Borrowing from Shareholders

If you and the other owners of your company want to put in additional cash, should it be in the form of a loan to the business (debt) or an investment of additional capital (equity)?

You as lender and the company as borrower enjoy tax advantages if the cash is treated as "debt." There are two reasons for this. First, the interest paid to you is tax deductible by the company; the same amount if paid to you as a dividend would not be. Second, repayments of the loan principal are not taxable income to you or the other lender–shareholders. This means that you get some cash out of the business tax-free. In short, debt financing avoids the "double tax" imposed on dividends (at the corporate level and at the shareholder level) *and* it provides tax deductions to the corporation.

As you might expect, the Internal Revenue Service is alert to abuses of the tax advantages associated with debt financing. Where there is abuse, the IRS will treat the "debt" as "equity" by denying the company's interest deductions and by taxing the shareholders for the principal payments they receive. The IRS debt-equity rules are new and extremely complex. If you want the benefits of debt financing, you should consult competent accountants and lawyers before you or other shareholders loan money to the company.

OTHER SOURCES OF MONEY: THE EQUITY MARKETS

Instead of borrowing money, your company could raise the needed funds through equity financing. Perhaps you want to strengthen the balance sheet so you can qualify for a larger credit line; or you want to avoid bank restrictions on the company's operations; or you simply can't handle the high cost of debt service.

Read chapter 12 for a full discussion of the legal pitfalls in the securities field. You will see that there are new federal rules governing securities offerings and that the registration process is now simpler and less costly than it once was. This is particularly true for "private placements" (stock sales to a limited number of investors); offerings to sophisticated investors; and offerings of small ($500,000) and modest ($5 million) size.

You should consult experts in the equity field, such as an investment banker who can help you determine whether a stock offering would be appropriate. You will also need the services of an experienced securities lawyer and accounting firm. None of this advice is cheap, and you should get written estimates before you hire anyone. Legal fees, even for a private placement, are rarely less than $30,000 and can easily be $50,000 or more.

Venture Capitalists

Another source of help and money is a venture capital company. It offers debt and equity financing but it is generally interested only in young companies with an excellent growth potential, most often the so-called high technology firms. Venture financing has its costs; the venture capitalist usually demands a substantial ownership interest and management role in the young company.

There are hundreds of venture capitalists. Consult Rubel, *Guide to Venture Capital Sources* for more information.

Small Business Investment Companies

Finally, small companies (less than $6 million in net worth and $2 million in after-tax earnings) can get equity capital from Small Business Investment Companies (SBICs). These SBA-licensed firms invest money they have borrowed from the SBA. Debt and equity financing are available, although the latter is preferred. A close cousin of the SBIC is the MESBIC (Minority Enterprises Small Business Investment Company) which invests in companies that are at least one-half owned by minorities, handicapped persons, or other categories of disadvantaged persons. You should contact your bank or local SBA office for a list of SBICs and MESBICs in your area.

A FINAL WORD ON MONEY MANAGEMENT

Our discussion of business finance assumes you have a well-managed business. If you don't, even the best negotiating strategy may not get you the loan you need. Sound business and financial management is vital to the success of any loan search. It should include:

- Accurate and complete accounting systems that show the cost to produce each line of goods or to deliver each type of service. Which aspects of your business are profitable? How can you improve profitability?

- Accurate cash flow projections that show you when to defer discretionary expenditures, cover projected deficits by borrowing, and wisely invest surplus cash until it's needed.

- Purchasing systems that prevent wasteful acquisitions but take advantage of volume discounts.

- Personnel programs that reduce employee turnover and inspire efficiency and productivity.

The money saved through good management can be the equivalent of one or two points of interest on your loan. The next time you review the company's financial records, pay as much attention to saving money as you do to borrowing it. If you can make your company more cost efficient, you may be able to reduce some of your need to borrow.

CHECKLIST OF FINANCING REQUIREMENTS

When you borrow, remember these points to keep the costs and legal risks low:

- Recall the most common bank borrowing mistakes.

- Be conversant with the Banker's Lingo.

- Be familiar with the types of standard bank financing including term loans, credit lines, and equipment and receivables financing.

- Put your loan request in writing; know how you will use the loan proceeds and how you will repay the loan itself.

- When you choose among different forms of debt financing, carefully evaluate the effect of any bank-imposed restrictions on company operations.

- Get professional advice from an accountant or lawyer before you sign long, complex papers. Even without professional advice, don't sign the documents if they differ in any way from your understanding of the lending arrangements.

- A complex financing arrangement may involve several documents and each one should be carefully reviewed for key provisions such as interest rates, repayment terms, defaults, and guarantees.

- Look to nonbank sources of funding, but be just as vigilant when striking a deal.

- Some of the greatest legal risks in business financing occur in the securities field. Read our explanation of this subject in chapter 12.

11. How to Avoid Common Tax Problems

by SHELDON S. COHEN

Sound tax planning has a twofold benefit: it saves money that might otherwise be paid in federal and state taxes, and it reduces the number and intensity of potential disputes that arise with tax authorities. This chapter provides some practical suggestions for realizing both these goals.

Tax disputes with the government can be traumatic for management and disruptive of business operations, particularly in a closely held corporation or small firm. This is true whether the result is a large tax deficiency or none at all: the cost in dollars and lost management time can be equally great.

This chapter describes certain preventive techniques you can adopt to avoid several tax problems common in closely held businesses, and ways to deal with the IRS in an audit. Specifically, you will learn:

- How to avoid the problem of excessive compensation of officers;
- How to avoid "constructive" dividends;
- How to avoid corporate penalty taxes;
- Important firm responsibilities for paying federal payroll taxes;

- How to avoid tax problems when a corporation or partnership is formed;
- How to handle a tax audit;
- The benefits of a periodic tax checkup; and
- The importance of maintaining thorough records.

Caution: This chapter is intended to give you a brief introduction to tax problems commonly faced by small businesses, and to suggest how to avoid them. It should not be viewed as a substitute for regularly consulting your tax advisor.

HOW TO AVOID EXCESSIVE COMPENSATION

The Problem: Excessive Compensation and Higher Taxes

Perhaps you recall from chapter 3 that there are tax problems for both the business and the employee if the corporation pays excessive compensation to an "owner–employee"; that is, a stockholder who is also an employee (usually an officer) of the corporation. The problems are of two kinds.

Double Tax on Corporate Profits. Corporate profits paid out as compensation are not subject to corporate income tax. A corporation can deduct "reasonable" compensation paid to its employees, even to those who are shareholders. In effect, every dollar of reasonable compensation reduces the corporate tax liability. However, if the IRS determines that the compensation paid to an owner–employee is excessive, there is an adverse effect: the corporation cannot deduct the excessive portion of the compensation. This is "double taxation"—both the corporation and the owner–employee pay tax on the same income. The combination of the two taxes can produce an effective tax rate on excessive compensation of as much as 73 percent.

Retirement Plan. Since compensation is the measuring stick for pension and profit sharing plans, retirement benefits usually increase when the compensation does. There might be a ripple effect if compensation is found to be excessive: the retirement benefits might be discriminatory and action might have to be taken to prevent a disqualification of the retirement plan.

Tips for Establishing Reasonable Compensation

For tax purposes, a payment will be treated as compensation only if (1) it is paid for services actually rendered, and (2) it is a reasonable measure of the value of those services. The IRS particularly scrutinizes corporate payments to owner–employees and their relatives. As with most business decisions, careful planning is the key to avoiding disputes over excessive compensation. Follow these guidelines to set compensation levels that will withstand IRS scrutiny:

1. Match the Money with the Job

- What duties and responsibilities does the employee have? Is he performing more than one role in the business, such as CEO and salesman?
- How much time does the employee devote to the business?
- What is his level of training and experience? Is he uniquely qualified for the position? Why?
- What compensation is being paid to employees with comparable positions in your firm and in similar firms?

2. Observe the Formalities of the Arrangement

As we discussed in chapters 3 and 4, all businesses must observe certain formalities. This is particularly true when they initially set and later adjust the compensation of an owner–employee.

- Use a written employment contract that describes in detail the duties and responsibilities of the employee and any other facts that were used to set compensation.
- The board of directors should review and approve all such arrangements; the minutes should reflect this and the facts that influenced its decision.

3. Don't Wait Until the Last Minute to Set Compensation

Set compensation in the year *before* the services are to be rendered. The IRS often views retroactive salary arrangements and big year-end bonuses as thinly disguised dividends that are designed to strip out corporate profits.

4. Avoid Sudden Increases in Compensation

A large, sudden increase in salary is sure to attract IRS scrutiny, particularly if the employee's duties and services have not changed. If the employee's duties remain the same, only gradual increases in compensation will ordinarily be justified.

Tip: New businesses frequently do not have adequate cash flow to fully compensate owner–employees. If this happens, the employment contract (and, in the case of a corporation, the board minutes) should recite the firm's inability to pay full compensation. When cash flow improves, you can increase salaries to cover past services that were not fully compensated. You should document the reason for the increase (additional cash flow) in both the employment agreement and the corporate minutes.

Do Annual Dividends Strengthen Your Case?

Some advisers suggest that closely held corporations pay annual dividends, regardless of amount, to demonstrate that the shareholders are receiving a return on their investment and that not all corporate profits are being withdrawn as salary. If the dividends are extremely small, this is not likely to be helpful. If the corporation has unneeded funds after it has compensated its employees and provided for its foreseeable business needs, then a meaningful dividend payment may help you withstand a charge of excessive compensation.

CONSTRUCTIVE DIVIDENDS: WHAT THEY ARE AND HOW TO AVOID THEM

Closely held corporations and their owners are often snared by the "constructive" dividend. Although never actually declared by the board of directors, it nevertheless has the same tax effect as an ordinary dividend—income to the recipient, no deduction for the corporation.

Constructive Dividend Defined

The IRS will "construct" a dividend for tax purposes whenever a profitable corporation confers an economic benefit on a shareholder without receiving *fair consideration* in return.

Examples of Constructive Dividends

1. *Shareholder Use of Corporate Property for Personal Purposes.* Suppose you as a shareholder make personal use of the company car, boat, or vacation property without paying a fair or "arm's length" fee for its use. In that event, the corporation is treated as having made a constructive dividend to you in an amount by which the full, fair rental value exceeds the amount (if any) that you actually paid.

2. *Excessive Rent Paid by the Corporation to a Shareholder.* For tax and other business reasons, corporations often lease rather than own certain business property. We mentioned in chapter 3 that shareholders in closely held corporations might lease property to the corporation as one way of attempting to avoid the problem of double taxation of corporate dividends. However, if the corporation leases property, such as office space, warehouse, machinery, or equipment, from a shareholder and pays an amount of rent greater than a fair rental, the excess will usually be treated as a constructive dividend by the IRS.

3. *Paying a Shareholder's Expenses.* If a corporation pays a shareholder's personal expenses, that amount will be treated as a constructive dividend unless it is part of a reasonable compensation arrangement between the shareholder and the corporation.

4. *Certain Sales Between Shareholder and Corporation.* Suppose a shareholder sells property worth $200 to his corporation but charges $300 for it. Result: The corporation will be deemed to have distributed a nondeductible

dividend of $100 to the shareholder. It works both ways: if the corporation sells property worth $200 to the shareholder for $50, the corporation has made a constructive dividend of $150.

With Related Parties. The same principle applies when the corporation purchases property from or sells it to a person or entity that is related to one of its shareholders. Example: if your corporation purchases property from your son or daughter or from another corporation that you control, and does so for a price that exceeds the property's fair value, the excess could be treated as a constructive dividend to you.

5. *Loans Involving Corporation and Shareholder.* The IRS often contends that a loan transaction involving a corporation and one of its shareholders creates a constructive dividend.

Guaranty. Suppose you as a shareholder borrow money from a totally unrelated firm such as a bank, and your corporation guarantees the loan. The corporation's guaranty could trigger a constructive dividend to you; the dividend would be equal to the fee that you would have paid an unrelated guarantor as a condition of obtaining the loan.

Loan to the Shareholder. Suppose instead that you borrow money directly from your corporation. The IRS may attempt to treat the loan as a dividend at the time it is made or at some later time depending on the facts and circumstances of the arrangement.

Loan to the Corporation. On the other hand, you might make a loan to the corporation. While this is often done, particularly in closely held corporations, there is some danger: the IRS might characterize the loan as a contribution to capital, which means the corporation's payments of principal and interest to you would be treated as dividends. We referred to this problem in chapter 3 (page 60). *Warning:* New and complex rules have been proposed concerning whether an advance to a corporation will be treated as debt (loans) or equity (stock). While the ratio of debt to equity (3:1 is often used as a benchmark) is an important fact, many others are just as significant. Be sure you and your tax adviser know beforehand the likely tax consequences of shareholder loans.

Tips to Avoid Constructive Dividends

The key to avoiding a constructive dividend is to attempt to deal with the corporation as if it were an unrelated party—at arm's length.

Loans. Loans between shareholders and corporations should be evidenced by a promissory note containing a fixed maturity date and market rate interest. The loan should be adequately secured and the borrower should be required to make (and should actually make) regular payments of principal and interest.

Purchase of Property. If you purchase property from the corporation or if it purchases property from you, be sure the sale price is approximately equal to the value of the property.

Use of Property. If you make personal use of a corporate auto, vacation home, or other property, pay rent to the corporation that is equal to what you would pay an independent party.

Corporate formalities. In all these "insider" transactions, observe the formalities you would normally honor in dealings with outsiders. Use written documents such as a promissory note or a rental agreement if they would ordinarily be used in a similar arrangement made at arm's length.

CORPORATE PENALTY TAXES AND HOW TO AVOID THEM

If your business operates as a corporation, you should be aware of two penalty taxes and the ways to avoid them.

Penalty Tax 1: The Personal Holding Company Tax

Holding and Operating Companies. This tax is imposed only on a personal holding company; that is, a corporation that primarily earns passive income such as dividends, interest, rents, and royalties and that fails to distribute its earnings regularly to the shareholders. A *holding* company is essentially an investment company, whereas an *operating* company derives its income by selling goods or providing services.

The Purpose of the Tax. The stated rationale for the personal holding company tax is that the relatively low tax rates for corporations (as compared to individuals) should be reserved for active businesses—operating companies—and should not be used by investment vehicles or holding companies. While the use of the corporate form principally for investment purposes is not prohibited, it comes at a price: the practical requirement that the corporation distribute its net earnings each year to its shareholders. The result is that tax is imposed on the same income twice—first at the corporate level, and then at the individual level.

The 50 Percent Tax. The personal holding company tax generally forces the corporation to distribute its earnings each year. It does this by imposing a 50 percent tax on undistributed profits (with adjustments). This penalty is in addition to the normal corporate income tax. As a result, the effective rate of corporate tax on undistributed income can reach 73 percent. This is thought to be sufficiently high to eliminate any incentive to retain earnings at the corporate level.

The Tests for the Tax. A corporation is subject to the personal holding company tax only if two tests are satisfied.

1. *Closely Held.* Only closely held corporations are subject to the tax. For tax purposes, this means five or fewer individuals own more than 50 percent in value of the corporation's stock at any time during the last half of its taxable year. (A person may be treated as owning stock that is actually owned by certain family members or related entities.)

2. *Income.* A corporation is a personal holding company only if at least 60 percent of its gross income (with adjustments) consists of passive income such as interest, dividends, certain rents, royalties, and other types of passive investment income.

Dangers for Operating Companies. An operating company can sometimes run afoul of the personal holding company tax. Suppose your closely held corporation owns a factory and stock in a bank. The corporation has a fixed price contract to deliver an entire year's production to one customer. If the cost of raw materials soars, it may be so high in relation to the gross receipts from sales that the corporation has little or no income from its manufacturing operations. In this event, the bulk of the corporation's income would be derived from dividends on the bank stock. Result: The corporation may be liable for the personal holding company tax if it has not made sufficient dividend distributions during the year.

How to Reduce the Adverse Impact of the Tax. A corporation can reduce or eliminate the amount of income that would otherwise be subject to the personal holding company tax by making a special dividend distribution after the close of the taxable year. This special procedure in the tax law is available only when the corporation's liability for the tax has been determined by a court or in an agreement with the IRS. Although the corporation can then distribute its earnings and escape the personal holding company tax, the cost is borne by the shareholders for they must pay taxes on those earnings.

Penalty Tax 2: Accumulated Earnings Tax

The Tax and Its Purpose. The purpose of the accumulated earnings tax is to force operating companies to distribute to their shareholders earnings that are not needed in the operation of the business. It does this by taxing unneeded earnings that the corporation retains rather than distributes. The tax rate is 27.5 percent of the first $100,000 of excess earnings, and 38.5 percent of excess earnings over $100,000. The combined rate of the ordinary corporate income tax and the accumulated tax can be as high as 66 percent.

Reasonable Accumulations Allowed. The accumulated earnings tax is not mechanically applied: it is imposed only when a corporation accumulates earnings beyond the *reasonable needs* of its business. Of course, there are many legitimate reasons for a corporation to accumulate earnings: to provide adequate working capital, to provide for expansion, to fund pension and other deferred compensation plans, to fund self-insurance, and to provide for a sinking fund to retire obligations. Unfortunately, there are no rigid rules for determining whether an accumulation is unreasonable. However, there are two benchmarks that, if not exceeded, will insulate the corporation from an IRS challenge.

The Code's Safeharbor: $250,000. The Internal Revenue Code itself allows a corporation to accumulate up to $250,000 ($150,000 in the case of a personal service corporation) of earnings without running afoul of the penalty tax. In effect, every corporation is presumed to have reasonable needs that require the accumulation of up to $250,000. Many small businesses need not worry about the penalty tax applying this test alone.

The "Bardahl" Formula. This special test applies to the entire accumulation, not merely the portion over $250,000; it is designed to measure a firm's need for working capital in the course of its normal operating cycle. For a manufacturer, the business cycle begins with the purchase of raw materials and ends with the collection of accounts receivable. IRS agents are instructed to utilize the formula as part of their audit procedures when reviewing a corporation's accumulated earnings.

Avoiding the Tax. A corporation that has accumulated earnings greater than $250,000 or the amount determined under the Bardahl formula will not, of course, automatically be subject to the accumulated earnings tax on the excess. As we said, there are many legitimate reasons to accumulate earnings even in substantial amounts.

Tip: The key to avoiding problems with this tax is to fully document in the corporate minutes and elsewhere the reasons for the accumulation, and to do it in advance. If you expect your corporation to accumulate more than the $250,000 statutory amount, consult your tax adviser to discuss how the Bardahl formula is applied, how you can properly accumulate earnings, and how to document the reasons for doing so.

YOUR RESPONSIBILITIES FOR
THE FEDERAL PAYROLL TAXES

The three federal taxes commonly known as "payroll taxes" are often a small company's biggest single tax obligation. The taxes, which are computed on wages paid to employees, are:

1. *Federal withholding tax.* Employers must withhold federal income tax from wages paid to their employees. Although the amounts are treated as payments of tax by the employees and credited against their federal income tax liability, the *employer* can be held liable for failure to withhold. (See "The Buck Stops Here.")

2. *FICA tax.* The Federal Insurance Contributions Act (FICA) imposes taxes to fund the social security system. The FICA taxes (more commonly called the social security taxes) consist of a tax on the employee and a tax on the employer. The employer is required to withhold the employee's portion of the FICA tax from his or her salary in the same manner that federal income tax is withheld.

3. *FUTA tax.* The Federal Unemployment Tax Act (FUTA) imposes a tax on the employer to fund federal unemployment compensation programs. A partial

credit against the FUTA tax may be allowed on the basis of taxes paid by the employer to state unemployment funds.

Warning. In addition to federal payroll tax obligations, an employer may also have state and local payroll obligations, such as withholding of state income tax.

The Payroll Taxes: On Wages to Employees

Federal payroll taxes are imposed on employers with respect to the "wages" they pay to "employees." These terms are defined in the Internal Revenue Code and elsewhere.

Wages. Employers are sometimes surprised to discover that some kinds of remuneration for services, such as transfers of property in lieu of money payments, are "wages" and subject to payroll tax. On the other hand, other forms of remuneration, such as certain sickness and disability payments, may not be "wages" for payroll tax purposes.

Employees. There is also the problem of determining who is an "employee." Sometimes, it is unclear whether a person performing services is (for payroll tax purposes) an employee or an independent contractor.

Tip: In order to minimize payroll tax obligations, review your busines operations with a tax adviser to determine whether the forms of compensation you pay are wages (and therefore subject to payroll taxes), and whether the persons who perform services for you should be characterized as employees.

Your Paperwork Responsibilities

Payroll tax laws impose on employers various collection, payment, and reporting obligations. These are described at length in several IRS publications such as the Employer's Tax Guide (also known as Circular E, Publication 15), and Employment Taxes (also known as Publication 539). It's best to consult your tax adviser, who can help you design and implement a system for fulfilling your responsibilities, such as with a tax "calendar" that will tell you the dates when certain obligations must be met.

The Buck Stops Here: Penalties for Noncompliance

The Internal Revenue Code contains civil and criminal penalties for failing to comply with payroll tax requirements. The "100 percent penalty" permits the IRS to collect unpaid payroll taxes from *any officer or employee* of a business who is responsible (directly or indirectly) for the payroll and who willfully fails to collect or pay the amounts due. Although this provision is called a penalty, it is actually a device to collect the taxes that should have been paid.

In general, unpaid payroll taxes can be collected from any person who had control over the funds that should have been remitted. If you have control over or supervise someone who has direct responsibility for collection and payment, the IRS can collect the taxes directly from you.

Warning: In a small business, the president usually will be held responsible for unpaid payroll taxes. Any person who has the duty to withhold and make payment, such as the secretary or treasurer, will also be held responsible unless he performs merely ministerial or clerical duties and has no discretion or involvement in making and implementing business decisions.

HOW TO AVOID TAX PROBLEMS WHEN FORMING A CORPORATION OR PARTNERSHIP

As we discussed in chapter 3, each of the three common forms of business enterprise—proprietorship, partnership, and corporation—has its pros and cons. Here we describe some of the tax requirements, perils, and planning opportunities in the formation of corporations and partnerships.

The Corporation: Tax Planning at Inception

Five Requirements for a Tax-Free Exchange

The incorporation of a business normally involves the transfer of cash and other property to the corporation in exchange for stock or securities. This exchange may produce a taxable gain, and in some instances loss, to you as the transferor (the person giving up the cash or property) unless the following requirements are met:

1. *Only Transfer "Property" to the Corporation.* The term "property" is broadly defined for this purpose and includes cash, accounts receivable, patent rights, trade secrets, leaseholds, and goodwill. However, if you receive stock or securities in exchange for the performance of personal *services* for the corporation, you will be taxed at ordinary income rates on the fair market value of the stock or securities.

2. *Transferors Must Have "Control" of the Corporation Immediately After the Transfer.* "Control" is defined as the ownership of at least 80 percent of the total combined voting power of all classes of stock entitled to vote and 80 percent of the total number of shares of each class of nonvoting stock.

3. *Transferors Must Receive Only Stock or Securities of the Corporation.* In order for the transfer to be wholly tax-free, the transferors must receive only stock or securities from the corporation in exchange for the property transferred. The term "securities" refers to certain instruments that represent long-term obligations of a corporation.

If you as a transferor receive cash or other property ("boot") in addition to stock and securities, you must report income equal to the lesser of (a) the cash plus the fair market value of other boot received, and (b) the excess, if any, of the fair market value of the property transferred over its tax basis.

4. *The Receipt of Stock Is Not "Substantially Disproportionate."* The value of the stock, securities, and boot that a transferor receives from the corporation must be approximately equal to the value of the property that has been transferred. If the values differ, the transaction may have other tax consequences for the transferor, and possibly the other stockholders or the corporation. For example, if you exchange $100 in cash for stock having a value of $90, you may be treated for tax purposes as having made a gift of $10 to the other shareholders.

5. *The Corporation Is Not an "Investment Company."* The transfer of property to an "investment company" may be a taxable transaction. In general, a corporation will be treated as an "investment company" if 80 percent (in value) of its assets (excluding cash and certain obligations) are readily marketable stocks or securities that are held for investment, or if it is a real estate investment trust or other type of investment vehicle. The type of transfer that will be taxable is one in which two or more transferors "diversify" their personal stock portfolios by transferring them to a closely held corporation in exchange for its stock. For example, assume that A owns stock of General Motors and B owns stock of Ford. If A and B form AB corporation and transfer their General Motors and Ford stock to it in exchange for AB stock, they will be viewed as having diversified their personal stock portfolios and the transfer will be taxable.

How Liabilities Can Produce a Taxable Gain

There are two situations when the transfer to a corporation of property subject to certain liabilities can produce a taxable gain.

Suppose you transfer to your new corporation a building that is worth $100,000 but is the subject of a $60,000 mortgage. Normally the corporation is liable for the payment of the mortgage debt; that is, the corporation takes the property subject to the mortgage. In this situation, the liability—in this case $60,000—is not treated as boot (and is therefore not taxable) with two important exceptions.

First, if immediately prior to the transfer of the building you borrowed funds for personal purposes and gave the $60,000 mortgage on the building as security, then that amount would be the boot in the transfer. The rule is that all liabilities assumed by the corporation will be treated as boot if there is no bona fide business purpose for shifting the liability to the corporation, or if the principal purpose of shifting the liability is to avoid federal income tax.

Second, if the sum of all liabilities assumed by the corporation (in this case $60,000) exceeds the tax basis of the transferred property (ordinarily the "basis" of property is its cost reduced by depreciation) then the excess is treated as boot and the transferor may be required to report income. In the facts given just above, there would be no boot; but if the property's basis were only $50,000, you would be required to report as income the $10,000 difference between the mortgage ($60,000) and the basis of the property ($50,000).

The Partnership: Tax Planning at the Inception

The formation of a partnership and the contributions of property to it by the partners in exchange for their interests is generally not a taxable event. But there are three important exceptions to this rule. *First*, the exchange of a partnership interest for services will have income tax consequences for the partner who performs the services, and in some instances for the other partners. *Second*, in some circumstances, the contribution of property subject to a liability (such as a mortgage) can result in the imposition of tax on the partner who made the transfer. *Third*, the contributions may be taxable if the partnership would be an "investment company" if it were incorporated.

An important legal concern at the time of the partnership's formation is the future income tax consequences to the partners. For this reason, the partnership agreement must be drafted with great care; it must specify each partner's interest in profits, losses, cash flow, and capital. In some cases, the partners may wish to include in the partnership agreement allocations to particular partners of items such as income, loss, or gain.

For example, assume that you and your partner form a partnership and that each of you has a 50 percent interest in profits. You contribute $1,000 in cash to the partnership and your partner contributes property worth $1,000 with a tax basis of zero. In the absence of a special allocation, if the partnership sells the property, you and your partner must each report gain of $500. In other words, you must pay tax on one-half of the amount by which the property has appreciated. You can avoid this problem by including a provision in the partnership agreement that allocates to your partner the first $1,000 of gain realized upon the disposition of the property. That way, when the property is sold, your partner must report as income the appreciation that accrued during his sole ownership, and each of you will report one-half of any subsequent appreciation.

HOW TO HANDLE A TAX AUDIT

How Returns Are Selected

When you receive a notice from the IRS informing you of an impending audit, your first question may be, why me? The IRS selects returns in many ways:

- By using criteria that identify returns that are likely to have many errors. Examples: high compensation to an owner–employee in a closely held corporation; a tax shelter; high deductions for travel and entertainment.
- By random selection.

- By using nontax characteristics, such as the identity of your tax preparer; the type of business you have, or industry you are in.

- By searching for discrepancies between your return and the data supplied by your corporation, partnership, or bank.

Three Types of Tax Audits

Correspondence Audit. This is used when it appears that only a minor adjustment may be necessary. The IRS sends a written inquiry, and if your response is satisfactory the audit is closed. Example: If you report $100 in bank interest but the bank reports $110, the IRS will probably use the correspondence audit to resolve the matter.

Office Audit. Here, you are asked to visit the local IRS office and submit in advance or bring with you identified records and business documents. The scope of an office audit is usually limited to the subject of the requested documents. The office audit is generally used only for individual (personal) and simple business returns.

Field Audit. This is the most comprehensive audit, conducted at your place of business. The revenue agent is likely to examine all books and records that relate to the items on the return.

Techniques for Handling an Audit

There is no assured way of emerging unscathed from an audit, but these seven techniques will put you in the strongest possible position.

1. Be Prepared

As in many other business matters, this common-sense principle is often the key to a favorable result. With an office and field audit, you are notified in advance and asked to furnish certain records; in some cases, the notice will identify the items the agent will examine. Prepare for the audit by assembling and carefully reviewing the documents.

Warning: It is essential that you be familiar with these records, just as you would any others you furnish to outsiders.

2. Keep Track of What You Give the Agent

Keep a list of the records you furnish the agent. An audit can take place over a period of several months or even longer; memory is fragile, and without a list you will turn over material that may already have been reviewed.

3. Don't Create a Hostile Atmosphere

Many taxpayers believe they can rid themselves of an agent by being hostile and uncooperative. This tactic often backfires; the agent has a great deal of discretion, and if he also becomes hostile he may closely (and perhaps unreasonably) review many more items than he originally intended to review. A cooperative attitude is far more likely to result in an expeditious and relatively favorable result. Be respectful and polite, and in the case of a field audit provide a clean and well-lit working place. Furnish records in an organized and professional manner; don't dump them on the agent and waste his and your valuable time.

Warning: There is sometimes a fine line between establishing and maintaining a good working relationship and wrongfully attempting to influence an agent. Exercise common sense. An agent is barred from accepting gifts and favors such as meals, the use of vacation property, and similar items. An agent may view an offer of such benefits as an improper attempt to influence the outcome of the audit.

4. Check with Your Adviser Before Meeting with an Agent

Check with your adviser before agreeing to meet with an IRS agent, particularly an agent of the Criminal Investigation Division (a "special" agent). At the meeting, the agent will normally identify himself; but if he doesn't, be sure to ask to see his identification card.

5. Centralize Communications

Designate one person from your firm to handle all the communications with the agent. This reduces confusion and the possibility that matters will be presented in a haphazard, contradictory, or unfavorable manner.

6. Use an Accountant or Lawyer

In some cases it is wise to have an accountant or lawyer handle the audit. Talk with your regular financial and legal advisers to get their views. The decision, which is ultimately yours, depends upon the nature and complexity of the case, your ability to answer the agent's questions without jeopardizing your legal position, your personality, and the cost of your time.

7. Carefully Evaluate the Wisdom of an Extension

The IRS normally has three years from the date you file a return to assess a tax deficiency against you. If it cannot complete its examination within that time, it may request that you agree to an extension of the assessment period. Should you agree?

Carefully consider the pros and cons. If you do not agree, the audit may be terminated, but you might be sent a hastily prepared statutory notice of deficiency. Once the notice is issued, the only way you can contest the deficiency is to initiate proceedings in the courts. For these reasons, it is usually advisable to give the IRS enough time to complete the audit so you will have an opportunity to respond to the agent's questions and settle unresolved issues without going to court. On the other hand, where the IRS is conducting a civil or criminal fraud investigation, it may not be wise to agree to an extension. In these circumstances, consult your tax adviser beforehand.

Should You Settle or Fight?

There are often matters that are not resolved by the time the audit ends. Should you try to settle with the agent, appeal to the Appeals Division (the next administrative level in the IRS), or litigate? In general, it is better to try to resolve the matter with the agent; it's faster and cheaper than the other methods. But there are many factors to consider:

- How strong is your case? The IRS's?
- Is the agent likely to agree to a settlement that you will accept?
- Would the Appeals Division (whose staff is generally more experienced and knowledgeable than the audit staff) be more, or less, inclined to settle on favorable terms?

In some cases, it's possible to settle with the agent on some issues and leave the balance for consideration by the Appeals Division. But an agent may be unwilling to make concessions that would adversely affect the Service's bargaining position at the Appeals level.

Agent's Report. Regardless of whether you settle at the audit level, the agent will prepare a revenue agent's report containing the pertinent facts and legal principles. This document is used as the basis for any higher level administrative review of your case. Take advantage of every opportunity to participate with the agent in the preparation of the report, since the agent's description of the facts can affect the outcome at the review stage.

USE A TAX CHECKUP TO AVOID TAX PROBLEMS

Spot Problems Early with a Tax Checkup

Careful tax planning makes good business sense: it contributes to profits and it prevents tax disputes with the government from arising. An important element of tax planning is the periodic tax checkup that can expose potential or existing tax problems before they become serious and costly to resolve. A tax checkup is a tax examination of your business operation, and it can be an exhaustive, sweeping examination or a more modest analysis of particular subjects. At the end, you should get practical suggestions for preventing tax problems and for reducing your taxes in proper ways you may have overlooked.

The cost of the checkup will be a function of its scope and depth. Some accounting firms offer the service as a means of attracting new clients, so you might be able to get a checkup for a modest fee.

How to Know if You Need a Checkup

Consider a tax checkup in any of these situations:

1. *When You Start a Business.* As we said in chapters 3 and 4, there are many tax issues to analyze when starting a business. Some questions must be addressed at the threshold as you decide whether to operate as a corporation or a partnership; the others must be answered as you plan the business and allocate its resources.

2. *As the Business Matures.* It's wise to have a tax checkup as the business matures so you can reexamine decisions made at the firm's inception. For example, it might be beneficial to incorporate a business that is now operated as a partnership; that way you can take advantage of lower corporate tax rates, compensation packages, and stock option plans, none of which is available to an unincorporated firm.

3. *When Business Conditions Change.* A checkup can help when industry or business conditions change. Example: If your inventory costs are escalating because of high inflation or shortages of materials, and if you use the FIFO (first-in, first-out) method of inventory accounting, a checkup may reveal that it would be advantageous to switch to the LIFO (last-in, first-out) method.

4. *New Markets, New Lines of Business.* A firm that penetrates new markets and introduces new products or services may face as many tax questions as would an entirely new enterprise. A checkup will confirm that you have made the right tax choices.

5. *When the Tax Law Changes.* There have been many recent changes in the tax laws affecting business. A checkup may reveal that you are not taking full advantage of them.

Any of these five circumstances might be reason enough to have a tax checkup. A tax checkup may also be advisable in the absence of these circumstances because it might lead to useful suggestions concerning your accounting and tax procedures. Any one of them can reduce your taxes and improve compliance with IRS requirements, and that way more than pay for the checkup. For example, your tax adviser may suggest:

- That you should change recordkeeping procedures and methods.
- That depreciable assets should be purchased rather than leased, or vice-versa.
- That one method of depreciation is preferable to another.
- That you should change inventory accounting methods.
- That you should change the form of business organization.
- That you can use special tax benefits such as energy tax credits, or research and experimental tax credits.
- That bad debt reserves are insufficient or excessive.

How to Choose a Professional to Make the Checkup

Consider these factors when selecting a professional to conduct a tax checkup.

- Your own accounting firm may be the right choice, particularly if it is a large regional or national firm with a solid reputation.
- If you use a small accounting firm, make sure it has a systematic checkup program.
- Does your accountant only prepare financial records and tax returns; or is he a business and tax adviser too, someone who makes creative tax saving suggestions and understands and furthers the business goals? The latter may be better for the job.
- Even if your present accountant is up to the task, you may want to get someone else to do it so you will have a second opinion.

AVOID TAX PROBLEMS: THOROUGHLY DOCUMENT TRANSACTIONS

Complete and accurate business records are essential for at least two reasons: they will help you withstand an IRS audit and the process of preparing them often makes for better company decisions.

Records for the Audit. An IRS agent will try to answer two questions: Did the reported transaction actually take place, and did you correctly report it? Documents are essential to the audit process because they substantiate your answers to both questions. Without records to support your responses, you must rely on memory; understandably, the IRS is skeptical of self-serving and after-the-fact explanations. Nonexistent or incomplete records can doom even the most legitimate business transaction.

Records Lead to Better Decisions. A documented tax analysis of business options often yields better decisions. Suppose your closely held corporation needs a new piece of equipment but does not have enough capital for the purchase. You might be tempted simply to loan funds to the corporation, but there are many other ways to finance the purchase and each one has different tax implications. For example, should the stockholders advance funds to the corporation? If so, should the advance be structured as a loan or a contribution to capital? Instead, should the stockholders purchase the equipment and lease it to the firm? A written analysis of the options should produce better decisions.

Board Minutes Are Essential Records. If your firm operates as a corporation, the most important records are the minutes of board of directors meetings. The board makes the most important corporate decisions and the ones with the greatest tax implications. The IRS knows this, and its audit of a closely held corporation will look to the decisions that were made, who made them, when they were made, and in some cases why they were made. The corporation that cannot provide the minutes to reflect the "what, who, when, and why" of its decisions will often be second-guessed by the IRS. In that event, it may face a substantial tax deficiency.

Warning: We discussed in chapter 4 the importance of observing corporate formalities to preserve the protection of the corporate shield; that is, to limit the shareholders' liability to the amount of their investment. Don't jeopardize the integrity of the shield or erode the strength of your tax position by drafting sloppy or incomplete minutes; in an audit, they can be more of a hindrance than a help.

Where Documentation Is Especially Important:
Transactions with Shareholders

Although good records should be kept for all business transactions, they are especially important for transactions (such as loans or sales of property) between the company and its shareholders. There are two reasons for this.

First, as we discussed in chapters 3 and 4, a corporation is itself a legal entity, distinct from its shareholders. For this reason, transactions between the corporation and any shareholders should be conducted with the same formalities as if they were transactions with another company or individuals unaffiliated with the corporation. These "formalities" include the preparation of records and documents.

Second, there are ample opportunities for tax abuse in transactions between a corporation and its shareholders. For example, you will recall that the payment of compensation is a means by which corporate profits can be distributed to shareholders with only one tax. This often leads owner–employees to pay themselves very high, and sometimes excessive, compensation. The IRS closely reviews company–shareholder transactions, and it places special emphasis on thorough documentation of them. Owners of small businesses should resist the temptation to act informally and dispense with the necessary corporate papers. This requires discipline, but the benefits are well worth the effort.

12. How to Comply with the Securities Laws

by CANNON Y. HARVEY

It is not simply the *Fortune* 500 that need worry about federal and state securities laws; any business that raises capital or has more than one owner should also be on guard. That surprises many businessmen, but consider just one example of the long reach of these laws: even the sale of a condominium can be a "security," and that means the seller has certain disclosure and perhaps registration obligations.

This chapter describes the reach of the securities laws and some techniques you can use to minimize corporate and personal exposure. This is not an instructional manual for writing your own prospectus or planning your own offering; presumably, you will pay someone else to do that for you. Instead, you will learn:

- How to distinguish a "security" from other investments;
- The elements of securities disclosure and registration;
- How to structure a capital offering so you are exempt from federal registration;
- The pros and cons of going public; and
- What happens when you do.

Warning: Securities laws are Byzantine and the penalties for violating them severe. This is an area where it's essential to obtain expert advice.

This chapter is divided into three parts. Part I, A Look at the Securities Laws, explains the basics including the important anti-fraud or disclosure requirements that apply even if a security is not registered; Part II summarizes federal and state registration and the exemptions from it that can save time and money; Part III concludes with answers to the often asked questions of When to Go Public, and What Happens When You Do?

PART I
A LOOK AT THE SECURITIES LAWS

The securities laws are increasingly fertile ground for litigation. The reasons are manifold. The definition of "security" has been extended as never before; investors are more knowledgeable and eager to assert their rights if an investment sours; private "class action" attorneys are eager to assist them; and more companies are stumbling over the protrusive laws and regulations. All this is ample incentive to know the legal risks.

Overlapping Federal and State Laws

The securities laws consist of overlapping federal and state statutes, regulations, and court decisions.

The two principal federal laws we discuss here are the Securities Act of 1933 ("Securities Act") and the Securities Exchange Act of 1934 ("Exchange Act"). All states, the District of Columbia, and Puerto Rico also have laws regulating securities transactions, so-called Blue Sky laws. State and federal laws are concordant but they are not identical, so compliance with one is no guarantee of compliance with the other: you must abide by both.

Tip: Don't make the mistake of spending a lot of time and money complying with federal requirements while ignoring the states'; the results may be disastrous.

Multiple Enforcement Agencies

The federal securities laws are administered by the Securities and Exchange Commission (SEC). It has a main office in Washington, D.C. and regional offices throughout the country. The Washington office processes most of the "registration" statements, which we discuss on page 246. The securities laws in the states are usually administered by a full-time Securities Administrator. Staff size and experience vary from state to state, although states with many securities offerings generally have an effective enforcement team.

Securities Laws Require Registration and Disclosure

The securities laws regulate a broad range of activities including the offer, sale, and resale of securities; proxy solicitation by public companies; reporting activities; stock trading by officers, directors, and other "insiders"; the operation of stock exchanges and the over-the-counter market; activities of brokers and dealers; operations of investment companies (mutual funds) and investment advisers; and tender offers.

For our purposes, the first subject is the vital one—the offer and sale of securities. There are two principal requirements, disclosure and registration:

Disclosure: There must be a *disclosure* of "material" information to prospective investors even if the security need not be registered. This "anti-fraud" provision may call for the disclosure of somewhat less information than is contained in a formal registration statement (see below), though the amount is still extensive.

Registration: So-called public offerings (which can be "public" even if made to only one investor) generally must be *registered* with the SEC and state agencies. A registrant must file with the applicable agencies a registration statement that includes a "prospectus" containing comprehensive, detailed information about itself, its management, and the offered security. The securities may not be sold until the registration statement is declared effective by the agencies.

These dual requirements of disclosure and registration exist under both federal and state law.

Consequences of Noncompliance: Assuring No Loss to the Investor

Government Suits. Both federal and state laws impose criminal and civil penalties, and a willful violation can result in a prison term and substantial fine.

Private Suits. A disgruntled investor can sue the company that issues the security (the "issuer"), other participants in selling the securities, *and* certain company directors, officers, and controlling shareholders.

Warning: The "corporate shield" discussed in chapter 3 cannot be counted on to protect senior company officials from liability. In fact, all directors and certain officers can be *personally liable* for material misstatements or omissions in a federal registration statement.

Recoveries in securities cases can be large; for example, the remedy for not registering a security (when registration is required) is for the investor to recover the entire amount he paid for it plus interest. Fraud or other wrongdoing need not be proved. The penalty for failing to make adequate disclosures ("fraud") is also high: the investor can recover the difference between what he originally paid and what he sold the stock for; or in some cases, if he still owns the stock, he can have the entire transaction rescinded ("rescission") and recover the full purchase price. Through these harsh remedies, the careless issuer—and sometimes its management—guarantees that the investor will not lose money, and company executives may find themselves having to make payments out of their own personal funds if the firm has inadequate reserves.[1]

WHEN THE LAWS APPLY TO YOU: S.O.S.

What triggers the dual requirements of registration and disclosure? Two elements must be present: there must be a *Security*, and there must be an *Offer* or *Sale* (S.O.S.). Many securities law violations occur because the company or individuals involved never imagined they were issuing a "security." Know how broad the term is so you can avoid an inadvertent violation.

Security: It's More Than Stocks and Bonds

To the astonishment of many businessmen, a "security" can be issued by an individual, partnership, and trust as well as a corporation. Although the definition varies among the federal and state laws, it is universally broad.

Everyone knows that stocks, bonds, and warrants (rights to purchase stock) are securities. But the following are also securities and as such are subject to regulation: limited partnership interests; subscriptions for stock or limited partnership interests; fractional undivided interests in oil, gas or other mineral rights; stock options; notes, and other forms of debt (with certain exceptions); interests in profit sharing agreements; voting trust certificates; interests in business trusts; interests in certain general partnerships and joint ventures; and virtually anything that can be characterized as an "investment contract."

Investment Contract. The last term, the investment contract, has been the basis for the greatest and most significant extension of the securities laws; it is also the source of greatest peril for the unwary executive.

An investment contract is created by any transaction in which a person invests funds in a common enterprise with the expectation of deriving a return primarily through the efforts of others. This sweeping definition has served as the basis for courts to declare that these can be (but are not always) securities: interests in real estate, fruit groves, and other properties; goods and animals; and some investments characterized as franchises or club memberships.

Tip: Use this three-part rule of thumb to determine whether an investment you offer creates a security:

---

[1]Another potential source of liability is the Racketeer Influenced and Corrupt Organizations Act, commonly known as "RICO." Fraud in the sale of securities is one of the illegal racketeering activities specified in RICO. Although the law is just beginning to develop, certain types of securities fraud (yet to be defined) may subject a person to liability under RICO. Private parties can recover triple damages plus attorneys' fees. This could result in substantially greater damages than would be available under the Securities Act or the Exchange Act.

1. If what you offer is *intended* in whole or in part as an investment vehicle;

2. If you (as the seller) or someone identified by you at the time of the sale will continue to have some *continuing responsibility to manage the investment*; and

3. If the investor is likely to *rely* on your continuing involvement when he makes the investment.

The following examples illustrate how an apparently routine investment can become a security.

The Condo. Suppose you are a condominium developer at a ski resort. You offer a unit for sale by describing its physical features and proximity to the lift lines. There is not yet a security, but the sales pitch with the next prospect is more fervid. You say many buyers use the units sparingly, preferring to rent them instead. You also offer the services of your condominium management company to handle advertising, rental, and maintenance. Result: This probably is a security because the three elements of the rule of thumb are present.

The Real Estate Venture. Now suppose you own a piece of real estate that you offer to sell to your neighbor. So far this is not a security. The same is true if the property has an apartment complex on it (assuming you have no continuing management responsibility); or even if you enter into a joint venture with your neighbor whereby he contributes the money to build the apartments, you contribute the property, and both of you have an equal voice in management. However, if you are the managing venturer for the project and your neighbor has no management rights except for a veto over major decisions (such as sale of the project), you probably offered a security when you invited your neighbor to participate. The same would be true if the deal is structured as a limited partnership with you as general partner and the neighbor as sole limited partner.

The Oil Well. You have not sold a security when you sell all of your 100 percent interest in a Wyoming oil and gas lease to one person, but if you sell a 1/3 interest in the lease to each of three people, that would generally be a security. Reason: oil, gas, and mineral interests are specifically included in the definition of security, so the three elements of an investment contract need not be present.[2]

The essential lesson is to remember the breadth of the security definition when you invite others to participate in your investment.

Offer: It Includes Informal Invitations

You need not actually sell a security to trigger the registration and disclosure requirements: in most cases a mere "offer" to sell is enough and even this term is broadly defined. It is vital to understand when an offer or sale occurs because a

---

[2]In some circumstances, the sale of all the stock of your company to one purchaser can be the sale of a security subject to the anti-fraud provisions.

premature offer—one made before the security is properly registered—can induce federal and state administrative sanctions or delays when you file the registration documents.

Warning: Even an inadvertent offer made before you have properly registered the security can violate the Securities Act and jeopardize the entire issuing process.

Under the Securities Act, an offer includes *every attempt* or offer to dispose of, or *solicitation* of an offer to buy, a security or interest in a security for value. This definition encompasses far more than the explicit, "I offer to sell you . . ." Example: You offer a security if you send a letter to a colleague requesting that he "let you know" if he would be interested in acquiring stock in your company. Reason: you are soliciting an "offer to buy" and that is part of the definition.

Warning: The vernacular meaning of "offer" is not the same as it is in the Securities Act. Even informal communications, casual remarks, and preliminary negotiations can trigger the Act. Be careful with oral and written comments before you file a registration statement.

Sale: It Is any Disposition for Value

If an offer triggers the securities laws, surely an actual sale does too. Not surprisingly, the word has a broad meaning: it is any disposition of a security for value. This includes a contract for the purchase or sale of a security; the conversion of one security into another (such as a convertible debenture to common stock); and the exercise of a warrant or option (even an employee stock option). Note that the exercise of a warrant or option could require the issuing company to deliver an updated prospectus, even if the underlying security was previously registered.

Other securities "sales" are more massive, such as general business combinations. For example, a merger, consolidation, or exchange of stock with a company's shareholders can be a sale. In addition, an exchange of stock for the assets of a company or partnership constitutes the offer and sale of securities to *all* of the shareholders or partners of that entity if the securities are distributed according to an existing plan or are in fact distributed according to a plan adopted within one year.

Your company's lawyer should be able to steer you clear of securities violations. But your role is a large one: prevent inadvertent violations by recalling the S.O.S. triggers of the securities laws—Security, Offer, or Sale.

WHAT THE LAW REQUIRES: ALWAYS DISCLOSURE

Recall that the two essential requirements of the securities laws are *registration* and *disclosure*. We take up the anti-fraud or disclosure provision first because it exists *whether or not* the security must be registered.

Warning: When you sell a security, you must make certain disclosures about it to the purchaser even if you are relieved of state and federal registration requirements. Though the latter are more onerous and often call for the disclosure of more information, the general anti-fraud standard is extremely important and the failure to follow it is a serious violation of the law.

Disclosure to Prevent Fraud

The federal Securities Act and Exchange Act as well as all the state laws prohibit "fraud" in connection with the offer or sale of *all* securities. These anti-fraud or "disclosure" provisions (so termed because the way to prevent fraud is to provide information) are embodied in several statutes and rules, of which SEC Rule 10b-5 is best known. Regardless of their location, the essential point is this: a securities sale is subject to both these federal and state prohibitions even if it is exempt from registration. A securities offering can be structured legally to avoid registration, but you still will have violated the law if you fail to make adequate disclosures.

Avoiding Securities Fraud: Disclose Material Facts

Securities fraud is like no other species of fraud in the law. Although the exact definition varies somewhat among the federal and state laws, essentially it means this: it is illegal to sell or purchase a security with a written document or by an oral communication that:

1. includes an *untrue* statement of a *material* fact or
2. *omits* to state a *material* fact that is necessary to make the statements that are made not misleading in light of the surrounding circumstances.

In short, you have two obligations: *not* to utter false statements, and *to volunteer* all important information.

It is clear from the legislative history and court cases that Congress intended to give investors much greater protection than was generally available to other marketplace consumers. *Caveat emptor* ("let the buyer beware") has no place in the sale of securities. This is a troublesome concept for many businessmen. Merchants who are fair in their business dealings and who would never lie in a negotiation are unsettled when they first encounter the detailed disclosures required by the anti-fraud rules. The irritant is the second disclosure element—the affirmative obligation to disclose every material fact that is necessary to make the other statements not misleading.

What is a "material" fact? It is one that would have been *significant*, though not necessarily controlling, in a reasonable investor's decision to purchase a security. Consider these examples and the significance of the undisclosed facts.

Sales Decline. Suppose in the third quarter of its fiscal year, your company sells securities (described either in a prospectus used in a registered offering or, where that's not required, a private offering memorandum) and states that last year's sales were $10 million, 200 percent greater than the year before. Although that's true, you don't disclose that in the first half of the current year, sales were only $2 million with few new orders in hand. You have committed fraud because the first statement is misleading without the second, and the second constitutes material information to the prospective buyer.

Supply Problem. Now suppose the first statement is the same ($10 million in sales, 200 percent gain) and sales and orders are running at the same level. But you have other problems: you can't get the raw materials you need to make your products, and though your executives are optimistic, you have yet to find alternative sources. You should disclose these facts even if you qualify them by stating that management expects the problem will shortly be solved.

Common Directors. Finally, suppose the prospectus or offering memorandum describes your company's valuable contract to do research and development for another firm. The contract is expected to account for a significant part of your company's business during the next two years. If you fail to disclose that one of your directors is also a director and substantial shareholder of the other company, you may have committed fraud. Reason: An investor might have declined to buy your securities had he known so much revenue was attributable to inside or "family" business.

The lesson is that if an investment is a security, you must disclose a good deal more information than if it were an ordinary product sale.

Though the dimension of the disclosure obligation may change, the task does not: examine all statements for accuracy and review them with all company officials having knowledge of relevant facts to see if there is more that should be said. The perfect disclosure statement or prospectus has never been written but it never hurts to try.

Tip: Use this rule of thumb to dig out material facts. What would you want to know about the company, its business, properties, personnel, financial position, and outstanding claims if you were purchasing it for cash with no representations or warranties from the seller (that is, he sells "as is") but with total access to information about the company before the closing? Presumably you would be eager to learn of anything that would adversely affect the company's financial condition, performance, and prospects. The law demands the investor be given the same information.

Remember that if you are sued for securities fraud, a judge or jury will have the benefit of hindsight in determining what is material. Today's seemingly trivial fact may look very important tomorrow. *When in doubt, disclose it.*

When to Make Disclosures: For a Purchase and a Sale

Purchase

Federal anti-fraud provisions apply to *both* the purchase and sale of securities, so a purchaser often has an affirmative obligation to disclose material facts to the seller. This is particularly true when a company repurchases its own securities or when an "insider" purchases from another shareholder.

Example: Suppose a brother and sister each own 50 percent of a company's stock. The sister has managed the corporation full-time for the past five years while the brother, a passive investor, has not even been on the board of directors. If the sister wants to buy her brother's stock, she must disclose facts that her brother would deem important in agreeing on a price for the stock. The existence of a valuable new contract is an example of such a fact. This obligation exists even if the purchase is initiated by the seller. (Note: The price of repurchased stock may have been fixed in a buy-sell agreement. See chapter 3, p. 65.)

Sale

Since the focus of this chapter is on the sale of securities, it should be apparent that this is when the anti-fraud provisions are most commonly invoked. Recall that "security" includes many different commercial arrangements and "offer" and "sale" are quite broad too, so your company may be obliged to make affirmative disclosures even if you need not file a registration statement.

PART II
WHAT THE LAW REQUIRES:
FEDERAL AND STATE REGISTRATION UNLESS
THE SECURITY OR TRANSACTION IS EXEMPT

Registration of a security is the second principal legal requirement we will discuss.

REGISTRATION

Every security that is offered or sold by an issuer (such as your company), an underwriter, or dealer must be registered with the SEC *unless* either the security or the transaction is exempt.

Federal Registration

If neither the security nor the transaction is exempt (more about exemptions later), a registration statement must be filed with the SEC in Washington, D.C. The key part of any registration statement is the "prospectus" that must be provided to all purchasers of the security. The required prospectus often contains more detailed information about the issuer, its business and financial condition, and the offered security than might otherwise be disclosed under the anti-fraud provisions. Further, there are requirements for updating the prospectus and delivering it to persons who purchase the security.

Warning: You may not complete the sale of a nonexempt security until the registration statement has been reviewed by the SEC staff and declared "effective." See page 246.

Exempt Transactions. A securities offering need not be registered if the *transaction* is exempt. (These are discussed beginning on page 237.) Routine unsolicited brokers' transactions executed pursuant to a customer's order are exempt. Normally, a member of the public who resells securities bought on the open market or in a registered public offering need not register the resale unless he is an officer, director, or controlling shareholder of the issuer.

Exempt Securities. Certain types of *securities* are exempt from the registration requirements including those issued by governments, banks, and certain charitable organizations. These are not discussed further in this chapter because most readers of this book are not likely to issue exempt securities.

Dual Requirement—State Registration

As we have said, there is a two-tier registration process, the second being in those states that require securities registration. When your company considers issuing securities, be sure to conduct a preliminary "Blue Sky" review to identify problems that may arise in the states in which you will offer the security. Three enigmas of federal-state securities laws provide the reason for this:

- Federal registration with the SEC does *not* guarantee that every state—or even the one state where you intend to sell—will register your securities offering.
- An offering that is exempt from federal registration may *not* be exempt from state registration.
- In some states if the offering is already registered with the SEC, it can be quickly registered using an abbreviated process.

So, the SEC is only part of your problem; the states are a hurdle too. In fact, many states go much further than the two federal laws (which principally require the disclosure of information) by permitting their securities commissioners to block an offering if in their opinion its substantive terms are not "fair" to investors. (See page 241.) In short, federal registration is important, but you can't overlook state requirements either.

AVOIDING FEDERAL REGISTRATION

There are several incentives to try to avoid federal registration:

- You save time and money;
- You discourage the growth of a public market for the security;
- If you are not public already, you can avoid incurring reporting obligations to the SEC; and
- Directors and the company itself can avoid special legal liability imposed on registrants by the Securities Act.

For these reasons, it is often wise to structure a transaction so that it is exempt from federal registration even if it must still be registered or qualified in one or more states. The savings in time and money can be significant, especially if your company has not previously been audited and the state permits the use of unaudited financial statements.

We now turn to a description of the most important federal exemptions for the offering of securities.

FEDERAL EXEMPTIONS

Most types of securities that companies issue (other than certain short-term commercial paper) must be federally registered unless they are exempt under one of the provisions we discuss next or another exemption.[3] *Warning:* Before you rely on these exemptions, have your lawyer carefully review the statutes, rules, and court decisions.

Private Offering Exemption—In General

The exemption that has been most commonly relied on is for transactions that do not involve "public offerings"; it is popularly known as the "private offering" exemption. (Section 4(2) of the Securities Act). To qualify under this general statutory exemption, all *offers* (not just sales) must be made to persons who can fend for themselves and who do not need the protection of the Securities Act; there can't be any general solicitation of sales; and resale of the securities must be restricted so that the initial offering is not simply one step in a broader distribution effort. (See p. 243.)

Unlike other exemptions, such as the one we discuss on page 238, the meaning of this one is found in court decisions and is not well defined. For example, an offeree (the person to whom you offer to sell a security) is deemed to be able to fend for himself if he is financially sophisticated (that is, able to evaluate the benefits and risks of the investment) and has access to adequate information about the issuer and its business (either through detailed information or by virtue of his bargaining power). The exact meaning of "general solicitation" is unclear, but it

---

[3]We do not discuss certain other transactional exemptions such as: the exemption under Section 3 (a) (10) of the Securities Act for securities issued in an exchange in which the terms and conditions have been approved, after a hearing, by a court, an agency of the United States, or a state agency; the exemption under Section 4 (6) of the Act for sales by an issuer solely to accredited investors where the aggregate offering does not exceed $5,000,000 and there is no public solicitation (note the overlap of this exemption with the exemption under Rule 505 discussed later); or the exemption under SEC Regulation A for offerings up to $1,500,000, which requires the filing of an offering statement containing specified information with the regional office of the SEC for prior review and delivery of an offering circular to all offerees, but which, unlike some other exemptions, permits general solicitation and enables purchasers to acquire freely tradable securities. Note that the availability of Regulation D and an abbreviated form of registration for small offerings have reduced the number of transactions for which Regulation A will be used.

certainly includes the use of newspapers, radio, and television advertisements, public meetings, and general mailings. One criterion, then, is the number of offerees (persons to whom you made an offer), but a court would also consider the offerees' relationship to the issuer.

Warning: Based on these tests, a transaction would not be exempt—that is, it would have to be registered—if securities were offered in a large, general mailing even though there was only one purchaser. The same may be true if there were an offer to only one unsophisticated investor or to one investor without restrictions on his right to resell.

Because of the uncertainties involved in relying on the private offering provision, most companies will find it safer to structure a transaction to fit within the more specific terms of the next exemption we discuss, Regulation D.

The SEC's New Regulation D: Three Exemptions

In March of 1982 the SEC adopted three new registration exemptions that will principally benefit small companies or those of any size that selectively market their securities. Unfortunately, the new exemptions are victims of awful legal jargon; they bear the label "Regulation D." The exemptions are:

- for offerings up to $500,000 (Rule 504);
- for offerings up to $5 million if limited to certain investors (Rule 505); and
- for offerings of any size if limited to certain investors (Rule 506).

The three exemptions are available only to the issuer of the securities, so they cannot be invoked for resales by "affiliates" (principal stockholders, directors, and executive officers) or other persons. But, in addition to cash sales, the exemptions can be used in connection with business combinations that would be considered offers and sales of securities as well as exchanges of securities for property. Furthermore, they are not exclusive; that is, you can claim a registration exemption under one of the three rules *and* under the previously discussed private offering exemption.

Common Requirements. With one exception, all exemptions under Regulation D provide that: no advertising or general solicitation may be used; resale of the securities must be restricted as it is with a private offering; and the issuer must file a prescribed notice with the SEC within 15 days after the sale. (The SEC has taken the position that simply accepting funds into an escrow account pending satisfaction of a minimum triggers the filing requirement.) Commissions may be paid in connection with sales. For sales under Rule 504 (under $500,000) the requirements regarding advertising and restrictions on resale are waived if the offering is carried out exclusively under a state law that requires registration and delivery of a prospectus before sale.

Accredited Investor. A definition common to Rule 505 and Rule 506 is the meaning of "accredited investor." Accredited investors, the theory goes, can make do with only the disclosures required by the anti-fraud provisions; they can fend for themselves. The definition is in the SEC regulations (Rule 501) so it may change from time to time. In general, the following are accredited investors: commercial banks acting for themselves or as trustee; certain insurance and investment companies; certain charitable organizations and employee benefit plans; directors, executives, and general partners of the issuer; purchasers of large amounts of the security (at least $150,000) for specified types of consideration, provided the investment does not exceed 20 percent of their net worth; individuals worth more than $1 million; and individuals with $200,000 of income for each year in a three-year period. Check the regulations to be sure your purchasers meet the exact definition. Issuers should establish methods for verifying the facts relating to the accreditation of an investor.

The Single Issue. A trap associated with these three exemptions, as well as the others discussed in this chapter, is the "single issue." This is the danger that several securities offerings will be aggregated and treated as one, so that together they will exceed the dollar limits or other exemption criteria. Result: the security must be registered. But at least Regulation D has a safe harbor: offers and sales made six months before or after the period of a Regulation D offering are not considered part of the issue as long as no other issues of the same or similar class are made during the period. If you plan to offer similar securities within a few months of one another, be sure to check first with a securities lawyer.

Single Purchaser. Rules 505 and 506 contain restrictions on the total number of investors. A corporation, partnership, or other entity organized for the specific purpose of acquiring a particular security is not counted as a single investor; instead, each shareholder, partner, or beneficial owner of that entity is treated as a separate purchaser.

Exemptions for Offerings Up to $500,000 (Rule 504)

This is the most liberal exemption in Regulation D. A securities offering is exempt if, during a 12-month period, the gross proceeds from the sale, sales under Rule 505, Regulation A, and sales in violation of the Securities Act do not exceed $500,000. Sales can be made to any number of purchasers; there is no requirement that the investors be sophisticated or accredited; and no specific information needs to be provided to the purchasers.

Warning: Remember the anti-fraud provisions. This exemption is not available to investment companies or any company that is already public and subject to SEC reporting requirements.

Exemptions for Offerings Up to $5 Million (Rule 505)

This rule, which applies to all issuers except investment companies, exempts offerings of securities if the gross proceeds do not exceed $5 million during any 12-month period. As with the preceding rule, other sales under this exemption, Rule 504, Regulation A, and those in violation of the Securities Act also are counted toward the $5 million figure. But note these other qualifications.

Investors. Sales may be made to an unlimited number of accredited investors but only 35 *non*accredited investors. (See the previous definition of accredited investor.) Unlike the first exemption we discussed, for private offerings, there is no requirement here that either type of investor be sophisticated in financial matters.

Sales and Information. The rule does not require you to provide any specific information to a purchaser if all sales are made to accredited investors. (Remember the anti-fraud disclosure requirements.) However, if you sell to any nonaccredited investors, then you must furnish certain information to *all* investors—accredited and nonaccredited alike. The information you must provide is similar to what is contained in a registration statement (see p. 246). Other information is required of "reporting" companies (see p. 247). Furthermore, if you provide any additional written information to an accredited investor, you must describe and offer it as well to nonaccredited investors. Finally, all investors must be given the opportunity to ask questions and receive supplementary information to the extent it is reasonably available.

Exemptions for Offerings in Unlimited Amounts (Rule 506)

This exemption, which may be relied on by *any* issuer, has no dollar ceiling—the amount of the issue is unlimited. This is really a special, secure niche carved out of the broad "private offering" exemption we first described.

Investors. Sales may be made to no more than 35 nonaccredited investors and to an unlimited number of accredited investors. There is one catch: the issuer must reasonably believe that each *nonaccredited* investor, either alone or with his purchaser representative (the qualifications of which are specified in Regulation D), has sufficient knowledge and experience in financial and business affairs to evaluate the merits and risks of the investment. This requirement applies only to actual purchasers, not to offerees. The requirements with respect to disclosure to investors are substantially the same as those discussed in connection with Rule 505, but if the offering exceeds $5 million and involves nonaccredited investors the disclosure obligations of a company that is not a reporting company are somewhat greater.

Federal Exemption for Intrastate Offerings

The intrastate exemption applies when the securities are offered and sold only to persons who reside within the one state or territory where the issuing company both resides and does business. If the company is a corporation or partnership, it must also be legally organized under the laws of that state. This

Securities Act exemption has no dollar ceiling on the value of the offering, nor does it limit the number of purchasers. Subsequent transfer of the securities is restricted only for nine months, and the restrictions need only prohibit sales to persons who are not residents of the state where the issue was made. Unlike the three Regulation D exemptions just discussed, this one permits general solicitation of sales. Carefully read SEC Rule 147 before relying on this exemption.

Now we turn to registration and exemptions in the states.

STATE EXEMPTIONS AND REGISTRATION

Variable Registration Requirements

Generally, unless there is an applicable state exemption, a securities offering must be registered in each state where the issuer intends to offer or sell even though the transaction is exempt under federal law. To complicate matters further, even if the securities are federally registered, there is no assurance that all states will permit you to sell in their jurisdiction.

Unlike federal registration, which is designed to provide information, in many states the purpose of registration is judgmental—to permit the state regulators to determine whether the offering is "fair, just, and equitable." The meaning of this standard varies greatly among the states, but it often limits sales commissions and the amount of "cheap stock" (stock obtained by investors shortly before the offering at less than the offering price to the public); and some states prevent sales where the underwriter's compensation is too large, the issuer has inadequate earnings or assets, or the shareholders or partners do not have legal rights meeting minimum standards applied by the states. All this is determined by the state administrator.

Many states have more particular and extensive requirements for real estate and oil and gas offerings.

If a securities issue is not exempt from registration, state qualification forms and a prospectus must be filed with the regulatory officials.

Different Standards for Granting Exemptions

States have widely varying standards for granting exemptions. A few exempt any offer or sale of securities if it is federally exempt as a private offering or under the SEC's new Regulation D. But in many of the states where companies are eager to sell their securities—such as California and Minnesota—exemptions are even harder to obtain than they are under federal law. Examples: A state exemption may depend on the number of offers or sales to residents within that state; or it may require that all *nonaccredited* and some accredited investors in an offering made under Federal Regulation D be financially sophisticated and able to bear the risk of the investment.

Anti-Fraud Laws Still Apply. An offering that is exempt from both federal and state securities laws is *not* relieved of the disclosure obligations discussed earlier in this chapter.

Tip: If the exemption (such as those under Regulation D) requires that the stock's resale be restricted, be sure to disclose the consequences of the restriction. For example, you should disclose that the stock is significantly less liquid than unrestricted stock. Consult your lawyer for other appropriate disclosures.

Registration as a Dealer. The broker/dealer laws of each state must also be checked because some states require that the securities issuer or one of its principals register as a dealer before the offer or sale. For example, New York does not require registration of offerings (other than those for real estate), but it treats the issuer as a dealer and requires it to register as such or obtain an exemption.

TIPS FOR HANDLING EXEMPT OFFERINGS

Screen Your Investors

Most securities lawyers and experienced issuers are conservative when it comes to exemptions from the federal and state securities laws. For example, it is good practice to screen in advance everyone to whom you intend to offer securities, even if it's not required by the particular exemption. Determine if they are financially sophisticated and whether they can bear the loss of the investment. This allows you to fall back on the general federal private offering exemption and it can prevent later complications with an investor who cannot afford the purchase.

Consider these other tips:

- Prepare a comprehensive disclosure statement in most cases, even if the exemption does not require one.
- Keep a list of all persons contacted in connection with the offer.
- Permit only certain trained employees to handle inquiries about the offering.
- Keep a list of the names of investors to whom you send the offering materials, and number the materials before you send them out.
- If you use a broker to help you sell the securities, be particularly careful: make sure the broker is registered in the states where that's required and its fees comply with applicable law; be sure the broker and its salesmen understand the exemption and disclosure requirements; and have the broker screen investors and keep track of offering documents.

- Do not be too eager to grant "registration rights" to purchasers as a way of making the offering more attractive. These give the purchaser the right to require the issuer to register the securities. This can present significant and unanticipated burdens on the company and force it public prematurely.

- Be equally wary of granting "piggyback rights" to purchasers. These allow the holder of restricted securities to include them in subsequent offerings registered by the issuing company. Although somewhat less burdensome, they can cause problems, particularly with later underwritten offerings.

HOW TO RESELL RESTRICTED SECURITIES: REGISTRATION OR EXEMPTION

You will recall from our discussion of federal exemptions that some of them (for private offerings and for those under Regulation D) require that the stock be restricted as to its resale. There is a good reason why federal law requires that exempt transactions have resale restrictions: it prevents an issuer from circumventing the letter and spirit of the law—providing detailed information to potential purchasers—by claiming an exemption and then using it as the first step in a broader scheme of stock distribution and resales. But the owner of restricted securities may want to sell them at some point; the question is, how is it done without violating the securities laws?

The restriction itself typically includes a representation by the purchaser that he is acquiring the securities only for himself and not on behalf of anyone else; and that the purchaser will not resell, pledge, or otherwise transfer the securities without either *registering* the transaction or satisfying the issuing firm that there is an *exemption* for the transaction. Generally, the certificate should include a legend to this effect. A lawful resale of restricted securities must meet one of these tests.

Registration. Of course, the resale of a security originally acquired in an exempt transaction could be registered with the SEC. But registration is usually not practical unless the purchaser has obtained registration or piggyback rights or the issuer otherwise cooperates, and registration may be contrary to the interests of the issuer. For these reasons, the resale of previously restricted stock is usually made under an exemption.

Exemption. The rules for being assured of an exemption on resale are complex, and a securities owner or company with outstanding restricted stock should certainly consult counsel before attempting it. In general, a restricted security may be resold through a private negotiated transaction if the new purchaser would qualify as a sophisticated investor for purposes of the private offering exemption, if he has access to adequate information about the issuer, and if the security continues to be restricted as to resale in the manner it originally was.

Rule 144. Although not the only way to do so, SEC Rule 144 is now generally used for selling restricted securities in a publicly traded company. Essentially, it provides a specific exemption for resales. In fact, any public sale, or sale through an established market, of a restricted security is very risky unless it is completed according to Rule 144. There are many prerequisites for a valid resale under Rule 144. For example, the securities must have been owned for at least two years before the sale; there are limits on the amount of securities that can be resold within a three-month period; there are restrictions on the manner of sale; the company whose securities are sold must be a reporting company under the Exchange Act or make comparable information available; and the seller must file a form with the SEC. Some of these restrictions do not apply if the securities have been held for three years and the seller is not an "affiliate."

Warning: Do not attempt a resale of restricted stock under this exemption, or any other for that matter, without expert advice.

PART III
GOING PUBLIC, AND WHAT HAPPENS WHEN YOU DO

The Pros and Cons of Going Public

For many companies, "going public"—selling stock to the public at large as distinct from a select group of investors—is a long-term goal. Some advantages are:

- You can create liquidity (a ready market for existing shareholders' stock);
- You can often raise more equity than in a private offering;
- Along with the stock, control is more widely distributed; and
- The value of the existing shareholders' stock may rise.

There are disadvantages too:

- Management must answer to many shareholders, not just themselves or another elite group;
- Directors and officers incur new legal liability under the securities laws (such as for misstatements in a prospectus) and the general corporate laws (such as for the protection of minority stockholders, see chapter 4);
- You must publicly disclose officer salaries and benefits, as well as a host of other facts about the business;
- Directors must forego personal business opportunities (chapter 4); and
- The public company must make periodic reports to the SEC and be audited annually.

A public company requires the constant attention of lawyers and accountants, so if you don't like such people you will hate being public. The process is expensive: a first time registrant can pay as much as $200,000–$500,000 for its first or "initial public offering" and the process can easily take four to six months.

How to Go Public:
Attorneys, Accountants, and Underwriters

Once you decide to go public, talk to the professionals you need to get the job done.

Attorneys, Accountants, and Others

This is one area where a company should not provide on-the-job training to its professionals; that's short-sighted and potentially disastrous. You will need experienced securities lawyers, auditors who know the SEC's accounting regulations, and perhaps other experts such as engineers and appraisers whose opinions may go into the prospectus.

Work with an Underwriter

Few companies make successful public offerings without an underwriter, a firm that markets or buys the securities. Before you talk to an underwriter, gather your audited financial statements, prepare a detailed operations plan, a two-three year cash flow estimate, and a description of the way the proceeds of the proposed offering will be used. Analyze your industry and describe how your company fits into it.

Underwriting Methods. In a "best efforts" underwriting, the underwriter agrees to use its best efforts to sell the securities but is under no obligation to buy any for itself. In a "firm underwriting," the underwriter buys all the offered shares and then markets them. Generally, the latter method is better for the issuer.

Underwriting Firms. Get the strongest, most respected underwriter you can—it should more successfully market your stock and lead to a more orderly aftermarket. There are local, regional, and national firms; some have been in business for decades, others have sprung up around the latest "hot issue" market. Many issuers doing their first public offering must use a local or regional underwriter. Though quality is not a function of size, many local firms do not have an adequate net worth to do a large "firm" underwriting. But size isn't the only fact you should consider: some underwriters are more successful selling certain types of securities, others in certain regions of the country, and still others specialize in particular industries.

Tip: Avoid "finders" who will put you in touch with an underwriter for a fee. Usually you can do just as well on your own, and because the permissible underwriter's compensation may be reduced by the finder's fee, a finder may decrease the chances of getting the desired underwriter.

Sign a Letter of Intent. After selecting an underwriter, the next step is to sign a "letter of intent" that describes such matters as the amount of the offering, the proposed price or method of pricing, the underwriter's fees, provisions for preparation of the registration, and sometimes first refusal rights for subsequent offerings. The fee may be in cash, or a combination of cash and warrants—options to purchase the stock later at a favorable price.

Warning: Even after signing a letter of intent, the underwriter has no legal obligation until the underwriting agreement is signed. Nevertheless, the letter of intent covers many financial and legal issues so it should be carefully reviewed by a lawyer.

How to Go Public: Register the Offering with the SEC and the States

Federal Registration with the SEC

The Registration Statement. Registration under the Securities Act occurs when a firm files a registration statement that is later declared to be "effective" by the SEC. The statement is in two parts: a prospectus, the document containing the narrative and financial information that must be delivered to prospective purchasers; and additional financial schedules, exhibits, and miscellaneous papers that are filed only with the SEC. The amount and type of information that must be disclosed is a function of many facts including the company's size and the amount of the offering.

Warning: Though the registration statement is the product of many hands, the directors and certain officers of the issuer are by statute *personally liable* for any material misstatements or omissions. Their only defense is that, after conducting a reasonable investigation (known in the trade as "due diligence"), they had reasonable grounds to believe and did believe that there were no misstatements or omissions. This requires more than a simple reading of the registration statement—and many directors will resist even that. Furthermore, the company itself is strictly liable for material misstatements or omissions.

SEC Action. The SEC comments on the registration statement, usually within 30 to 60 days of filing. During this time, a preliminary prospectus or "red herring" is used to inform prospective investors about the issuer and to generate interest in the offering. After amendment to conform with SEC comments, the statement is declared "effective" by the SEC. This means only that it may be used in selling securities, *not* that the agency has approved or endorsed the securities.

State Registration as Appropriate

The registration procedures and the nature of the substantive review of the offering vary greatly among the states, but most require the filing of a copy of the federal registration statement plus some additional forms. As we have said, many states have great leeway to block registration based on the "fairness" of the offering.

Sale of Securities

After the SEC declares the registration statement "effective" and the states have cleared the offering, the issuer and underwriter sign their "underwriting agreement" and sales commence. If it is a firm underwriting, closing of the sale of the securities to the underwriter occurs a few days later.

Warning: Do not "precondition" the market during the registration process (even after the "effective" date) by engaging in abnormal publicity about the company. Limit press releases, interviews, and public statements to information that could properly be included in the prospectus. Have all such communications reviewed by your attorney.

Another Registration Requirement—
Even Without a Public Offering (The Exchange Act)

There is another registration requirement that is widely misunderstood: certain firms must register with the SEC even if they *never* made a public securities offering. While the Securities Act imposes the registration requirement on specific transactions—offerings of securities—the Exchange Act requires that publicly held companies register with the SEC and provide certain information about themselves.

Mandatory. Whether or not a company has had a public offering, it must register with the SEC if (1) it has *total* assets of $3 million or more and a class of securities held by at least 500 holders of record; or (2) it has securities listed on a national securities exchange. (Stock might be widely held due to many private offerings or numerous transfers.)

Voluntary. Any company can voluntarily register under the Exchange Act and many do: underwriters often require it of the companies for which they underwrite; in some states, registration facilitates the trading of a firm's stock; and it permits the sale of restricted stock and stock held by affiliates.

Consequences. A firm with securities registered under the Exchange Act must periodically provide certain reports to shareholders and have its financial statements audited annually. It is also subject to special rules on tender offers, proxy solicitations, and a variety of other matters. There are also restrictions on the purchase and sale of company stock by directors and officers.

Registered Companies Must Report to the SEC and the Shareholders

One "cost" of registration under *both* the Securities Act (for the registration of a public offering of securities) and the Exchange Act (for the mandatory or voluntary registration of a public company's securities) is that the registered company must file various reports with the SEC. (In some circumstances, companies can be relieved of these reporting obligations.)

SEC Reports. The annual "10-K" is the most comprehensive report that must be filed with the agency. It must contain audited financial statements and be filed within 90 days of the end of each fiscal year. Other reports must be filed, including the quarterly "10-Q" that contains unaudited financials.

Shareholder Reports. Companies registered under the Exchange Act also must provide their shareholders with annual reports containing audited financial statements and certain other information from the company's 10-K. Registrants need not provide quarterly reports to shareholders, although the SEC encourages companies to do so.

How Much to Tell? Suppose your company obtains a valuable new contract, perhaps worth millions of dollars. Is there an obligation to announce it publicly? This is the subject of much debate, although the SEC staff has suggested that a firm should announce any material development that could affect decisions by buyers and sellers of the stock, even if the company is not then involved in buying or selling its own stock. Many companies make prompt public announcements of such matters unless there are good business reasons not to. Of course, what is material for a small company may be routine for a large one. *Tip:* Whatever you announce, make sure it is accurate and factual; don't include predictions or projections except under unusual circumstances and where there is a reasonable basis for the projections.

Special Rules for Insiders: Stock Transactions

Federal law imposes special restrictions on stock transactions by corporate insiders. Legally, these people are "affiliates"—principal stockholders, directors, and executive officers of a firm.

Transactions. An affiliate may not sell stock in his company without registering the sale under the Securities Act or establishing that the sale is not part of a "distribution" of the stock. Rule 144 can be used for sales by affiliates, and there is no two-year holding period if the stock is not restricted. There are technical rules for complying with both of these requirements, so it's important to see a lawyer before selling.

Inside Information. Neither the company nor any affiliate with material inside information about the company should buy or sell the company's stock until that information has been made public. To do otherwise is a violation of

SEC Rule 10b-5, and it can subject the company or affiliate to serious liability. Although the law is still developing, the same restriction can apply to certain other people who receive the inside information from an affiliate.

Tip: Do what many firms do; establish procedures to prevent stock transactions by insiders at times when the company is aware of information that could affect the price of its stock but which has not yet been released to the public.

Ten Percent Shareholders, Directors, and Officers. Ten percent shareholders, directors, and officers of companies with securities registered under the Exchange Act must file with the SEC reports of all their transactions in the company's stock. In some circumstances, they must disgorge any profits on such sales whether or not they used inside information.

PERILS AND POTENTIAL OF SECURITIES LAWS

Securities is an intricate and specialized area of the law. We have seen the long reach of federal and state laws—how a security can be, with some minor exceptions, an apparently ordinary investment—and how some special disclosure obligations—the anti-fraud provisions—fall on issuers of securities even if the security need not be registered with the states or the SEC. In the matter of registration and exemptions, you have some idea of the complexity of the field; do not try to structure your capital offerings or make any kind of stock sales without consulting professionals. Finally, consider the pros and cons of going public; the capital raising advantages can be substantial, but there are many reporting and recordkeeping requirements and some loss of operational flexibility.

13. How to Extend Credit and Repay Debts

by ROBERT JOEL ZAKROFF

One day you receive a notice from the United States Bankruptcy Court advising you that one of your best customers has asked for relief under the Bankruptcy Code. The notice states that you will probably not receive anything when the court distributes the assets, even though the customer owes you thousands of dollars. The reason: you are an unsecured general creditor and there is no collateral to pay off the debt. Though this is bad enough, it could be worse: you could be the one filing for bankruptcy.

In our present economic climate, few companies are without credit problems of one sort or another—whether as creditor or debtor. The well-known financial problems of Chrysler, International Harvester, Braniff, and thousands of smaller companies are proof that the loss of a valued client or customer, a change in the public's taste or buying habits, the erosion of a previously strong market, or plain mismanagement can cause a business downturn. This chapter discusses some of the consequences of a financial crunch from two perspectives:

- *As a Creditor:* If you extend credit, be it to a retail customer or large manufacturer, what precautions should you take to guarantee you will be paid back or to preserve your legal rights?

- *As a Debtor:* If your company is in debt, what steps can you take to protect the company either by restructuring the firm's debts or by changing its method of doing business?

Both sides of this equation are important, for with careful planning and foresight you can reduce the risks of extending credit; and if you run into financial trouble, you can take advantage of laws that allow you to devise a sensible way to repay the debts. Either way, you protect yourself and the company.

Part I of this chapter takes the creditor's view, Part II the debtor's.

PART I
RULES FOR THE CREDITOR:
HOW TO KEEP THE RISKS LOW
WHEN YOU EXTEND CREDIT

The lifeblood of any business organization is cash: you want to assure a steady, predictable flow. Most businesses extend credit, whether it's only to one long-time and valued customer or to thousands of smaller accounts. But there are three rules you should follow to protect your financial position and reduce the legal risks.

Rule 1: Use a Comprehensive Credit Application and Do a Follow-Up Investigation

A top-notch credit department is essential for any company extending credit; without it, a firm will sputter and fail because it won't be able to collect on its accounts receivable. The difference between an effective and a useless credit department is the information it requests on the credit application; that will largely determine whether credit is extended and the debts are collected.

A comprehensive credit application should:

- Properly identify the firm applying for credit;
- Demand references;
- Set proper credit limits;
- Obtain personal guarantees;
- Require the debtor to pay interest, collection costs, and attorneys' fees.

1. Properly Identify the Credit Applicant

Certainly you must know to whom or to what you are extending credit. But you would be astonished at the number of businesses that do not go beyond "Name of Company: _____" on the identity line. Yet it's imperative to go further—to ask about the legal form of the business—or you may not be able to collect the debt.

Confirm Details of Corporate Existence. You will recall from chapters 2 and 3 that a corporation must observe certain statutory formalities or it will not legally be deemed a corporation. In that event, creditors could not look to the corporate assets to satisfy the debt; they would have to go after the shareholders instead. If the shareholders have few personal assets or the total of all creditor claims exceeds the shareholders' worth, no one creditor will ever be fully paid. In short, the corporate shield will have been lifted but to little avail.

To avoid this, if a credit applicant identifies itself as a corporation ask for:

- The state of incorporation;
- The date of incorporation; and
- The name and address of the registered agent.

Most states will verify the accuracy of this information free of charge over the telephone.

Tip: If the state of incorporation is not the state in which your business is located, ask the applicant and the appropriate official in your state (usually the office of the secretary of state or the corporations bureau) whether the applicant has registered to do business in your state. You will recall from our discussion in chapter 4 that the failure to observe this formality often means the shareholders are doing business personally in the state; the corporate shield is lost.

There are other reasons for confirming these corporate details:

- You will be extending credit to a legally constituted entity, not someone who is trying to defraud you.
- The date of incorporation gives you an idea how long the company has been in business. Although a date many years ago is no assurance of a good track record, a recent date means the company has just started up; you may want to keep its credit limit low.
- Find out if the registered agent (the person who officially receives the legal notices for the corporation) is in fact available; if he is, that is usually a good sign the rest of the application is accurate.

Warning: If your preliminary investigation shows that the corporation does not exist, the prudent course is to deny credit. If there are less serious errors on the application or if through inadvertence the business was improperly characterized, get personal guarantees from the principals (p. 254).

Identify Partners and Their Authority. As we discussed in chapter 2, the liability of the principals in a partnership and sole proprietorship is very different from a corporation: in the former, they are personally liable for business debts. Determine the identity of the other partners and their credit history.

Warning: If the application is in the name of a partnership, find out if the partner signing the application or placing the order for the goods has the partnership's authority to do so. While in theory any one partner can bind the partnership, litigation is common on this issue; credit managers often discover that a customer's ex-partner placed the order without authorization, so the present owner refuses to pay.

2. Obtain a Complete List of References and Check Them

Whether the applicant is a corporation, partnership, or sole proprietorship, it should provide you with a complete set of references. With them, you can assess the applicant's credit worthiness and commercial reputation. But a list of references is useless unless you do more—call and find out:

- Whether the applicant pays bills on time (usually within 30 days);
- Whether the applicant has ever passed a check that was later dishonored by the bank;
- The nature of the applicant–reference relationship; and
- How long the applicant and reference have been doing business.

It is no surprise that applicants supply the names of references who will provide favorable reviews. That is why the first and second questions will almost always be answered in the affirmative. But answers to the third and fourth questions may expose the reference as a biased source.

Reference the Reference. If the answers to any of these questions are not satisfactory, take the next step and reference the reference. Frequently, applicants will identify as references some of the most notorious debtors in the area. If they do, it is possible that the reference and the applicant may themselves be associated, in collusion, or perhaps are one and the same company.

Use a Credit Bureau. Use a credit management organization to give you more detailed information about the reference or applicant; it specializes in collecting debts and informing its members of the credit worthiness of firms. Membership costs from $200–$500. It provides credit information as requested and circulates bulletins on a weekly or monthly basis.

Use a Crisscross Directory. Consider using a street and telephone crisscross directory, usually found in the public library. It lists telephone numbers and street addresses and often indicates how long the company has been at that address and listed in the same name. This is another measure of stability.

3. Set the Proper Credit Limit

Now that you have determined that the applicant is worthy of credit, you must decide how much to extend. As a general rule, don't extend any more than you can comfortably afford to lose. This is a vague guideline, but the amount in each case will be a function of your own cash needs, whether the loan or product sales are secured with collateral, and the amount of credit you have extended to other customers.

If you have reviewed the information in the credit application and followed up on references, you should know the applicant's payment habits. A satisfactory credit history generally continues absent events beyond the applicant's control. If the enterprise is a new one, establish a low credit limit unless you obtain an assurance of payment, such as a personal guarantee.

4. Get Personal Guarantees

A personal guarantee means the individual who signs for credit on behalf of a business is personally responsible for the debt if the business fails to repay it. (We also discuss personal guarantees with commercial loans. See chapter 10, p. 203.)

Credit to a Sole Proprietorship. A sole proprietor is personally liable for the debt so a personal guarantee is superfluous. But consider obtaining a guarantee from the applicant's spouse; this will permit you to proceed against property held by both husband and wife in the event of a default.

Credit to Partnerships. We have already mentioned here and in chapter 2 that partners are personally responsible for their partnership debts, and this is true (unless there is a provision in the partnership agreement to the contrary) even if the partner has a small percentage interest in the partnership. Although an additional personal guarantee is for this reason not necessary, make sure the partner–applicant understands his personal liability and acknowledges it in writing, preferably at the bottom of the credit application.

Credit to a Corporation. It is always best to get personal guarantees from the shareholders in a closely held corporation. This will protect you in the event the enterprise is merely a corporate shell—a fly-by-night operation intended to insulate the shareholders from personal liability. With a personal guarantee from the principals, nothing short of their personal bankruptcy will prevent you from collecting in the event of a corporate default. It is also wise to have the signatures of the principals notarized or witnessed so they cannot later claim there was a forgery.

5. Provide for Collection Costs

Despite strenuous private efforts to collect on a debt, creditors must sometimes ask the courts for assistance. By planning ahead, you can pass on many of these collection costs to the debtor.

Most states will not permit a creditor to pass on its attorneys' fees or to charge interest above the legal rate (which is typically 8 percent to 18 percent) unless the debtor has agreed to this in writing. Without this agreement, the creditor would have to pay the legal costs for collecting his own money, and the allowable interest may not fairly compensate the creditor for the loss in use of the funds. The solution is the credit application. Most courts would approve of provisions assessing 15 percent to 25 percent of the principal amount of your claim for attorneys' fees if you have the written permission of the debtor. A court will often permit you to impose an interest rate that's higher than normally permitted for judgments in that state, again if the debtor has agreed in writing.

Tip: By imposing collection costs on the debtor, you can increase his incentive to pay the debt before you reach the courthouse door.

6. Beyond the Credit Application

The credit application is the best tool for weeding out high-risk customers and reducing credit losses. Though it's the most reliable and comprehensive source of information, try using two other methods to measure credit worthiness.

Make a Personal Visit. If the customer is in your area, personally visit the premises so you can evaluate his operation firsthand. When this is too time-consuming for senior management, have members of the sales force do it for you.

Get Credit Records. As mentioned earlier, a number of commercial credit reporting firms will provide credit reports for a modest fee. Sometimes the report will already be in the firm's file, but often an investigation will have to be made and a special report prepared. The reports typically include information on outstanding judgments, tax liens, and any financing statements on file against the applicant. Similar information can also be provided by title companies who offer a "rundown"; that is, a search of the public records to determine whether there are any liens or judgments against the applicant or its property. These usually cost $60 to $100.

Rule 2: Secure Your Financial Position

The work that you have done in investigating and analyzing the credit worthiness of an applicant will not ensure payment of the debt: history is not an absolute predictor of future performance, and the personal guarantee allows you to proceed only against *personal* assets in the event of a default. You need further assurances of payment in the event of the debtor's insolvency. The way to protect yourself is to "secure" the credit you have extended. There are at least four ways to do this.

1. Obtain a Security Agreement and Financing Statement

Security Agreement. When you extend credit, you should obtain both a "security agreement" and a "financing statement." As you will recall from chapter 10, the former gives the lender an interest in and rights to certain property, such as accounts receivable, contracts, inventory, fixtures, cash, or any property in which the debtor has rights. The interest that is conveyed is in exchange for the money or property that is loaned. In short, the security agreement describes your collateral; it "secures" your position because if the debt is not repaid in cash, you can take the collateral instead.

Financing Statement. The financing statement is a close cousin of the security agreement; it gives notice to other potential lenders that you have a security interest—a "secured position"—in the debtor's property that is described in both documents. The financing statement must meet a number of legal requirements, but essentially it identifies the collateral, the debtor, and the lender (also called the "secured party.") The financing statement should be written so it also covers cash received from the sale of the collateral as well as new property the debtor subsequently acquires. Talk with a lawyer about the proper drafting and filing of these statements. (If you are a borrower, recall our discussion in chapter 10 about the importance of careful planning before giving up collateral.)

2. *Obtain a Lien on Motor Vehicles*

You can also secure your position by getting a lien on the debtor's motor vehicles. The manner of obtaining this lien varies among the states, so you must consult your state's department of motor vehicles.

3. *Obtain a Mechanic's Lien*

You can obtain a mechanic's lien even if the debtor does not expressly agree to it. If you provide materials or labor for the improvement of an existing building or property or for the construction of a new building, you are entitled to a lien against the owner of the property for the value of the services rendered and materials supplied. In some states this right to a lien exists as soon as the work is commenced or the materials supplied. But all states have special requirements for notifying the owner or contractor as well as the creditor's intention to claim a lien.

4. *Obtain a Lien on Real Estate*

You can also get a lien on real estate owned by the debtor. The method varies among the states but it generally involves obtaining a "deed of trust" (also called a mortgage) from the debtor and recording it in the land records of the court where the property is located. If you obtain a court judgment against the debtor and record it in the court's records, that too becomes a lien on the real estate.

Rule 3: Know the System to Make It Work for You

If you have followed the first two rules by wisely extending credit and securing it with collateral, you should be ready to withstand the emotional and financial trauma of a debtor who doesn't pay his bills. To get the most from your spadework, you must (1) use effective internal collection procedures, (2) be prepared to seek the assistance of collection agencies and attorneys, and (3) understand the nature of your protected position even if the debtor files for bankruptcy.

Develop an Effective Internal Collection Procedure

Develop a rigorous internal collection policy and procedures to implement it; do not deviate from either one. When an account becomes delinquent be ready to deal with it promptly because time is on the debtor's side: the longer you wait to begin the collection process, the longer the debtor has to use your money for his own purposes. If the debtor has serious cash flow problems, you probably are not the only creditor who isn't being paid on time. *Tip:* The creditor who applies legal pressure properly will generally be paid first.

A well-run collection department should take these actions when an account is 30 days overdue:

- Promptly send a letter advising the debtor that the account is overdue.
- If payment is not received within 10 days, call the debtor and demand a reason for the nonpayment.
- Be prepared to give the debtor a 30-day grace period to pay.
- If payment is still not made, place one last call and demand immediate payment in cash or by certified check.

If all these efforts fail, take the next step.

Seek Outside Assistance

From a Collection Agency. There are thousands of agencies around the country, some specializing in commercial collections (business vs. business), others in consumer collections (business vs. consumer). Check their credentials with the Better Business Bureau before hiring any one of them. The agencies generally charge 25 percent to 50 percent of the value of the claim, though this commission is contingent on collection.

From an Attorney. If the agency is unable to collect the claim, it may request your permission to refer the matter to an attorney in the debtor's locale. Although a lawyer may be able to collect the debt without going to court, all too frequently this is not the case, so you will be asked to make an advance to cover court costs. If you decide to do so, keep in mind that if you included in the credit application the provision on attorneys' fees and interest, the debtor will ultimately bear the lion's share of court costs. Furthermore, the detailed information on the application should make the attorney's job that much easier; and if you have also secured a personal guarantee, the attorney can proceed against the debtor personally.

It may take some time for a collection matter to wind its way through the company–agency–attorney collection process. Some firms prefer to short-circuit matters by going from their own collection department directly to an attorney, bypassing the agency. This can increase collections and reduce agency commissions and the time needed to collect. But it doesn't make economic sense in all cases. If you try this approach, be sure to get an estimate of attorneys' fees and try to gauge the odds of collecting the debt using all three methods—collection department, agency, and lawyer.

Know Your Rights if the Debtor Files for Bankruptcy

Suppose as a result of all this pressure from your company, the collection agency, the attorney, and the demands of other creditors the debtor files for relief under the federal Bankruptcy Code. What happens now? Do you write off the account, take a tax loss, and turn your effort to the next delinquent?

If you have followed our suggestions, you don't have to do that because you have prepared the company for this eventuality: by obtaining the credit application, investigating the information on it, and—most importantly—getting a security agreement and filing a financing statement or obtaining another lien. As a secured creditor you obtain the value of your security while most other creditors get nothing.

With your credit secured, you have a vested interest in the debtor's property—be it real estate, equipment, or inventory. This means you are in a far stronger position to collect on the debt than is an unsecured creditor; it generally means that the secured property is sold and the proceeds distributed to you. But your specific rights to the property depend on the type of bankruptcy protection the debtor has requested.

Chapter 7: Liquidation. The debtor's property is being liquidated in a Chapter 7 Proceeding. The court will permit the sale of the secured property (with the proceeds going to you) if the debtor does not have any "equity" in the property; that is, if the value of your lien is greater than the fair market value of the property. If the property is more valuable than the lien, the property is sold and the proceeds are first applied to your claim.

In a Chapter 7 proceeding the debtor has the right to *redeem* the property or *reaffirm* the debt. In the former case, the debtor pays you the fair market value of the property and then takes it free of your lien; in theory you get what you would have received in the event of an actual sale. If you agree, the debtor can reaffirm the debt—continue to make payments to you until the entire contractual obligation is satisfied.

Chapter 11: Reorganization. This is a business reorganization proceeding: with the court's approval, the debtor continues to operate the business but must provide the court with a plan of reorganization, generally within 120 days of the filing of the petition. Since the debtor's business is being reorganized, not liquidated, you cannot automatically sell your collateral; if the property is necessary for the effective reorganization of the company, the debtor will be permitted to use it although your interest in it continues.

Chapter 13 Proceeding. This is a proceeding used by an individual wage earner who seeks to repay his creditors either in part or in full over a specified period of time, generally three years.

Bankruptcy Procedure: Recovering the Debt. As a general rule, you and your attorney can reach an agreement with the trustee (the person appointed by the court to oversee the mechanics of the bankruptcy process) and with the debtor for the release and sale of your property. The agreement is put in a consent order signed by the court. You are generally entitled to have the property for the purpose of sale if (1) the property is not necessary for the effective reorganization of the debtor (chapter 11 of the Bankruptcy Code) and (2) the debtor does not have "equity" in the property, that is, if the value of your lien is greater than the value of the property (chapter 7). You must account for the proceeds from any sale of the property.

Warning: The court must approve all acts against the debtor's property after the debtor has filed for protection under the Bankruptcy Code. Failure to get the court's approval can result in the entry of a contempt order against the creditor.

There are two other situations when your rights to the debtor's property may not be honored in a Bankruptcy Proceeding.

Ninety Days. The Trustee in bankruptcy can abolish (or "void") someone else's rights to the debtor's property if the rights came into existence 90 days before the filing of the bankruptcy petition. If your secured position to the property came into existence before that time, your rights are generally preserved.

Insider. The Trustee can also abolish rights to secured property if the creditor holding those rights is an "insider"; that is, someone whose close relationship with the debtor demands careful scrutiny of the transaction. The term is defined in the statute, but for a corporation it includes anyone holding a controlling interest in the corporation and a relative of any such person.

We now turn to the other side of the equation—the problem of the overextended debtor.

PART II
THE DILEMMA OF MOUNTING DEBTS:
TIPS FOR REPAYING THEM

With the acute economic problems of the last few years, it's no wonder that thousands of companies have sought protection under the Bankruptcy Code and thousands more have made out-of-court agreements with their creditors to restructure their debts. Firms become overextended in the best of times; when the entire economy is weak more companies teeter on the edge or fall over, and creditors become less willing to grant extensions. We have no solutions to economic malaise, but we can offer five tips for coping with excessive debt.

For most companies, the problem becomes acute when cash flow is cut off or severely reduced; accounts payable soar, the company can't meet the payroll, creditors regularly call, and demand letters outweigh the rest of the mail. Suddenly a firm views bankruptcy, not as a dubious technique for debt avoidance, but as the sole means of survival. We will consider bankruptcy later in this chapter, for it offers a "safe harbor," or at least one that is more placid than the churning ocean of debt. Before you run to the courthouse door with bankruptcy petition in hand, consider taking these steps that are cheaper and perhaps equally effective in preserving the business.

Tip 1: Meet with Your Creditors and Work Out a Repayment Plan

A large and common mistake of financially burdened companies is to hide from creditors. This is counterproductive: when a company refuses to discuss repayment, the creditor gets worried and will probably refer the account to a collection agency or attorney. This puts more pressure on the debtor to make even larger payments.

The better course is to meet with all your largest creditors with two goals in mind: rescheduling your debts and staying out of court. This can ensure your survival and placate the creditors. There are several elements to this approach:

Hold a Meeting. Arrange a meeting as soon as you fall seriously behind. This is the best way to answer your creditors' inquiries and to enlist their support in solving your problems. Do not be haphazard; hold the meeting in a pleasant facility away from your office in a room large enough to accommodate your creditors' representatives. Make sure your attorney, accountant, and chief financial officer are present.

Tip: Be sure to stress the importance, for both you and the creditors, of the freedom to operate without lawsuits; they would inevitably imperil the company's existence. Seek a moratorium on lawsuits for some period of time; this will permit you to reorganize your affairs for the benefit of all creditors, not just the belligerent one or two.

Describe the Financial Picture. Be prepared with a financial statement that reflects your costs of operation and present condition. Make sure the statement is accurate and that your accountant and chief financial officer are prepared to fully explain it.

Devise a Repayment Plan. If you were able to devise a repayment plan before the creditors meeting, by all means describe it and ask the creditors for their approval. It is often possible in these meetings to convince creditors to accept something less than they would otherwise be entitled to. Usually a plan calls for payment of indebtedness on a pro-rata basis (for example, every creditor gets 90 percent of the amount due) either as a lump sum or in installments.

Tip: You increase the odds of having your repayment plan accepted if you can show that its rejection will push you into bankruptcy where creditors will receive an even smaller percentage—fewer cents on the dollar.

Invite Alternatives. After you have described your financial condition and the repayment plan, invite your creditors to give their opinions and suggest alternatives. It's unlikely that all creditors will agree to the same repayment terms: some will be unsecured and essentially at your mercy, while others will be secured with some of your company's assets. As you recall from our earlier discussion, the secured creditor is entitled to the value of his security even in bankruptcy so he may take a harder line.

Tip: You must be able to give the secured creditor an opportunity to recover in an informal proceeding what he would be entitled to in a court-supervised liquidation.

Establish a Creditors' Committee. The meeting with creditors presents an excellent opportunity to have them establish an informal committee with a chairman to coordinate its work. The committee serves several purposes. First, a smaller creditor group can more quickly make a consensus recommendation and convince the obstinate creditors to go along in the hope of salvaging your business. Second, if all the creditors agree on a plan, the committee will supervise its implementation; it is with their cooperation that you continue to operate the business. Third, in the event you are forced into bankruptcy, this committee would likely be the official creditors' committee established by order of the court.

Tip 2: Get Advice in Running the Business

If you are confronted with a serious financial challenge, obtain professional counsel. Change is often a painful process, but it will probably be necessary if the company is to survive. Get help so the problems can be identified and solutions devised. There are at least three available sources.

The Creditors' Committee. Look first to the committee for guidance. Remember, the members are still your creditors so they want to protect their financial investment in your firm. Furthermore, their own companies may be managed by experienced professionals who may have encountered similar problems and devised reasonable solutions.

Business Consultants. There are many private business consultants who are trained in commercial or accounting matters. They can quickly study your company and submit recommendations for overhauling its operations. Many of the major national accounting firms also provide this service.

Government Agencies. Your local office of the Small Business Administration may be able to advise you or suggest private consultants who could help. The SBA can also put you in touch with the Service Corps of Retired Executives whose members provide advice for free or at reduced rates.

Not surprisingly, the recommended solution to the problem often calls for an infusion of funds, either for additional inventory and equipment or working capital.

Tip 3: Obtain Additional Financing

We discussed in chapter 10 the many types of debt financing. Of course, if you still have corporate assets that are free of any liens you can use those assets to obtain more money; but if your company is in serious financial difficulty, it may not have any such "unencumbered" assets so it may be difficult to secure conventional financing.

Warning: If you can get a bank loan under these circumstances, it will probably be conditioned on the personal guarantee of the stockholders or a pledge of their personal assets. Scrutinize these loans and make sure you are prepared to suffer the consequences if the corporation cannot make the payments.

In addition to the debt financing techniques in chapter 10, there are two others that often come into play in times of financial stress.

Subordinate a Claim. If you have inventory that is secured, you may be able to convince the secured creditor to "subordinate" his claim to the claim of a new investor if this will not reduce the value on the first lien. This means the new investor has a preferred status over the earlier creditor. Example: You have inventory worth over $500,000 but your supplier has a security interest valued at $400,000. If the supplier will agree to subordinate his claim to the first $100,000, he will still be fully protected but an additional $100,000 in inventory value is now available to use as security for another creditor.

Sell Assets. Another way of obtaining additional funds is to sell off part of the firm's assets. The goal is to scale down the size of the operation, not to liquidate it. Although the purpose of this "bulk sale" is to protect creditors, merchants have sometimes used it to defraud creditors by selling the assets to a friend or relative for a nominal price and subsequently using the assets to operate the business. To prevent such abuse, all states now have laws that require the seller to notify all creditors of the impending sale if the assets, such as fixtures or equipment, would not be sold in the ordinary course of the business. These laws also require that the purchaser be supplied with a list of the creditors.

The sale proceeds are applied to pay off the debts to the creditors on a pro rata basis. But often the proceeds do not cover all the debts so the unsecured creditors are not repaid in cash; instead, if they do not receive notice of the sale, they have certain rights to reclaim the goods.

Warning: A bulk sale is not recommended for a partnership or a sole proprietorship because the individuals remain personally liable for the unpaid debts. A bulk sale is used by corporations that do not intend to continue their operations, that cannot pay their debts, and where there are no personal guarantees.

Tip 4: Get Creditor Approval for Your Repayment Plan

If you are able to obtain additional capital to finance your repayment plan, or even if you are not and must make do with existing resources, you should present the plan to all the creditors for their approval. Ideally, the plan will be worked out with the creditors' committee and will be presented to all creditors with the committee's blessing. You should distribute to the creditors a copy of the plan and a written acceptance form for their signatures. The creditors should be instructed to mail the acceptances back to you by a specific date. The creditors' written acceptance of the plan means you have a binding contract; if you perform under it as you have contracted to do, you will be released from any further liability for the debts you incurred.

If you are unable to get the creditors to agree to your plan, steer for the safe harbor of bankruptcy.

Tip 5: Don't Flinch from the Bankruptcy Code

Faced with one or more recalcitrant creditors, you may have no alternative but to seek the protection of the Bankruptcy Court; that may be the only way to restructure the company. While bankruptcy is viewed by many as the "end of the line," in fact its purpose is not to bury a firm but to resuscitate it. As we said, once you file a petition, creditors are barred from taking any action to force a payment of the debt. We have already looked at the three different bankruptcy proceedings from the creditor's side; now we take the debtor's view.

Chapter 7 Liquidation. In this straight liquidation proceeding, you throw in the towel and in effect say to the court, "I can't make a go of it, here are all my assets, distribute them pro rata among my creditors to satisfy their claims." While this sounds hopeless, a Chapter 7 proceeding offers the debtor the chance to begin his credit life anew, unburdened by the heavy debts that crushed his company.

Chapter 11 Reorganization. As an alternative to liquidation, a company can ask the court for interim protection against creditors while it attempts to restructure itself and devise a plan of repayment. This can be viewed as a time of rethinking, and it would not be available without the Bankruptcy Code. The firm's operations and finances are reorganized, and there is a repayment plan that protects the interests of both the firm and the creditors. In fact, the plan may be the same one that was rejected during the informal, out-of-court meetings.

Anything that sounds this good must have its disadvantages, which it does: your company's daily operations are subject to the scrutiny of the creditors' committee which is composed of your ten largest creditors. After 120 days they have the right to propose their own plan of distribution or to suggest to the court that the company be liquidated if it can't be successfully reorganized.

In short, the Bankruptcy Code offers protection where other self-help methods fail. It should be looked on as your second wind, not a sign that the race is over.

Index